DATE DUE

MAY 0 6 2000	
DEC 1 0 2002	

GAYLORD   PRINTED IN U.S.A.

AGE OF
CONTRADICTION

Twayne's American Thought and Culture Series

Lewis Perry, General Editor

AGE OF CONTRADICTION

American Thought and Culture in the 1960s

HOWARD BRICK

Twayne Publishers
An Imprint of Simon & Schuster Macmillan
New York

Prentice Hall International
London • Mexico City • New Delhi • Singapore • Sydney • Toronto

Age of Contradiction: American Thought and Culture in the 1960s
Howard Brick

Twayne Publishers
An Imprint of Simon & Schuster Macmillan
1633 Broadway
New York, NY 10019

Library of Congress Cataloging-in-Publication Data

Brick, Howard, 1953–
    Age of contradiction : American thought and culture in the 1960s /
Howard Brick.
        p.   cm. — (Twayne's American thought and culture series)
    Includes bibliographical references and index.
    ISBN 0–8057–9080–2 (alk. paper)
        1. United States—Civilization—1945–   . 2. United States—
Intellectual life—20th century.   3. United States—
History—1961–1969.   I. Title.   II. Series.
    E169.12.B6946   1998
    973.92—dc21   98–18965
                                                                              CIP

10 9 8 7 6 5 4 3 2 1

Printed in the United States of America

Part of chapter 3 appeared in somewhat different form in *American Quarterly* 44 (1992).

For Debra
"like a sunrise that rose without warning"
(Laura Nyro, 1966)

Contents

Contents

EIGHT
The Push and the Shove 168

Illustrations

Foreword

The American Thought and Culture Series surveys intellectual and cultural life in America from the sixteenth century to the present. The time is auspicious for such a broad survey because scholars have carried out so much pathbreaking work in this field in recent years. The volumes reflect that scholarship as well as valuable earlier studies. The authors also present the results of their own research and offer original interpretations. The goal is to bring together books that are readable and well informed and that stand on their own as introductions to significant periods in American thought and culture. There is no attempt to establish a single interpretation of all of America's past; the diversity, conflict, and change that are features of the American experience would frustrate any such attempt. What the authors can do, however, is to explore issues that are of critical importance to both a particular period and the whole of American history.

Today the culture and intellectual life of the United States are subjects of heated debate. While prominent figures summon citizens back to an endangered "common culture," some critics dismiss the very idea of culture—let alone American culture—as elitist and arbitrary. The questions asked in these volumes are directly relevant to that debate, which concerns history but too often proceeds in ignorance of it. How did leading intellectuals view their relations to America, and how did their compatriots regard them? Did Americans believe that theirs was a distinctive culture? Did they participate in international movements? What were the links and tensions between high culture and popular culture? While discussing influential works, creative individuals, and major institutions, the books in this series place intellectual and cultural history in the larger context of American society.

In this volume, Howard Brick interprets American culture in the 1960s. It will take no argument to convince most readers of the cultural importance of that decade, which many remember as a radical break from American traditions. In the course of the decade's civil rights struggles and antiwar protests, scholars and artists were certain that major changes were occurring in their fields of knowledge and expression. Brick quotes the historian Richard Hofstadter, for example, as describing "the rediscovery of our violence" as one of the "important intellectual legacies" the decade would be remembered for. The shift by the end of the decade from hopeful discussion of nonviolence to escalating scenes of violence in American cities and Vietnam provides one example of the cultural conflicts and transformations that lead Brick to present the 1960s as an "Age of Contradiction."

Although Brick stresses the polarization—and in the end, the fragmentation—of intellectual life, his use of the term *contradiction* goes far beyond simply noting intellectuals' divergent reactions to political events. In searching chapters on problems of affluence and alienation, scientific objectivity, modernization and industrial change, artistic authenticity, and urban community, this volume considers links between the intellectual endeavors of the 1960s and earlier periods of American history. Brick finds connections, for example, between the famous Port Huron statement of the Students for a Democratic Society and John Dewey's vision of democratic community. And he is suitably cautious about oversimplifications offered by later movements seeking to claim affiliation with, or express contempt for, movements of the 1960s. There are many books on the 1960s, but no one has previously studied the intellectual life of that decade with the care and subtlety that Howard Brick has brought to important works by a wide range of authors and artists. His book is a model showing how close study of a short period can illuminate both enduring conflicts and shifting patterns in American culture.

LEWIS PERRY
Vanderbilt University

Preface

It is remarkable that "the sixties" remain so vivid today after some 30 years, still exciting controversy and appearing as a backdrop, a point of origin, or a foil whenever current trends in thought, art, politics, and religion are discussed. No decisive historical boundary obscures those years from view, and they remain part of present dilemmas. As their consequences linger over time, so their origins stretched back to earlier decades. In the political debates of the 1960s, for instance, we easily recognize analogies and epithets recalling the depression and war years: those defending the Vietnam War recalled "lessons of Munich"; their opponents labeled war leaders "fascists."

More significantly, the ill repute of capitalism stemming from the 1930s had not entirely been wiped away by the conservative revival that followed World War II or by the fervent anticommunism embraced by all mainstream political factions with the beginning of the Cold War. Few defended capitalism frankly. The most potent ideologies of the 1940s and 1950s justified the prevailing economic order in popular or democratic terms, touting productivity as a boon to the many; they refrained from old bourgeois apologetics that spoke for the few by defending the sanctity of private property or the legitimacy of profit as reward for risk. To be sure, the postwar reaction had done its work: McCarthyite repression struck hard at the main force on the political left, the Communist Party (before a broad disenchantment, spurred by Khrushchev's 1956 speech denouncing Stalin's crimes, dispersed more of the party's members), and subdued other left-wing organizations and activists as well. Liberalism, meanwhile, learned to tread lightly in its demands for change. Yet the postwar reaction had only contained, and did not roll back, the limited welfare state commenced by the New Deal, the democratic egalitarianism spawned by wartime ideology, or even the more general sense that the old world of bourgeois society (an order governed by a business class and devoted to principles of hardy economic individualism, family piety, stringent moral restraint, and respect for superiors in private and public life) was doomed to fade away. Heady hopes for a "new world" had flared briefly at the end of the war, just before the conservative mood settled in like a long postwar hangover; when its pall lifted, after the mid-1950s, the world again seemed fresh with possibility. Intellectuals and activists then approached the coming decade of the 1960s as a chance to realize far-reaching goals of social progress. They aimed to redefine and enrich democracy, eliminate poverty, enhance popular participation in government, expand opportunities for self-fulfillment, put reason at the helm of public policy, and make flexibility and variation keys to a new order of social roles.

Here lay all the ingredients for an era of sharp contradictions. Although not usually posed as part of an overarching program for change, these ambitious goals, taken together, posed challenges to the American status quo almost as revolutionary as any leftist of the 1930s and 1940s might have imagined. For the most part, however, and especially in the early years, reformers of the 1960s did not at all think that revolution was necessary to achieve their goals but considered all of them to be achievable within the progressive framework of a modern society. In the 1930s and 1940s, radicals as well as many reformist liberals saw the working class, or organized labor, as the strategic force capable of demanding and forcing social change; in the 1960s, coming after the postwar reaction had broken the continuity of labor and left-wing traditions, that conviction was lost, and no other coherent strategy emerged. The greatest contradiction of this new era, then, lay in the deceptive ease with which reformers thought great change could be achieved: that kind of confidence fostered dramatic aspirations for a new society but failed to recognize or nurture the social and political means that could bring change about.

The idea of postindustrial society, first discussed during the early 1960s, illustrates some of these strains. Its proponents argued that organized intellectual activity in universities and research institutes, along with the growth of public services, was pushing mechanical industry out of its leading role in modern society. In the offing there appeared, they said, a more collective organization of social life than that allowed by the classic economic ideology of the market. Optimistic liberals promoting this idea generally soft-pedaled the inequitable distribution of American wealth and power and the concentrated interests in American life that would resist such far-reaching change. Instead, they suggested that theirs was a time not to fight economic battles but to fashion the purely "social" resources of education, welfare, health, and collaborative effort that promised to all a future of innovation and security. Here truth and illusion mingled. Everyday life was indeed more and more "socialized"— organized in institutions of a large scale, integrated in a way that broke down barriers between different groups of people and different walks of life, and dependent on public resources. Yet alongside the growing bounds of socialized experience persisted an economic order geared to private benefit, adding to the accumulation of private wealth and promoting a growing apparatus of consumer culture. The stress between a mass society integrating the affairs of all, and economic norms insisting that each take care of one's own, is a perennial contradiction of modern capitalism. It became acute in the 1960s, though, when new forms of socialized experience made palpable at least the potential for a different way of life.

Further contradictions followed. Although holding to an enormously optimistic view of future possibilities, reformers were haunted by two dark undercurrents of pessimism: a sense, lingering from the conservative mood of the 1950s, that the American status quo was after all stolid and immovable, and the fear, stemming from atrocities of the past war and the threat of nuclear weaponry, of an apocalyptic end to things. Still, that bleak tone did not overcome the general affirmative sense of the times. Meanwhile, conservatives nursed their resources for political battles in years to come, though they were denied a paramount role in intellectual and cultural life for most of the 1960s. Thus a stout argument for the legitimacy of existing inequalities was, for the most part, an absent contender in debate, and reformers rarely had to acknowledge the obstacles to social change. Debate and conflict flared mainly between liberal reform and a renewed but callow radicalism. Both these currents were full of inspired hopes but largely blind to the sources of social power they would have to combat to win their goals, and both were unprepared for the turbulence, anxiety, and resistance their programs of social change would excite by the decade's end.

Contradiction could appear in very concrete forms. A sharp social torsion governed American life in the years after World War II, as trends toward a more democratic social and cultural life continued in the face of political and economic forces retarding change. Trends toward the emancipation of women, for instance, had some continuity through midcentury (especially after the mid-1950s), measured in rising proportions of women in wage work, increased college attendance, emphasis on women's self-fulfillment in careers, and more egalitarian ideas of marriage. But those trends strained against the normative conservatism of the Cold War era and what Betty Friedan and Kate Millett called a sexual counterrevolution, working since the 1920s to push back women's liberation. Likewise, the social emancipation of African Americans was fostered by migration out of the rural South, the nationalizing and liberalizing pressures of mobilization for World War II, and the dawning of black communal power in postwar southern campaigns against Jim Crow. These trends, however, had to contend not only with a white racist backlash against black progress but also with the perverse consequences of capitalist development, which denied urban blacks in the 1960s the kind of job opportunities that the immigrant poor had found during industrialization. Black Power, a form of collective self-assertion echoed in movements of other oppressed "racial" groups such as Mexican Americans and American Indians, can be understood as an attempt to shore up community resources in the wrenching context of urban decay.

The principle of contradiction also offers a way of studying intellectual life and the arts. A phenomenon could assume two opposed guises. The socialization of intellect in the new mass universities, tied to centers of power in government and the business world, struck some observers as the onset of a new Enlightenment but others as the demise of free critical thought. A nonconformist "counterculture" espoused both uninhibited individualism and communalism. Moreover, distinct trends and antithetical values seemed to thrive at once. Thus the pursuit of personal "authenticity" *and* a fascination with calculated means of "impression management" marked the 1960s. Finally, in some instances, one set of motives turned into its opposite as elements of protest movements built on principles of pacifism or nonviolent tactics turned to embrace armed violence as a means of struggle, or even a cathartic end.

This study recognizes contradiction in the forms of contending interpretations, coincidence of contrary trends, the transformation of opposites. It focuses on a number of polar opposites or antinomies in the thought and culture of the period—on authenticity and artifice, the appeal of systematic organization and the distrust of order, the urgency of peace and the uses of violence—while refusing to fix on one style or disposition as a key to the decade. The study's organization is not strictly chronological, event driven, or even topical. As it examines these antinomies, certain events, ideas, and authors encountered in one context may reappear in another light, as in the study of language by Ludwig Wittgenstein, in which one is called "to travel over a wide region of uses, criss-cross in every direction, the same use being approached again and again, each time from a different direction, from a different point of view, from a different use." The goal is a set of "sketches" arranged "so that if you looked at them you could get a picture" of the field and get to "know your way about."[1]

Despite variation and volatility in the sphere of ideas, some common modes of thought appeared. A typical political critique emerged, along with heightened democratic aspirations, predicting that American society was turning toward a new kind of elite domination, more concentrated, rigid, and *less* democratic than in times past. A common cultural critique claimed that society was losing its moral ballast and heading toward a normless order, called "the therapeutic society" by sociologist Philip Rieff or recognized as "the heat-death of society" by novelist Thomas Pynchon. Similarly, a new psychological analysis identified a "narcissistic" malady among individuals incapable of finding meaningful order within themselves or forming strong bonds to others. Finally, in social terms more or less compatible with these criticisms, it was said that the stringency of social control over behavior was increasing, or that organized society threatened to turn persons into automatons. In recognizing these tropes, however, contradiction remains a touchstone. Each of them was politically indeterminate, figuring in both right- and left-leaning criticisms of American life. (The critique of elites, for instance, figured in the analysis of concentrated power promoted by radical sociologist C. Wright Mills and his followers, as well as the neoconservative theory of the late 1960s and early 1970s that a "new class" of adversarial intellectuals undermined social stability.) Given the range of contrary tendencies in the 1960s, however, each critique taken alone could be profoundly one-sided and misleading.

Two generalizations do hold for the course of American thought and culture in the 1960s. The first is a trend toward an enriched sense of social context—a growing recognition of how deeply embedded in complex social relations were all practices of science, art, literature, and education. Purist and formalist notions were subject to assault. In the philosophy of science, an old argument for the distinctive character of the "scientific method" and the rules governing it fell before historicized and contextual views of scientific practice, such as Thomas Kuhn's analysis of the social organization and dogmas of experimental science. In the arts, formal barriers between different modes (painting, sculpture, theater, etc.), as well as the reputed self-sufficiency of art itself, fell before artwork made in mixed media, the imitation of commercial artifacts and use of industrial materials, and the embrace of political relevance. The second trend moved not toward wider terms of social coherence but toward the rupture of intellectual community. By the end of the decade, the intelligentsia tended to polarize into rival camps, and dissenting caucuses and disputes over basic methods upset the stability of academic disciplines. Lost was the kind of intellectual authority and self-confidence of the early 1960s that accompanied a stout belief in the maturity of modern disciplines and the virtue of serving public agencies, whether the Defense Department or the antipoverty program.

This book is more or less limited to the realm of formal ideas and artistic trends, with little focus on popular culture. Furthermore, attention focuses to a large extent on the social sciences, since the 1960s were marked by the preeminence of "the social sphere" in experience and in thought. Still, the book aims to touch on many of the most significant issues in the intellectual debates of the time. It begins with a discussion of economic ideas and expectations of social change associated with the promise of prosperity. From that baseline, chapter 2 considers the infrastructure of intellectual life—the new system of mass universities—and the questions arising in that context about how we know, and why knowledge matters. Given the prominence of academic institutions in public affairs, intellectuals in the 1960s were acutely self-conscious about their "social role," inclined either to glorify or decry it, and their debates on this point were closely bound up with competing interpretations of the course of contemporary social change and the value of progress. In treating that topic, chapter 3 completes the presentation of the most general issues at stake in American thought of the time. Thereafter, focus shifts to ideas about the status of the person and the nature of communities in a mass society before returning to the large, abstract issue of how "systems" structured experience (chapters 4 through 6). Chapters 7 and 8 come closest to a chronological perspective on the period, addressing the problems of peace and violence that became especially acute as the debate over the war in Vietnam intensified and, finally, the climactic struggles in scholarship and art that capped the decade as a time of conflict and close engagement with social and political affairs.

Acknowledgments

I would not have written this book if Lewis Perry had not phoned to suggest it or offered such steady advice and encouragement. Daniel H. Borus and Joseph G. Fracchia also gave me counsel, and productive argument. Casey Blake, Alice Echols, Marilyn Farwell, Robert Kyr, Kathleen Rowe, Cheyney Ryan, Laurence Schneider, Quintard Taylor, and Carl Woidek gave me important tips and pointers. Casey Blake, George Cotkin, Susan Henking, Ellen Herman, Daniel Horowitz, Robbie Lieberman, James Maffie, Christopher Phelps, Daniel Pope, Sandra Silberstein, Quintard Taylor, and Alan Wald offered comments on a draft manuscript, helping enormously to improve the book. Having tried to save me from errors, they cannot be held responsible for them.

The University of Oregon provided sabbatical leave, and Washington University research funds, that helped me complete the project. I also had the support of very able research assistants at both institutions: Mike Boles, Jennifer Slosar, and Isaac Green. I must thank many people I do not know personally, having encountered their remarks and advice on electronic discussion lists, particularly the "Sixties list" established by Kali Tal of *Vietnam Generation*. Jessye Rose and Michael Perry Schwartz Brick, wondering why I had to write the same book more than once, graciously bore with me as I plunked away on the keyboard.

one

Contradictions of the Affluent Society

"The problem of production has been solved." This assertion, voiced often in the years around 1960, can be counted as one of the great conceits of the new decade, announcing the arrival of something radically new—a society of abundance. Ten or 20 years later, the claim appeared to some observers a mark of the complacency, excessive optimism, or even utopian folly of the 1960s; nevertheless, the idea was a potent one, part of a provocative discourse on the problems of modern society. From the theme of abundance came a critique of alienated work, economic logic, consumerism, and environmental destruction. Abundance suggested ways of imagining a society where the uses of leisure, the impulses of creativity, and the integrity of communities had priority. Above all, it called attention to the growing salience held by the *social* sphere of human action: by extrafamilial social institutions that shape everyday life, by experiences enjoyed in public, and by demands for services and forms of human interaction that transcend the individualism of economic markets.

The primacy of the social sphere in the consciousness of the 1960s followed the real drift of American life toward the organization of skills, services, habits, and interactions on a large scale of coordination, pressing against the barriers of private, local, and sheltered experience. In this sense, American life became more and more "socialized." Socialization was a trend especially marked during the 1960s in intellectual life and the arts, where institutions of higher learning and aesthetic experience emerged that were open to, and intended to address, a vaster public than ever before. By inviting more of the American people into a common social life, this trend had a democratic dimension to it, but the institutions it created often seemed more like ponderous, impersonal forces than means of popular involvement in social affairs. Likewise, while the socializing trend provided conditions for new kinds of collective action in American life, it accompanied a growing capitalist economy that still emphasized the action of lone individuals. These were some of the contradictions of the affluent society, posing acute problems for thinkers of the time: the prospects of abundance opened vistas of social change but also reinforced a sense of personal alienation, aroused hopes for a greater degree of democratic participation in public life but also suggested a growing concentration of effective power in American life.

The Promise of Affluence in the Age of Automation

Celebration of the American status quo for its productivity—judging Americans to be blessed, in David Potter's words, as a people of plenty—is so familiar that we may forget that the discourse of abundance circa 1960 was more a criticism of conventional thought and practice than an endorsement of it. John Kenneth Galbraith's *The Affluent Society* (1958) was one book among others, such as *The Challenge of Abundance* (1961) by dissenting economist Robert Theobald and *Challenge to Affluence* (1963) by the Swedish observer Gunnar Myrdal, that greeted prospects of a bountiful economy as an occasion for changing the standards of economic thought and policy.

Galbraith argued that classical and neoclassical economics, rooted in conditions of scarcity and mass poverty, were rendered obsolete by the unprecedented economic growth after World War II. Yet his message was misunderstood if taken as a call for the dismal science to wake up and be happy. His claim that "the problem of production was conquered" meant not that long-term economic stability was assured but merely that "given a sufficiency of demand, the responding production of goods in the modern economy is almost completely reliable." Galbraith thought the point simple but profound: now it was "not total output but its *composition* [that becomes] the critical matter" in economic affairs, and "the problem of social balance" between goods produced and distributed through private means and services made available through public channels came to the fore. "Social goods" such as public thoroughfares, clean air, and scientific knowledge must be provided to all if they would be available to any and could hardly be exchanged as merchandise; they were persistently shortchanged, however, by the outmoded premium economic dogma placed on producing commercial goods and keeping public expenditure to a minimum. The result was not only, in Galbraith's famous phrase, a glaring contrast between "private opulence and public squalor" but also neglect of the conditions for growth in an economy dependent on public resources such as basic science, generalized knowledge, and highly qualified labor.[1]

Because Galbraith gave political support to the presidential campaign of John F. Kennedy and later accepted an ambassadorial appointment from him, it is sometimes assumed that Galbraith's *Affluent Society* provided the ideology for the new, forward-looking administration. Yet Kennedy was a relatively conservative figure who sponsored few initiatives in generating social goods and built an economic program on a policy of tax cuts that Galbraith opposed.[2] Galbraith's ideas actually placed him to the left of the political center in the United States. Since the American economy, at the very least, had cultivated expertise in engineering output, he argued, the "urgency of production" rightfully surrendered its place as the central concern of social policy; thus the old imperatives to maximize capital available for private investment and maintain harsh "incentives" driving workers to labor—the watchwords, that is, of bourgeois economic faith—lost their force.[3] Whether owing to a liberal confidence in the capacity of reason to promote change, or to a bit of rhetorical guile, Galbraith himself did not clearly acknowledge the potentially radical conclusions stemming from this broadside against economic orthodoxy. Others, such as his disciple Robert Theobald, argued more insistently that idolatry of economic growth, at least in prosperous countries, could be set aside as social and communal needs such as enhanced welfare services and a humanistic assessment of the benefits and dangers spawned by new technologies took the helm in public policy.[4]

Focused on a whole new level of productivity, Galbraith's discussion of affluence alluded to the advent of "automation," a subject that preoccupied observers of social and economic affairs for a decade after the mid-1950s. That was when the term, possibly coined by a Ford executive, came to describe the use of self-regulating machines in integrated sequences of continuous-process production, centrally controlled by computers; fittingly, the United Auto-workers (UAW) became a leading voice for labor in discussing the social consequences of the new techniques. Anticipating Galbraith's rhetoric, UAW head Walter Reuther was not reluctant to embrace the prospects of lavish output: "Science and technology," he stated in 1954, "have at last given us the tools of economic abundance, and we are confronted no longer with the need to struggle to divide up scarcity." Liberal allies of labor, such as the University of Chicago sociologist Warner Bloomberg, who wrote a pamphlet titled *The Age of Automation* for the social democratic League for Industrial Democracy (LID), also tended to be upbeat. Automation made possible a more "easy-going shop life" as workers shifted from in-line production to jobs involving superintendence, and it promised declining status distinctions between "blue-collar" and "white-collar" employees, shorter hours, and a greater "sense of power" as workers played a part in commanding an integrated production apparatus.[5] But although "radical productivity increases" could provide for "security and abundance," the UAW and its allies warned, automation spelled "unemployment and misery" unless corporate and public policy devised new ways of sharing available work (by reducing the standard workweek) and new means of providing workers with income outside the customary wage. The fear of widespread "technological unemployment" as automation destroyed industrial jobs troubled many observers in the early 1960s. Still, theorists of abundance preferred to speculate on the liberating prospect of reduced work time. Theobald cited predictions of a 15-hour workweek by the century's end, and in 1965 the sober LID discussed "redistributing the new productivity" and "how to determine payments for a four-hour day."[6]

Automation and its effects remained high on the agenda of public debate until the mid-1960s. Skeptics insisted that expectations of massive labor displacement due to automation were far exaggerated, and that technological change offered grounds neither for euphoria nor for despair. The inaugural 1965 issue of *The Public Interest*, the journal founded by Irving Kristol and Daniel Bell to spur "professional" discussion of the issues raised by an age of reform, gave top billing to "The Great Automation Question." Economist Robert Solow argued that there was no clear evidence that technological innovation as such outraced the economy's capacity to create new jobs. Robert Heilbroner, on the other hand, saw reasons to expect burgeoning unemployment and, finding no convincing alternative to "public employment-generating" policies, saw a growing need for "a whole new attitude toward the appropriate public-private mix for the peace-time economy." Reporting in 1966, a National Commission on Technology, Automation, and Economic Progress sought like Solow to allay fears of massive unemployment but still regarded the balance between innovation and jobs delicate enough to warrant new social policies—a guaranteed minimum income, public job creation, and improved public services in health, transportation, and housing.[7]

Those who doubted that automation would profoundly disrupt social affairs proved correct, for in the 1960s automation was implemented at a rather slow rate. As Charles R. Walker showed in *Toward the Automatic Factory* (1958), many labor-saving innovations touted as automation hardly deserved the name. The continuous-process steel-pipe mill Walker studied had reduced the labor force to only nine workers, but the process remained wholly mechanical. Although several workers were freed from exhausting physical labor to take up superintendence and maintenance, some jobs were still "hot and heavy and wholly physical"—resulting in a type of "partially automated" factory that "will remain for many years characteristic of the greater part of the American economy." Early speculation also overestimated the ability of mainframe computers to master the complexity of integrated processes and control them from a single point; genuine "cybernation" became more realizable only after a further chain of technical advances in the 1960s and 1970s: the integrated circuit, microprocessor, and distributed processing, which permitted more flexible systems of computer control and human intervention at several points in production.[8] Greater automation was hobbled too by social and economic factors, as the war-fueled economic boom of the mid-1960s, with its easy profits—and the wave of mergers in new "conglomerate" corporations—helped divert funds away from investment in technical innovation.

Still, it was the prospect of a post-scarcity society that propelled a great deal of the ambitious progressive, or utopian, ideas of that period. That prospect underlay the views of Herbert Marcuse, an advocate of libidinal liberation from work, whose *Eros and Civilization* (1955) claimed that the "surplus repression" demanded by a society governed by the "performance principle" (i.e., production for production's sake) was obsolete; the same idea led him in 1970 to declare the "end of utopia," since the age-old dream of cornu-copia was now, simply, realizable. It filtered into Betty Friedan's call for a new era of women's individuality, *The Feminine Mystique* (1963), when she claimed that in the prior 15 years, "the very nature of human reality has become increasingly free from biological and material necessity."[9]

Apostles of abundance who claimed "the problem of production has been solved" did not claim that American life would move from a culture of work to a culture of consumerism. Rather, the thesis of abundance often carried with it the claim that commercial consumption was reaching its limit and declining as a motive. The reason "production for the sake of goods produced is no longer very urgent," Galbraith wrote, was not only that productive effi-ciency was rather easily achieved but also that as output reached the point of abundance, the marginal utility of goods in several branches of production began to diminish. Perhaps consumers were acknowledging a sense of surfeit. Sociologist David Riesman claimed the professional middle classes had lost "the zest for possessions," and Theobald argued that the decline in purchases of consumer durables that helped spark the 1957 recession might be related to a waning "desire ... for additional goods." Thinking of the Volkswagen "bug" already winning popularity, Theobald noted the growing preference for func-tion over status and argued, "the contempt for material goods is already more widely spread than is generally realized and ... a real revolution in this field can be expected within a relatively limited time." Later, Albert O. Hirschman suggested that dissatisfaction with the private life of consumerism grew around the start of the 1960s, "shifting involvements" away from consump-tion toward public action and commitments.[10]

The "rediscovery" of poverty in America during the early 1960s, further-more, posed less of a critical challenge to the discourse of affluence than it appeared. Renewed attention to poverty came in many forms, including Edward R. Murrow's 1960 television documentary on migrant farm laborers, *Harvest of Shame*, the income-distribution statistics developed by Robert J. Lampman starting in 1959, and a spate of specialized studies such as David Caplovitz's study of low-income consumption, *The Poor Pay More* (1963). Michael Harrington's well-known book *The Other America* (1962) challenged Galbraith's view that poverty was now an "insular" phenomenon limited to small "pockets" of underdevelopment such as Appalachia, claiming instead that a large minority remained poor. Still, Harrington concurred with Gal-braith in viewing this phenomenon as a "new poverty" precisely because it included only a minority, not a majority, of the people and thus left the poor mired in "social invisibility." Harrington was joined by Gunnar Myrdal, who calculated in 1963 that as many as 40 percent of Americans were left on the outside looking in. While he condemned "the creeping complacency that America is now an affluent society," however, Myrdal conceded Galbraith's main point by noting that there was "so much solid truth in the appreciation of the technological revolution under way and of the capacity of the American economy to expand production of material goods in almost every field." That was why, Myrdal said, achieving economic balance required public efforts to boost the purchasing power of the poor.[11]

Rather than dwelling in complacency, the discourse of affluence implied greater confidence in prospects for significant social change than did the new writing on poverty; in the latter, the poor appeared saddled by a unique degree of pessimism or despair. Unassisted by New Deal programs that sustained "the middle third" of the people, lacking a voice or the sympathy of the contented majority, Harrington's new poor were shunted aside and demoralized. Myrdal coined a new term when he called the American poor an "underclass" that was "not really an integral part of the nation but a useless and miserable substratum." The impression of the poor mired in despair received its strongest impulse from the writings of anthropologist Oscar Lewis, who claimed to have discovered a universal "culture of poverty" in the slums of Mexico City: feelings of personal inferiority and helplessness, a narrow scope of consciousness limited to the local neighborhood and the present moment, acute status jealousy, spontaneous violence, and habits of dependency. Harrington adopted Lewis's phrase in his own book and added the psychic shortcoming of passivity to the elements fostering a "vicious circle of impoverishment" in America. Another element of fatalism entered the portrait of American poverty as Harrington, Myrdal, and others claimed that automation augured ill for the poor, who lacked the educational qualifications for getting on the job track in an economy requiring high levels of expertise. The automation skeptic Solow argued, though, that unemployment among the poor should be attributed not to their lack of skills but to weakness in the economy, as insufficient aggregate demand kept the rate of growth and job creation below full potential.[12]

Another way to cut across the currents of optimism and pessimism in the automation debate came from the corner of American intellectual life still held by Marxism. In 1958 the Trinidad-born historian, cultural critic, and political philosopher C. L. R. James, long a resident of the United States then exiled to Great Britain, treated automation as "a new stage of technology," driven by the interest business had in cutting the number of recalcitrant workers needed in production. While labor-saving innovation threatened to "put the majority of the population on the shelf," he wrote, it also led workers to recognize that they needed control not merely of their own machine but of "the whole work process, [the] method and tempo by means of which machinery is to be developed and put into use." Thus automation enabled them "to visualize a new society."[13] Marx had also looked to a time when the displacement of labor from direct production made the *social* basis of all wealth blatantly evident and subverted the system that built earnings on the backs of wage-paid workers:

[T]he human being comes to relate more as watchman and regulator to the production process itself.... He steps to the side of the production process instead of being its chief actor. In this transformation, it is neither the direct human labour he himself performs, nor the time during which he works, but rather the appropriation of his own general productive power, his understanding of nature and his mastery over it by virtue of his presence as a social body—it is, in a word, the development of the *social individual* which appears as the great foundation-stone of production and of wealth. The theft of alien labour time, on which the present wealth is based, appears a miserable foundation in face of this new one, created by large-scale industry itself.[14]

For Marx, capitalist development ultimately made the social dimension of human experience more and more pressing a reality. This insight reappeared, somewhat altered, in the discourse of affluence. The emphasis in the 1960s on enhancing public services of education, health, and welfare and (as we shall see) on exploring matters of identity, community, and power in intimate relationships focused on a "social" realm—of culture, personality, and human interaction—distinct from economics and politics, strictly speaking. So insistent was this focus, it might have seemed that social life was already virtually free from the economic constraints characteristic of capitalism. In Galbraith's optimistic view, the power of bourgeois wealth per se had declined in comparison to the power of office-holding corporate managers, a public policy consensus on providing economic security for the masses was secure, and the reserve army of labor no longer served to restrain workers' expectations. Neither James nor Marx would have shared this confidence, but in their terms, the very emergence of such "utopian" ideas signaled the arrival of a stage of development in which abundance made the differentiation of social from purely economic concerns at least conceivable. That is, it was possible to recognize in current conditions the chance for great change in the makeup of modern society, even to the point of surpassing the limits of capitalism. In this sense, the discourse of abundance raised the possibility of bringing "postmaterialist" or "posteconomic" values into public affairs and personal life, providing a boon to creative and critical thinking in the 1960s.

The Conditions of Knowledge and Sensibility

The expansion of the social sphere was especially marked in the trend toward socializing the conditions of thought and expression. From the late 1950s to the late 1960s, there was a massive expansion in the institutions and media involved in the pursuit of knowledge and the cultivation of sensibility. Higher education became a broad-based, organized social resource, available to large numbers of young people on a more democratic basis than ever before, and became closely integrated with both public agencies and organized private interests outside the academy. Cultural experience also became more public as grand municipal arts centers were built, federal funding of the arts began, universities became hothouses of creativity, audiences for popular arts assumed new forms, and the communications media chased after them with an expanding output of expressive goods.

In retrospect, the creation of a new system of mass higher education seems to have begun with the mobilization of science for World War II, postwar appeals for more public funding of research, and the GI Bill's educational entitlements. In the 1940s, however, it was not immediately evident that American colleges and universities would or should be so quickly transformed. Most educationists, still thinking of college graduates as a natural elite, were surprised first by how many veterans took advantage of the GI Bill and then by the persistence of high enrollments in the 1950s. (Even as the postwar influx of men quickly shrunk the proportion of college students who were women, the number of women attending and graduating college also kept growing through the 1950s.) Then, as observers in 1955 first discerned that an "impending tidal wave of students" would hit campuses around 1960, it became clear that the late 1950s would mark a watershed. Soviet success with the Sputnik satellite, by arousing American fears of falling behind in technology, occasioned a dramatic increase in government funding for higher education, while admissions applications to colleges and universities jumped. Then, from 1960 to 1970, enrollments more than doubled again; at that point, roughly a third of high school graduates went on to college. Such growth was absorbed by the creation of new institutions and the addition of more branch campuses to public universities, especially in California, which planned three new university campuses in 1958 and opened them, with high ambitions for pedagogical innovation, in 1964 and 1965. The proportion of students attending public rather than private institutions rose from 59 percent to 73 percent during the 1960s, and with that, access to higher education was democratized to a degree, as more lower-middle-class and working-class youth appeared on campus.[15]

In the context of massive growth, higher education was linked with government and corporate institutions. Federal funding of university research doubled from 1955 to 1959 and then grew almost six times over by 1968. The Department of Defense (DOD) and Atomic Energy Commission (AEC) built close ties with academic scientists in a number of new national laboratories and "contract centers" dedicated to military projects (such as Johns Hopkins's Applied Physics Laboratory). With the addition of the National Aeronautics and Space Administration (NASA) in 1959, the large "defense establishment" occupied a prime place in university life. Private corporations, many of them symbiotic with the defense establishment, also built their own laboratories or sponsored university research.[16]

The burgeoning "scientific estate" witnessed several major intellectual innovations in the 1960s, from the debut of the "big bang" theory of the universe's origins to the establishment of molecular biology as an independent field and a number of breakthroughs identifying new subatomic particles (quarks, "charmed" quarks, as well as W and Z particles). Some fields, such as electrical engineering, aeronautics, and early computer science, were dominated by research agendas fixed by government programs of weapons development.[17] In time, however, even defense-sponsored research moved away somewhat from narrowly conceived weapons projects toward more open-ended "basic science." By the late 1960s, too, increased funding by agencies such as the National Institutes of Health (NIH) and National Science Foundation (NSF) meant that the public funds given to civilian research rivaled those spent on military work. In any case, military interests could have ramifying effects in knowledge: a naval research program of mapping the ocean floor, for instance, provided data for the revolutionary theory of plate tectonics in geology. Cold War policy also motivated government funding for other fields such as language training, area studies (on Russia and China, for instance), and certain aspects of political science, but it could not shape these fields completely: the Center for International Affairs, led by strategic arms theorist Thomas Schelling, also supported peace advocate Gene Sharp in writing his three-volume treatise *The Politics of Nonviolent Action*.

The socialization of resources in knowledge also showed itself in the growing prominence of private, extra-academic research institutions devoted to providing information and consultation to public policy makers. Study groups such as the RAND Corporation and the Hudson Institute had spun off from the contract centers in weapons development created by academic, government, and corporate organizers early in the Cold War. As the Kennedy and Johnson administrations, aiming to adopt "rational" means of evaluating options and outcomes of policy initiatives, sought counsel from these new organizations, the reign of the "think tanks" began. The RAND Corporation was the biggest, using engineering, mathematical, and economic analysis to assess the cost-effectiveness of different options in weapons deployment for Robert McNamara's Defense Department. The 40-year-old Brookings Institution, recently rejuvenated by Ford Foundation grants, studied the effects of tax cuts and the value of United Nations aid programs to U.S. foreign policy aims. Think tanks did not always rest on such close government ties: conservative philanthropists reinvigorated the American Enterprise Institute to propagandize for laissez-faire doctrine in 1960, and in 1963, on the other hand, Marcus Raskin and Richard Barnet, two disarmament advocates who had served briefly in the Kennedy administration, founded the Institute for Policy Studies (IPS) to provide a counterweight to the entrenched military attitudes that promoted the arms race.[18]

The social organization of knowledge, however, did not necessarily make it a genuine public resource or democratic domain. Indeed, a few economists began to study the production and consumption of knowledge as merely another exchange of private resources among individuals. In *The Production and Distribution of Knowledge in the United States* (1962), the Austrian émigré and neoliberal economist Fritz Machlup estimated that the economic value of those activities that composed "the knowledge industry"—the whole gamut of activities (educational institutions, research and development, communications media, computers, information services) that involved conveying information to others not yet aware of it—was growing faster than the gross national product, suggesting greater demand for more highly skilled, educationally qualified workers. Considering education primarily as a resource for qualified "manpower," Machlup urged a more intensive, accelerated high school regime that would send about half of all young people on to college and the rest out to work by age 15.[19]

The economic perspective on education prevailed also in the new theory of "human capital," that is, the study of human skills and capacities as a form of capital, something that could absorb investments and yield returns in enhanced productivity. Early work by the University of Chicago economist T. W. Schultz portrayed human capital in some senses as a general social resource, the "secular improvements in workers' skills based on education, training and literacy ... improved health and longevity ... the capacity of a more educated population," which explained modern economic growth better than conventional accounting of the concrete labor and capital units added to production. In *Human Capital* (1964), Gary Becker, another Chicago economist, effectively converted the concept to an individualistic basis, a way of assessing the equilibrium achieved in the labor market between personal investments in education and the return they brought in greater lifetime wages. Extended schooling for Becker was a matter of individual economic advantage and rational calculation. His work, following that of his teacher, Milton Friedman, whose libertarian manifesto *Capitalism and Freedom* (1962) helped revive conservative intellectual life, showed how the trends that Galbraith believed drove beyond conventional economic logic might nonetheless be reduced to the terms of market exchange.[20]

The expansion of the university system, however, had other subtle effects that partly countered militaristic and economistic uses of knowledge. Paradoxically, as college education became both a popular route for social mobility and a training and recruitment agency for high-tech employers, the academic seriousness of the undergraduate actually increased. According to Christopher Jencks and David Riesman in *The Academic Revolution* (1968), the early 1960s witnessed dramatic growth in the proportion of entering students who declared an intention to undertake graduate studies after finishing their four college years, and thus, with college performance a priority, the lackadaisical attitude of the "gentleman's C" became outmoded. The academic model of training in formal scholarship rendered baccalaureate programs "more intellectual, abstract, and conceptual," and the proportion of undergraduates engaged in business and preprofessional programs declined while the liberal arts major, for both men and women, became increasingly predominant. At least for some students and their teachers, a humanistic view of the value of ideas for their own sake militated against crude utilitarian views of knowledge, and a brewing critique of industrial, military, and bureaucratic uses of information took off from such sentiments.[21]

Along with public investments in knowledge came public funding of the arts in what was sometimes grandly called a new democratic era in culture. A boom in building municipal arts centers began in 1962, when construction was going on in 69 cities from Minneapolis to Yakima; and by 1969, when more than 170 such centers had been completed, a like number were still in the making. The most lavish of these, New York City's Lincoln Center, boasted an opera house, finished in 1966, that seated more than the great halls of Paris and Vienna. Meanwhile, state universities such as Iowa and Illinois built emporiums of performing arts. The claim made in 1963 by University of California president Clark Kerr that the academy was "ready to bloom" as a base for artistic creativity seemed borne out in cases such as Indiana University, host to 600 concerts and recitals a year. The growing tendency of artists to support themselves partly or fully by academic appointments, and the multifold increase throughout the 1960s in the number of fine-arts degrees awarded, made it clear that colleges and universities were becoming a principal center of cultural as well as intellectual life. The academy became a social center of the arts in another way, too, as colleges and universities served as magnets around which grew vital communities marked by bookstores, taverns, music halls, and other gathering places, attracting a good number of determinedly nonacademic artists and musicians.[22]

Government-sponsored efforts to bring art to the public were not unknown before this time, and sociologist Diana Crane points out that the community arts centers built by the New Deal in the 1930s had some lingering effect in building a bigger public audience for the arts. More important, however, was the burgeoning number of college students and college graduates who made up a new arts audience by the 1960s, and Crane suggests that this was the principal factor that drove the cultural expansion of the era, calling forth new expenditures by federal and state governments, philanthropic foundations, and corporate donors. Beginning roughly in the mid-1960s, when the National Endowment for the Arts (NEA) was established and efforts such as the Ford Foundation's multimillion-dollar grant to municipal ballet companies got under way, these new funding sources revealed the organized form of patronage that replaced the increasingly unreliable model of art support by families of the old urban bourgeois elite. Initially, the NEA had only a pittance at its disposal, less than the Defense Department spent each year on military bands. Still, the NEA's appropriations, like those to state arts councils, grew slowly but steadily in the coming two decades, providing seed money that helped to expand considerably the availability of, and audience for, cultural events, broadly speaking.[23]

Neither the intentions nor the outcomes of this activity were always democratic in a populist sense. In the late 1950s and early 1960s, those who called for new federal expenditures on the arts rested the case for culture partly on a Cold War–inspired wish to boost the grandeur and dignity of the nation and partly on old-fashioned pious notions that art was needed to refine the sensibility in the face of harsh modern life. The building of Lincoln Center was promoted by a mixture of philanthropic narcissism, urban planners' distaste for the poor Latino district occupying those West Side streets, and business interests in real estate and tourism. Audiences there grew in size but remained more or less limited to members of the middle and upper-middle class. Still, there was at least something of a sincere democratic ethos dwelling amid the growing public presence of the arts. The televised Young People's Concerts conducted and narrated from the late 1950s to early 1970s by Leonard Bernstein, maestro of Lincoln Center's New York Philharmonic, were successful ventures in popularization not lacking in musical sophistication, reflecting some of the egalitarian cultural views Bernstein brought with him from the Popular Front sentiments of his youth, and never, according to music historian Joseph Horowitz, suggesting a "patronizing or sanctimonious" posture.[24] Likewise, a producer of plebeian origins, Joseph Papp, offered free Shakespeare performances in New York City parks starting in the late 1950s, intending to reach "a great dispossessed audience" unfamiliar with elite theater.[25] Some artists evoked Galbraith's notion that, in an affluent society, social and cultural needs legitimately rivaled economic imperatives. When poet Robert Frost, in 1959, called for a cabinet-level Department of Arts, he remarked, "I want our poets to be declared equal to—what shall I say?—the scientists. No, to big business."[26]

At the same time, commercial presentation of cultural artifacts was transformed, too, as some media expanded their scope, and others, straining to cope with mutations in the entertainment market, were opened to new artistic impulses. The expansion of book publishing that began with the "paperback revolution" of the late 1940s, the establishment of new postwar houses such as Twayne, Grove, and Praeger, and the appearance of trade paperback imprints such as Anchor and Vintage helped remake literary conventions. The 1957 Supreme Court decision *Roth v. the United States* started to lift the heavy hand of censorship when Justice William Brennan's decision defined obscenity (unprotected by the First Amendment) as only "prurient" writings about sex lacking "ideas having even the slightest redeeming social importance." Confident of meeting that standard in court, Grove Press, under Barney Rosset's editorial control, broke the ban on publication of D. H. Lawrence and Henry Miller novels. Grove went on to play a leading role in constructing a new dissenting literary canon of avant-garde and left-wing writing for the 1960s by importing the work of Bertolt Brecht, Alain Robbe-Grillet, Jean Genet, Eugène Ionesco, Marguerite Duras, Jorge Luis Borges, and Frantz Fanon and publishing a mixed bag of American outsiders such as John Rechy, LeRoi Jones, and Denise Levertov in the bohemian *Evergreen Review*. In another field, court decisions challenged movie censorship and Hollywood's monopolistic theater practices. In their wake, the stress that television and suburban migration put on American movie companies, combined with the growing availability of new European films, helped foster a "new American cinema" in the mid-1960s that was formally sophisticated, self-consciously critical of social and political conventions, and franker in portraying sexual relations.[27]

While decline of the industry fostered the stress and diversification that helped revitalize American moviemaking, rapid growth of the youth market for popular music occasioned a degree of instability and aesthetic renewal in the recording business. In the mid-1950s, the new "crossover" music of rock 'n' roll challenged the color line as a high school–based peer culture found more discretionary income at its disposal, and a bevy of small-scale producers worked to capture regional styles and young performers on record. Following this bloom in new firms with hit records, the big labels reestablished their industry dominance by the early 1960s, a development blamed by some observers for sustaining the bland and treacly pop fare of those years. Meanwhile, more localized milieus of folk, blues, and soul music, combined with the so-called British invasion of bands that recovered the styles of the first wave of rock 'n' roll, nurtured a mass audience that unsettled the recording industry once again in the mid-1960s. The big labels that fared best in this environment, such as Warner Brothers, benefited from the activities of talent scouts and producers with a bohemian or freelance flair who insisted on "following the artist" (not the money) in pursuit of new acts.[28] Meanwhile, young performers and their audiences continued to feel that they shared a kind of intuitive communication beyond the ken of an uncomprehending cultural establishment. Of course, this consumer market exerted a strong pull on entertainment industry moguls, so that the rising youth culture gained mass exposure in the commercial media. Even though television, the newest, most centralized of the mass media, gave the impression that communications in the affluent society were narrowly limited to a set of homogenized images approved by broadcasting elites, the networks helped let out the news of this turbulent new field of creativity. In its own way, television played out one version of the contradiction between concentrated organization and popular expression.

Alienation, Individualism, and Community

In many respects, the growing priority of social relations in the affluent society took the perverse form of imperious social organizations shaping the course of everyday life: institutional behemoths such as corporations, mass universities, service bureaucracies, and the military establishment. Coordinated action in a society of abundance might as well swamp as liberate the individual. Cultural criticism in the 1940s and 1950s had responded to such prospects by mounting a common critique of "conformism," but the 1960s opened with a subtle shift of perspective to focus instead on "alienation." Although these two concerns were not antithetical, and survived together as two sides of the same coin, the advent of the idea of alienation can be traced to the importation of two streams of thought, French existentialism and Marxist humanism, that achieved great currency in American intellectual life during the years just before and after 1960. Given the awkward relation between these two intellectual currents and the problems of interpretation posed by each of them, it is hardly surprising that the significance of alienation remained ambiguous. The concept promoted both a search for personal freedom from unfulfilling routine and a search for community to assuage a pressing sense of personal isolation. Observers often misconstrue the tone of intellectual life in the 1960s, however, by failing to recognize how cultural criticism turned from the complaint that everyone was too securely wedded to the given order of things toward a greater insistence that individuals were far too divorced from others and from the consequences of their own actions.[29]

The work of the French existentialists, particularly Jean-Paul Sartre and Albert Camus, first came to attention in the United States right after World War II, but except for winning a small group of champions, existentialism was widely dismissed in popular and academic philosophical circles as a nihilistic doctrine hostile to science and moral values. The existentialists' second chance in American letters, from 1956 to 1960, was far more successful. The number of people familiar with Sartre "dramatically increased" with the first complete translation of *Being and Nothingness* in 1956 by University of Colorado professor Hazel Barnes and the appearance of compelling surveys such as Walter Kaufmann's *Existentialism from Dostoevsky to Sartre* and William Barrett's *Irrational Man*. Camus's *The Rebel* was also reissued in a revised translation, followed by several volumes of his essays. By 1965 existentialism remained "the hottest thing in town" for philosophy students, wrote one college teacher.[30]

A basic existentialist proposition was the putative loss of meaning in the world. For the German philosopher Martin Heidegger, who began writing in the 1920s, the crude, instrumentalizing norms of modern civilization had irredeemably wrecked a prior world suffused with, and ordered by, spirit. Sartre's left-wing sympathies ran contrary to the conservative import of Heidegger's cultural critique, but Sartre assumed no less desolate a view of modern experience, propounding a robust but bleak atheism. For Camus, a chastened socialist activist, the world war had revealed a world gone mad, events run amok, making no sense on any scale of human understanding. The conviction, then, that the world at large offered no meaning one could embrace gave rise to a sense of exile, loneliness, or homelessness—a condition deemed permanent. "Man feels an alien," Camus wrote. "His exile is without remedy, since he is deprived of a lost home or the hope of a promised land. This divorce between man and his life, the actor and his setting, is ... the feeling of absurdity."[31] Existentialism's better reception in the late 1950s, however, rested in part on the more affirmative image of it provided by interpreters such as Barnes, who approached the subject partly under the influence of William James. Although not inclined to embrace reason and science as American pragmatists did, the existentialists resembled them at least in rejecting absolutes, first principles, and the search for certainty, describing experience as something varied, contingent, and open-ended. On that basis, the existentialists fashioned a doctrine of freedom and responsibility that emphasized one's need to act, in the endeavor of constructing a world, and to face squarely the consequences of those actions. Freedom itself, however, was an absolute. Choice was a duty, the means of creating oneself in the world; flight from choice, on the other hand, was the mark of "bad faith." Acting to conform with the expectations of others or to win their esteem, pretending that one's life was determined by social, political, or psychological forces beyond one's control, meant accepting the status of an inert object. Such "bad faith" denied the basic truth of human existence, freedom of the subject, and rendered the person "inauthentic." Hence the dual aspect of alienation in Sartre's view: freedom was to be accepted "not in ecstasy but in anguish … a realization of one's isolation" and thus was understood as the condition of being permanently alien in the world; however, the common experience of dependence, or conformism, was alienation too—alienation from self, from the freedom of the subject, and hence lack of authenticity.[32]

Sartre's doctrine of existential loneliness suggested an extreme form of individualism and even perhaps a measure of political quietism, but the heroic sense of freedom that won Sartre his newfound American appeal actually derived from his experience of struggle against the Nazi occupation of France. Largely written before or during the war's early years, *Being and Nothingness* mingled moods of despair and action; Sartre's recognition of the "weight of history" and the experience of collective solidarity during the war led him later, in the 1950s, to attempt a fusion of existentialism and Marxism. Camus likewise recognized in the Resistance a potent sense of fraternity that helped transcend absurdity, and whereas *The Rebel* criticized Promethean revolutionism, it was intended to vindicate a concept of collective political action that could provide meaningful order to the human world. Some readers in the United States found in Sartre a demand for undiluted nonconformity and saw in Camus's pained call for limits to human aspiration a withdrawal from political engagement. But many others, encountering existential individualism in the late 1950s and early 1960s, took it, as Camus and the later Sartre would have wished, as a doctrine of heroic resistance that entailed political commitment and collective endeavor.[33]

Different emphases figured in the simultaneous importation of Marxian writings on alienation. This theme had come to play a significant part in the understanding of Karl Marx only in the 1920s and 1930s, when European writers such as Georg Lukács and Karl Korsch explored the Hegelian elements of Marx's thought, and Marx's Paris manuscripts of 1844 concerning the phenomenon of "estranged (or alienated) labor" were discovered and published for the first time. The issue had hardly any impact in American discussions of Marxism, however, until around 1960. It was then that the first full English translation of the Paris manuscripts appeared coincidentally with word of a new "Marxist humanism" that had been stirring among European leftists since the events of 1956, when Khrushchev both admitted the scope of Stalin's crimes and sent Soviet troops to crush the Hungarian revolution. Led by figures such as the Polish philosopher Leszek Kolakowski, who defined authentic communism as a "moral duty" to join "the side of the oppressed against their oppressors, the side of the poor against their masters, the side of the persecuted against their persecutors," the new humanism protested Stalinist repression and pseudo-Marxist orthodoxy while evoking the accents of Camus's rebel. In the coming years, other Eastern European dissenters, such as Alexander Solzhenitsyn and Milovan Djilas, were also received in the United States not merely as opponents of dictatorship but also as advocates of a socialist humanism that promised to rejuvenate the Left.[34]

The issue of alienation brought to the United States a small-scale version of the debate simmering since the writings of Lukács and Korsch in the 1920s over the relation between the "young Marx" of the Paris manuscripts and the "mature Marx" of his masterwork, *Capital*. Writing in 1959, the sociologist and former socialist activist Daniel Bell thought all the current talk of alienation in Marx was "indeed strange," not only because modern sociology had long plied the theme effectively in its analysis of bureaucracy and anomie but also because the real "historical Marx" had (to his detriment, Bell said) left the critique of alienation behind as he focused more narrowly on workers' exploitation. Erich Fromm, however, in a long 1961 introduction to selections from the Paris manuscripts, insisted on the essential continuity of Marx's work and its foundation in an ethical critique of capitalism that denounced "its destruction of individuality and its enslavement of man." Indeed, Fromm declared Marxism a form of "humanist existentialism" more relevant to the social and psychological plight of middle-class individuals seeking fulfillment than to current proletarian struggles.[35]

A third alternative in this debate might recognize the way Marx's concept of alienation mutated into the mature critique of "commodity fetishism" in *Capital*. Here Marx sought to show how conventional economic theory served as an ideology of capitalism, falsely portraying historically specific practices of market exchange as unchangeable features of nature ("economic laws") while reflecting accurately the way capitalist economy works in a fashion beyond the control of the humans who make it up. Capitalism is, for Marx, a peculiar form of society in which individuals are subject not so much to other people who obviously wield force but to social relations that appear in impersonal, abstract form—in the form of the market (the force of price fluctuations and business cycles), in the demands of technological change that reorganize jobs in unanticipated ways, and in economic "development" that follows a course all but impervious to human choice and control. Marx's target, Moishe Postone writes, is capitalism as "an alienated form of society."[36]

The coincidence of existentialist and Marxist currents of thought produced a fruitful muddle including dual notions of alienation, one concerning the plight of the individual in pursuit of meaning and the other addressing the nature of society as a thing apart, beyond control. Further variations appeared. The Beat writers who came on the American literary scene in the mid-1950s continued to hold influence into the early 1960s, promoting alienation in the mode of romantic protest against a militarized mass society. Their desire to break free, achieving libidinal release and expanded consciousness, gave them a Dionysian flavor but one qualified by a deeply religious temperament (Allen Ginsberg's and Gary Snyder's orientation to Buddhism, Jack Kerouac's devout Catholicism), a sense of solidarity with the poor, oppressed, and outcast, and an urgent longing for tenderness. A distinct style of alienation, graced by the name "existential," was propounded by Norman Mailer, especially in his 1957 essay "The White Negro": here, desire to free all momentary passions of sex and violence reflected the individual's desperation in facing a mad world hell-bent on crushing freedom and wreaking mass destruction. Lacking the religious temperament that led the Beats to identify with what Ginsberg called "the lamb in America," and the insistence on responsibility that gave French existentialism an austere moral rigor, Mailer's stance was more heedless, intent on projecting the will beyond bounds.[37]

The concept of alienation could spawn a variety of motives, ranging from an antinomian individualism to an ardent desire to build intimacy and community. Here lay another contradiction in the culture and intellectual life of the 1960s. When, in 1965, J. Glenn Gray tried to explain to the middle-class parents he imagined reading *Harper's* "why existentialism is capturing the students," he persisted in describing his students as "rebel-without-a-cause" individualists. "To a man," he wrote, "Existentialists are against group activities."[38] Yet others who responded to the vogue of alienation saw in it the imperative to reconstruct social bonds. The idea of alienation weighed heavily on the young activists who converted the student affiliate of the League for Industrial Democracy into Students for a Democratic Society (SDS) and those who founded the Student Nonviolent Coordinating Committee (SNCC), both in 1960; in both these camps, the idea of "community" as an answer to isolation and powerlessness stood as a vague but potent lure. The idea of alienation remained current in the critique of "dissociation"—a disabling, demoralizing distance between self and others, between actions and consequences—that became one of the watchwords of intellectual discussion throughout the decade. Thus the rebellion against constraint and in pursuit of independence was only one side of the contradictory ambience of the 1960s, and not always the weightiest one. Looking back on that decade from afar, we might recognize how, amid the ambiguities of alienation and the demands of

17

the affluent society, thinkers and actors muddled their way toward something that might look like a kind of social individualism, promising both autonomy and engagement.

A More Social Democracy or Rule by Elites?

The reformist promise of affluence, combined with the critique of alienation and the desire for an alternative to it, helped frame the most telling political contradiction of the time. Galbraith and like-minded writers suggested the need to move toward a more social democracy, in which public resources would be marshaled by democratic government to meet a wide range of social needs. Yet the specter of alienation in a highly organized society suggested a different vision, one that perceived an antidemocratic drift in American life toward rule by elites. For the rest of the decade, tension between these two prospects created one of the central preoccupations of American intellectual and cultural life, the problem of democracy—what it meant and what it took to realize democracy in American life.

The intellectual debate had taken some curious turns in preceding years. Ironically, one of the most incisive observers of the American democratic temperament was an ardent opponent of popular democracy, the Austrian émigré economist Joseph A. Schumpeter. Professor at Harvard University from the early 1930s to his death in 1950, Schumpeter believed as fervently in the heroic qualities of the entrepreneur as he did in the depravity or inferiority of the masses. New Deal interference in economic affairs and its demagogic populism stirred in him some disgust, and though he believed capitalism itself remained a powerful engine of economic growth, his influential 1942 book *Capitalism, Socialism, and Democracy* concluded that capitalism would not likely survive in the United States, for the democratic temper of the country militated against those essentially aristocratic virtues, such as the frank defense of great property identified with a family lineage, that were necessary for the bourgeoisie to rule in its own name on behalf of free enterprise. Still, Schumpeter would make the best out of a dismal prospect: socialism, which he believed to be the wave of the future, might work if understood as central planning of the economy by experts and could be compatible with democracy if democracy was understood as a system in which the role of "the people" was strictly limited. "The democratic method is that institutional arrangement for arriving at political decisions in which individuals acquire the power to decide by means of a competitive struggle for the people's vote." Furthermore, "the voters outside of parliament must respect the division of labor between themselves and the politicians they elect. They must not withdraw confidence too easily between elections and they must understand that, once they have elected an individual, political action is his business and not theirs."[39]

Nothing could be further from the assumptions of John Dewey, the leading American philosopher of the early twentieth century. Dewey pictured democracy instead as the political norm of a great community, a body increasingly conscious of itself as a unit, knit together by free communication and offering all individuals the opportunity to realize their creative and rational capacities that would come with a sense of belonging. Ironically, some of Dewey's young disciples in the 1940s went on to purvey what appeared like Schumpeterian theories of democracy on the eve of the 1960s. Political sociologist Seymour Martin Lipset, for instance, had belonged to a group of young socialists who left the Trotskyist movement around 1940 on the grounds that, however acute its criticisms of Stalinist tyranny, Trotskyism had failed to assimilate the culture of democracy as Dewey defined it. Although continuing to view himself as a socialist, Lipset's concern after World War II to define the social conditions that rendered democracy stable and resistant to totalitarian movements led him to a position that echoed a large part of elitist democratic theory: democracy survived, it seemed, where there was a wide umbrella of consensus among leading political players, no astringent debate between political parties over fundamentals, lack of sharp divisions among elements of the population at large, and consequently a popular willingness, aside from electoral participation, to let politics go of its own momentum.[40]

Political scientist Robert A. Dahl had also appealed to Dewey in a 1940 dissertation that promoted a model of "economic democracy" based on pragmatic reform and the planning theory of market socialism. But by the time he came to the fore of American intellectual life, with his *Preface to Democratic Theory* (1956) and *Who Governs?* (1961), Dahl limited himself to a modest defense of what he called "polyarchal democracy." Dahl adopted Schumpeterian views in stating that a "numerical majority is incapable of undertaking any coordinated action" in public affairs and that democracy was defined by electoral competition among politicians. What won electoral contests was a politician's ability to assemble a numerical voting majority from many particular constituencies backing one or another of several planks, no one of which necessarily reflected majoritarian sentiment: hence the "rule by minorities" that Dahl named "polyarchy." Dahl refrained from trumpeting the virtues of this system but claimed that "it does nonetheless provide a high probability that any active and legitimate group will make itself heard effectively at some stage in the process of decision [and this] is no mean thing in a political system." Dahl was no conservative opponent of democracy, for he admired the political tradition of social reform that sought to meet popular needs in the teeth of opposition from conservative elites. It was, however, the very modesty of his claims on behalf of American democracy that showed, almost poignantly, how far American reformers had pulled in their horns after World War II.[41]

Dahl also played a part in the empirical debate over the distribution of power in the United States, a question reopened almost single-handedly by the sociologist C. Wright Mills and his 1956 book *The Power Elite* for the first time since investigations of economic concentration in the late 1930s. Mills caustically argued that any significant power—that which decided the major issues of national and international consequence—was increasingly remote from the people at large and instead concentrated in a narrow elite, a number of conversant individuals sitting atop institutional bureaucracies in three orders of American life: the great corporations, the federal government, and the military apparatus. Mills's portrait was fairly crude, lacking any convincing account of the dynamic forces in society that shaped *what* the elite aimed to do, and *how* (or how far) it accomplished its ends. But his opponents were not too convincing either. Talcott Parsons, the reigning chief of American sociology, responded to Mills with a combination of theoretical sophistication and social apologetics, arguing that power in the United States was now distributed with far less reference to inherited wealth and social standing than in the past and in much closer proportion to expertise and demonstrated skill in institutional leadership. Dahl's *Who Governs?* described a "pluralist" political situation in which decisions were made by politicians who lacked the social glue of an elite caste and instead responded piecemeal to a variety of special interests in the community. His account, however, admittedly failed to address the question of concentrated power on a national level and concurred with Mills in describing a hollowed-out public sphere in which "most citizens use their political resources scarcely at all."[42]

Debate in political science and sociology seemed split between Mills's elite and Dahl's pluralist analyses, the latter dominating the academy, but this conventional way of distinguishing schools of thought does not really grasp the drift of opinion in the 1960s. Before long, it was common coin to argue that a new form of elite domination had straitjacketed American political life, and this typical critique took off as much from pluralist premises as Millsian ones. To be sure, the analysis of the new elite society could take many forms. Sharing Galbraith's optimistic view of the evanescence of classic capitalism, the iconoclastic lawyer David Bazelon wrote in his *Power in America* (1967) that "organizational power has replaced the problem of property" and that organizations (or "bureaus administering technology") were owned by a new class of planners that gained power and prestige from education and office rather than wealth. "American society is closing up," he wrote.[43] Bazelon was actually one of the more sanguine observers, counting on this "new class" to cultivate a leadership ethos that would put national power behind majoritarian interests and turn aside the regressive force of old private business interests. Much more disconsolate was Theodore Lowi's critical pluralism in his 1969 book *The End of Liberalism*. According to Lowi, the United States had become virtually a "corporate state," in which organized groups brought their particular interests before administrators who viewed public affairs solely as a process of bargaining among elites. In such a system that "shut out the public," Lowi concluded, "the citizen has become an administré, and the question is how to be certain he remains a citizen."[44]

The currency achieved by these critiques of the new elite society showed how much the concept of democracy was transformed and renewed in the 1960s by aspirations for popular participation in self-government. In the realm of practical affairs, nothing gave a greater impulse to reshaping the democratic idea than the black freedom struggle beginning in the mid-1950s. From the start, this struggle entailed not only an attempt to bring an ostracized group under the purview of citizenship rights but also a substantial redefinition of citizenship itself. City movements such as the bus boycott in Montgomery, Alabama, from 1955 to 1956, and the regional campaign begun by the Southern Christian Leadership Conference (SCLC) in 1957, showed that demonstrators had great capacities for organization, commitment, and solidarity. Moreover, popular applications of social knowledge, such as the alternative transit system created by and for Montgomery blacks during the bus boycott and the uncredentialed neighbor-teachers recruited by SCLC organizer Septima Clark to run literacy schools, provided a striking riposte to the conventional view that modern society was too complex for forms of direct democracy to be practicable.[45] The movement goal of "self-determination" was defined by both the achievement of personal dignity and the vitality of collective action. In years to come, some movement leaders, furthermore, concluded that establishment of genuine racial equality required fuller social services, income redistribution, and economic planning. In all these respects, the struggle pushed the definition of democracy beyond old associations with a market economy and minimal state.

Under the force of this impulse, a group of young radical intellectuals, meeting in 1962 as Students for a Democratic Society (SDS), issued *The Port Huron Statement*. In the *Statement*, they performed the remarkable feat of leaping back over 20 years of Schumpeterian liberalism to recoup something like John Dewey's ideal of democratic community. In their model, which they called a "democracy of individual participation," or more simply "participatory democracy," the SDS intellectuals imagined individuals finding fulfillment as citizens in an ongoing process of self-government. Surely, not all advocates of a revitalized democracy in the 1960s advocated a participatory model: the views of Bazelon and Lowi, for instance, might be described instead as "national progressive," calling for a more purposeful, central polity responsive to majoritarian interests. But the SDS idea found echoes among writers such as Hannah Arendt and Sheldon Wolin, who relied on the ideal of the polis in classical political philosophy to call for a renewal of citizenship. Wolin's *Politics and Vision* (1960) insisted that politics per se dealt with "what is general and integrative to men, a life of common involvements," a view he thought was lost to a modern society dominated by organizations that represented special interests and recognized only "the specialized roles assigned the individual." "Citizenship" restored wholeness to the person and society; thus democracy served as an answer to alienation.[46]

Still, Schumpeter was most incisive when he discerned, despite his own preference for an elitist conception of democracy, a *popular* democratic temper in American life that treaded on the prerogatives of wealthy elites needed for capitalism to work. Indeed, the sharp conflicts marking the 1960s derived from the convergence of vibrant democratic forces with a range of social demands that were out of tune with the standards of a capitalist society. This tension was evident in the black freedom struggle, whose demands for social equality ultimately called for the redistribution of economic resources; in the growth of universities cultivating a sense of social responsibility that student and faculty protesters turned against military-industrial research; and in the popular youth culture, where commercial entertainment coexisted with a communal sensibility. Galbraith's diagnosis of affluence, by recognizing social imperatives that pushed against the limits of bourgeois economic dogmas, had something of the same spirit. Yet while the discourse of affluence pointed to the contradiction between new social forms of experience and the private power of capitalist wealth, it also helped downplay the intensity of that conflict. For Galbraith and Bazelon, capitalism per se was on the wane: wealth had surrendered power to office, profits no longer were the absolute desideratum of production, poverty was more a matter of public neglect than economic necessity. Indeed, liberal faith in the gradual victory of social principles over private prerogatives both helped excite expectations of far-ranging change and obscured the limits to change imposed by the entrenched inequities of American life: here lay another crucial contradiction in this new age of reform. In the end, the established forms of wealth and power went largely undisturbed. Nonetheless, as greater possibilities at least reached the awareness of many, American thought and culture grew turbulent and rife with contention; the realm of ideas and arts became more subject to instability than the foundations of American social structure itself. For that very reason, what was then new and provocative in American intellectual and cultural life not only warrants historical attention but has lost little of its critical edge in the years since.

two

Knowledge and Ideology

With the postwar academic revolution, intellectual life became more thoroughly socialized—organized in formal institutions relying on public funds as well as private (corporate) resources, dependent on the course of public policy, and often involved in making it. Writers, scholars, and critics, forced by these new circumstances to confront the relation of ideas to their social context, of intellectuals to public affairs, and of knowledge to ideology, debated the social status and purpose of intellectual activity throughout the 1960s. All these questions became acute in what Russell Jacoby has called the "age of academe." Each age, it seems, has a characteristic mode of organizing intellectual life and shaping its preoccupations. The primacy of the ministry and political philosophy in early America, the romantic mode of the artist-moralist amid antebellum reform, and, later in the nineteenth century, the elite mode of the critic dedicated to preserving the highest achievements of culture: these mark off distinct periods and styles of work. The university model, based on rational criticism, scientific procedure, and disciplinary specialization, first appeared on the eve of the twentieth century but coexisted with a competing model—the "independent intellectual" or freelance critic spawned by the growth of magazine publishing, new popular entertainments, class struggles, and radical movements that together formed an alternative pole of attraction. Only after World War II did the expanded university system swallow the independent, becoming home to the great bulk of those claiming an intellectual vocation.[1]

Debate over the character of this new arrangement tended to polarize into two positions: one described the organization of intellectual life and its integration with social affairs as the onset of a new Enlightenment in which the uses of reason would not only guide policy making but also take the lead in remaking society; the other described the socialization of intellect as the decline of critical thought—a loss of intellectual autonomy, the withering of dissent, and the impoverishment of public discourse. Yet neither camp could resolve the key problem posed by the new conditions of knowledge, namely, the relation between the practical relevance and the objectivity of ideas. Ideas no longer dwelled within a sheltered preserve but appeared to be social arti- facts having a definite utility, and new justifications for their truth and integrity were required as their "disinterestedness" became much less certain.

Contradictions of Socialized Intellect

In 1963, when Clark Kerr delivered the lectures that became *The Uses of the University,* he had more than 10 years' experience as a top administrator in the country's most dynamic center of public higher education. As former chancel- lor of the University of California at Berkeley and then president of the entire university system, Kerr trumpeted the promise of a new Enlightenment as he tried to square intellectual service to powerful social organizations beyond the campus gates with the doctrine of disinterested scholarship. His background and temperament suited him for this delicate task. A lifelong Quaker eager to ensure harmony in social affairs, Kerr was trained in the 1930s by the Berke- ley economist Paul Taylor, who did pioneering studies on the plight of migrant farm workers. After serving on the War Labor Board, Kerr built a career as a labor arbitrator and a scholar of labor-management relations.

Although his associations with Berkeley scholars moonlighting at the Pop- ular Front–inspired California Labor School raised some eyebrows, Kerr signed the anticommunist loyalty oath demanded of University of California faculty in 1949. The controversy over the oaths, however, left him anxious about California's conservative social and political elites and their hostility toward academic life. A man of liberal, mildly social democratic views chas- tened by the Cold War red scare, Kerr regarded the conditions of social order with jealous concern while championing the virtues of democratic progress in an organized society.

Kerr saw the late 1950s and early 1960s as a watershed in academic devel- opment, a "hinge of history" that sent universities "swinging in another direc- tion" away from the models of the past.[2] The new university—like Berke- ley—was neither a humanistic college nor a scientific institute but both of these and more (a center of public discourse and the arts, a base for new exten- sion services). Kerr called it a "multiversity" for its variegated form, coining the term that critics would use scornfully for years afterward to label the new university a bureaucratic monstrosity or a kind of degraded, commercialized sprawl—an "L.A. of the intellect," as critic Edgar Friedenberg put it. Kerr did not deny that the new university was an unwieldy creature, but he admired its unique combination of values: a "German" commitment to scholarly research, an "American" egalitarian commitment of popular access to higher education, and a kind of practical engagement he called the "socialist" principle of "service to society," an aim distinct from the elite traditionalism that used to govern respectable American colleges.[3]

Friedenberg recalled the "traditional" purposes of the university as "liberal study, the cultivation of a socially responsible intellectual elite, and a sense of continuity with the culture of the past," purposes that made the university "society's specialized organ of critical self-scrutiny" rather than a company "servile in [its] readiness to accommodate to immediate social demand." Friedenberg and Kerr held very different estimations of the past. Kerr's view of the old bourgeois college, the sort dominated by conservative trustees and faculties more devoted to hierarchical values of learning than to practical knowledge, was the one most current in liberal and left-wing circles when Kerr came up in the 1930s. In his ardent progressivism, Kerr was unembarrassed to embrace a more instrumentalist vision of the university. Still, he admitted that the new university faced a problem in maintaining "internal" control over its own affairs in the face of influence wielded by grant givers from government, foundations, and "the surrounding and sometimes engulfing industry." The mild and polite manner in which Kerr raised this issue soft-pedaled the real dilemma at the heart of his argument: how to justify the social engagement of academic work while upholding the principle of professional autonomy, or "academic freedom," premised on the disinterestedness or objectivity of scholarship.

This was the problem facing those who viewed socialization of the conditions of knowledge as a new Enlightenment. The problem was addressed in four ways, which appeared prominently in Kerr's account. First, to justify the social engagement of research, the doctrine of the new Enlightenment supposed there existed in society a robust consensus of views and purposes, so that research in principle need not fear subordination to the biases of special, or abusive, interests. Second, it made an "engineering" conception of science the model for all disciplines, whereby the conclusions of research would be regarded as objective, usable knowledge available to all, regardless of the particular purposes motivating an inquiry or the intended application of its results. Kerr's commitment to the premise of stout social consensus was apparent in his strident Cold War patriotism; he mocked the Marxist idea that class struggle divided American society and lauded the university as a crucial support to the nation in its contest with the Soviet Union for power and prestige. The second premise, a kind of positivism that stringently separated means and ends (knowledge and its applications), was implicit in Kerr's title, *The Uses of the University,* and his failure to ask whether the meaning of ideas was shaped by the "uses" they fulfilled.[4] Thus even engaged knowledge appeared autonomous in principle, at least in the sense that it remained the same for all comers.

Advocates of the new Enlightenment hedged their bets by adding to their assumptions of social consensus and engineering positivism a third principle: that in the merger of universities and social life at large, academic values assumed priority or vied for hegemony in guiding affairs. For Kerr, the very economic dynamism Fritz Machlup ascribed to the "knowledge industry" gave education a leading role in shaping society. Those "who fear the further involvement of the university in the life of society," distressed that "the university and segments of industry are becoming more alike," could rest assured, for although they worried "that the university will lose its objectivity and its freedom," Kerr expected academic norms to triumph: "Society is more desirous of objectivity and more tolerant of freedom than it used to be." Others shared Kerr's evolutionary confidence in the demise of vested interests. In *The Academic Revolution,* David Riesman and Christopher Jencks claimed that the new university helped disseminate meritocratic norms throughout society, and that graduate and professional schools served as an advance guard advocating proposals for social reform (such as collectivized forms of medical care) that before long seeped into normal professional belief and practice.[5] Finally, from the first three principles of the new Enlightenment came perhaps the most vulnerable postulate of the whole piece: that it is possible to accept the social involvement of the university in extra-academic affairs while excluding political conflict from campus. All four elements in the notion of a new Enlightenment would be challenged sharply in the 1960s, but the last two, regarding educational primacy and an apolitical academy, will be examined first.

The principle of educational primacy was hardly new to the 1960s, for the view of universities as pacesetters for social change reflected a historic American conviction that schooling had a transformative power in shaping the fate of individuals and the moral conduct of society as a whole. A test of this premise could be found in the 1966 report by a federal commission, headed by sociologist James S. Coleman, on the state and consequences of racial segregation and desegregation in public schools. Based on a massive nationwide survey of school conditions and student achievement, *Equality of Educational Opportunity* was the most talked-about social scientific study of public policy ever issued in the United States, next to Gunnar Myrdal's *An American Dilemma.* Commissioned and funded by an act of Congress, the Coleman report illustrated the public uses of knowledge in a new age, but its findings also challenged liberal confidence in several ways. The report concluded that equalizing resources devoted to racially segregated schools did not erase large gaps in measurements of academic performance by black and white students, and that the modest positive effect school integration had on performance by black students stemmed primarily from their being exposed to white students from more affluent homes. The report suggested that factors other than the level of educational resources as such, notably the social class of students' families and other features of their homes and neighborhoods, had far more power to explain differences in student performance. Such findings disappointed civil rights advocates, who cited decrepit conditions in ghetto schools, along with teachers' racism or indifference, as causes of black students' poor grades and graduation rates; to some antiracist activists, Coleman's conclusions seemed to resemble the arguments of those who defended ghetto schools on the grounds that their deplorable results were really due to "adverse influences of the home and the streets"—a case of blaming the victim rather than the institution.[6]

Yet the Coleman report was misconstrued if taken as an attack on integration or an excuse for persisting inequality. Rather, its findings implied that dramatic social change had to *precede* educational innovation if equality was to be achieved.[7] Writing in defense of the Coleman report, Christopher Jencks, an independent critic of social policy, reached the startling conclusion that almost nothing schools did (establish better school libraries, add more or newer books, raise teacher salaries, reduce class size, add classroom auxiliary personnel) reliably improved student performance. Jencks sympathized with critics of conventional schooling, such as Paul Goodman, Herbert Kohl, and John Holt, who argued, among other things, that competitive learning and hidden or open practices of labeling (or ranking) students reinforced failure.[8] School resources alone did not explain performance variations, and American schools—rich or poor—did little to help weak students become better learners. Later studies would reassert a correlation between inadequate school funding and student failure in areas populated by members of racial minorities, but Jencks's main point remains compelling. When "a comprehensive picture of inequality in American life" became available, he predicted, it would find that "educational inequality is of marginal importance for either good or ill" and such things as "control over capital" were much more central. Inequality in social class laid roots for inequality in school performance, and modifying schools could not fix the underlying fault. Contrary to Kerr's view of a new Enlightenment, schools bore the impress of society far more than vice versa.[9]

If the Coleman report implicitly undermined one principle of the new Enlightenment, the doctrine's keystone—its hope of accepting the social involvement of higher education while excluding political conflict from campus—was bluntly challenged by the start of large student protests with the Free Speech Movement (FSM) at Berkeley in the fall of 1964 and the Vietnam teach-ins the following spring. Led by activists in local civil rights campaigns, Berkeley's FSM won wide support in its attempt to challenge a new university rule banning political activity from a sidewalk strip just outside campus gates where students customarily set up tables to distribute protest literature and circulate petitions. For the first time, students brought mass civil disobedience to campus and used it effectively: the spectacle of heavy-handed police dragging more than 800 students from an administration building sit-in swung faculty sentiment to the students' side and compelled the university to give up all attempts to regulate campus political activity. Meanwhile, Kerr's refusal to brook any challenge to the administration's rule-making authority, his misguided and fruitless pursuit of compromise solutions, and his duplicity in negotiations tarnished his reputation and helped convince protesters that liberal reformers were enemies, not proponents, of social change.[10]

The rapid spread of the Vietnam teach-ins a few months after this break-through showed how alive the universities were to present political issues. The first teach-in, organized by faculty at the University of Michigan in response to Lyndon Johnson's announcement of bombing raids on North Vietnam and the buildup of U.S. troop strength in South Vietnam, brought 3,000 students to a series of lectures and discussions lasting through the night of March 24–25. Circulars for the event were headed, "Viet-Nam and U.S. Policy: Learn about It/Protest It." Teach-ins at about 35 other campuses led up to the biggest event, the Vietnam Day at Berkeley, on May 21 and 22, during which more than 10,000 people heard FSM leader Mario Savio, the Marxist writer Isaac Deutscher, Senator Ernest Gruening, the independent journalist I. F. Stone, the young historian and radical pacifist Staughton Lynd, and a tape-recorded message from British philosopher Bertrand Russell. Under the aegis of a Vietnam Day Committee (VDC) led by an energetic community activist, Jerry Rubin, the Berkeley gathering assumed a more left-wing tone than earlier teach-ins. Speakers condemned the "myths and legends" of American Cold War policy and called for "militant direct action ... so massive and publicized that everyone will be speaking of Vietnam protests, and how best to end the war, at every mealtime." "American society is well organized—we must be too," the VDC declared. Here, integration of the campus with social affairs assumed quite a different guise than in Kerr's *Uses of the University.*[11]

Dominating the teach-ins was a rhetoric of "responsibility" that looked back to the Nazi campaign to exterminate European Jews and determined not to let public indifference give sway to official barbarity again.[12] In the late 1950s and early 1960s, a burst of Holocaust literature had appeared, including survivor memoirs by Elie Wiesel and Primo Levi, books about the German pastor Dietrich Bonhoeffer, who had been martyred for his participation in an assassination plot against Hitler, a play *(The Deputy)* about the failure of Pius XII to speak out against the Judeocide, and the first major English-language history of the so-called Final Solution, by Raul Hilberg.[13] No single piece of writing gained such notoriety, however, and raised the issue of responsibility so forcefully as Hannah Arendt's *Eichmann in Jerusalem* (1963). Arendt portrayed the 1961 Israeli prosecution of the Nazi fugitive as a kind of show trial that misrepresented the nature of Adolf Eichmann's crime. He was neither the mastermind of the Final Solution—though his job as executive in charge of Jewish deportations and transport throughout German-occupied Europe gave him a crucial role in carrying it out—nor the "monster" of murderous intent the prosecutors described. Rather, he was a man who had no sense of vitality, no human feelings, outside of belonging to an organization and faithfully carrying out, with the greatest expertise, his instructed duties. Claiming to abhor anti-Semitism and mass murder, Eichmann nonetheless remained proud of his record of "loyalty," obedience, and efficacy and thus demonstrated an obdurate disconnection, or ability to distance himself, from what he knew perfectly well was the purpose and result of his actions. "That such remoteness from reality and such thoughtlessness can wreak more havoc than all the evil instincts taken together which, perhaps, are inherent in man—that was, in fact, the lesson one could learn in Jerusalem." This is what Arendt meant by saying Eichmann illustrated "the fearsome, word-and-thought defying *banality of evil.*"[14]

Combined with Arendt's acid portraits of some Zionist leaders and the notorious Judenräte dragooned into collaboration with the Nazis, this misunderstood phrase helped rouse a storm of protest among critics (led by the Anti-Defamation League of B'nai B'rith and some, but not all, of the prominent New York Jewish intellectuals) who accused Arendt of minimizing Eichmann's crime or blaming the victims of Nazi extermination for their own plight. Arendt deserved neither charge. She intended to reveal the weird dislocation that accompanied Eichmann's commitment to executive skill, the bureaucratic mentality of an archetypal alienated man distant from the real world of consequences, and to describe the "hollowness of respectability" as "the good people" of Europe, "not only among the persecutors but also among the victims," conceded to disaster or sought excuses for the futility of resisting it. These lessons weighed on the minds of dissenters in the 1960s, as did the saving exceptions, the instances of resistance in Denmark and elsewhere to Nazi policies, the actions that showed, Arendt wrote, that "under conditions of terror most people will comply but *some people will not.*" Such resistance counted a great deal, for "humanly speaking, no more is required, and no more can reasonably be asked, for this planet to remain a place fit for human habitation."[15]

In contrast to the psychological dissociation, social indifference, and organized collaboration Arendt described, responsibility—acknowledgment of the consequences of one's action or inaction—weighed heavily as an injunction guiding American intellectual life. At Berkeley's Sproul Plaza, FSM leader Mario Savio sarcastically urged students not to blame the policemen trying to arrest CORE activist Jack Weinberg, for "they have a job to do ... like Adolph Eichmann." "He fit into the machinery," Savio said, but the students had the duty to "put your bodies upon the gears and upon the wheels ... and ... make it stop."[16] Leaders of the first teach-ins spoke similarly. The University of Michigan psychologist and teach-in organizer Marc Pilisuk reported that faculty felt "transformed" by a "heightened sense of responsibility" as they "chose to make [their academic work] count" in public action. A Washington University philosophy professor who helped organize the teach-in there commented, apparently in response to charges of unprofessional bias in the conduct of the teach-ins, "There is nothing improper in what we are doing here. We are just covering up for, or updating a poorly designed curriculum. We forgot to have courses on Southeast Asian politics in the curriculum this year. The academic community failed in Germany during the 1930s. We are not going to let it happen here."[17]

Such rhetoric gave only one instance of the self-consciousness exhibited by American intellectuals amid a widespread sense that the postwar academic revolution had profoundly altered the terms of creative thought. German sociologist Karl Mannheim had described the modern intelligentsia as "free-floating" or "socially unattached" *(freischwebende)*, a term that, though taken out of context, seemed in American parlance to recall the "independent intellectual" of the early twentieth century who occupied a marginal position outside the academy and was often affiliated with radical politics or modernist aesthetics. When Lewis Coser inverted Mannheim's phrase to write of the "attached intellectual" firmly rooted in universities that were closely bound with the institutions of society at large, it appeared that the new type was one whose intellectual autonomy, and hence capacity for social criticism, was compromised by organizational obligations. To some observers, the trend suggested nothing less than the decline of critical thought in their time, and the socialization of intellect signaled not the liberating sway of reason but the same kind of political "coordination" that ruined the universities of the Third Reich.[18] Yet if one were to resist the corruption of truth by the concerted interests of the powerful organizations the university served, to whom or what did one owe responsibility: a higher standard of disinterestedness or some alternative kind of commitment in intellectual work?

Issues of disinterest and commitment were broached in a series of debates among historians. In a 1960 book on industrial sociology, a field that had grown up since the renowned "Hawthorne experiments" of the 1920s to provide managers with insight into the psychology and social control of workers, Loren Baritz claimed that academic experts, increasingly "absorbed into society," were now less social scientists than "servants of power." The intellectual's "most essential job rests on resistance to his society," Baritz wrote, and one could be either "*intellectually* responsible" or "*socially* responsible," that is, tied to special interests. Put so starkly, Richard Hofstadter objected, the ideal of "criticism" ruled out any respect for "the social usability of a body of ideas" and seemed to demand that intellectuals avoid any "taint of concern with practice." Furthermore, Hofstadter was rankled by Baritz's suggestion that critical integrity required "repudiation" of society as it existed; openness to the society's virtues as well as its faults, Hofstadter wrote, fit better with their common conviction "that the essential business of the intellectual is ... the disinterested pursuit of truth." The young Marxist David Eakins, writing in the new University of Wisconsin journal of radical scholarship, *Studies on the Left*, provided a kind of rejoinder to both Baritz and Hofstadter, merging their different emphases on criticism and practicality while challenging the norm of disinterestedness they shared. More important than that, Eakins argued, was "objectivity," understood as "the honest use of the most relevant evidence," and in that sense, objectivity was not incompatible with "partisanship or commitment" to definite social and political values, particularly those opposed to the status quo.[19]

Activists in the 1965 teach-ins mulled over the question of partisanship. Berkeley professor Robert Scalapino had charged that the Vietnam Day program was so "unbalanced"—pretending to educate people about Vietnam while presuming opposition to the war—that "no self-respecting intellectual" would attend; in response, the radical pacifist and historian Staughton Lynd scorned a moral sensibility that could denounce the sin of bias while defending American brutality in South Vietnam. "Some day," Lynd declared, "the entire academic community of this country will look back on the few professors who have publicly protested our Vietnam policy and say, 'They kept the spirit of truth alive.' " Outlining plans for a major antiwar campaign of civil disobedience, Lynd suggested intellectual life was not corrupted but inspired by some kinds of power, namely, "the power of non-violence."[20] Even some of Lynd's allies remained uncomfortable, however, with a tight link between truth and commitment. Historian Christopher Lasch, for instance, joined the antiwar teach-ins; like Baritz, Lasch denounced a group of liberal anticommunist writers who had received undercover CIA funds for "serv[ing] the interests of the state, not the interests of intellect." At stake, however, was not merely the question of whether to serve the status quo or change it. Indeed, in his complex book *The New Radicalism in America*, Lasch criticized radical intellectuals of the Progressive Era for their longing to make ideas effective in the "real" world of political power: precisely that desire for engagement, he argued, motivated reform in one era and Cold War apologetics in another. With poignant ambivalence, Lasch urged intellectuals to adopt the vocation of political criticism yet avoid the lure of activism.[21]

A similar ambivalence about commitment and disinterestedness marked the work of an even more prominent activist, MIT linguist and antiwar organizer Noam Chomsky. Chomsky had established an international reputation in the late 1950s with his formulation of a "transformational generative" grammar, a theory intended to account for people's capacity to use grammatical form in producing an unbounded variety of proper sentences and to recognize the relation between variant forms of sentences (for instance, in the active and passive voice). A sharp critic of B. F. Skinner's behaviorist analysis of language learning, Chomsky distinguished himself as a humanist who stressed the key role of individual creativity in language use. By 1966, when he published his first philosophical book, *Cartesian Linguistics*, Chomsky had concluded that the relatively rapid acquisition of language by children showed that the human mind holds an innate grammatical element that sustains universal human linguistic capacities. It was this "rationalism" that led Chomsky to term himself a "child of the Enlightenment" who believed humans have

31

instinctive inclinations toward freedom, reason, and morality.[22] As anthropologist Dell Hymes, a leading proponent of sociolinguistics, pointed out, however, Chomsky's rationalism overlooked the social and cultural dimensions of language use and structure.[23] Language was far more embedded in particular kinds of social interaction, more bound to the practical needs of users in their distinct communities, than Chomsky allowed.

There was a clear parallel between Chomsky's linguistics and his politics once he became deeply involved in antiwar agitation after 1965. His rationalistic rhetoric always made it appear that his antiwar convictions stemmed from nothing but abstract intellectual principle, rather than any particular social interests or ideals. The title of his best-known political essay of the time, "The Responsibility of Intellectuals" (1966–1967)—the very title evoked the most urgent concern of dissenting academics in that time—suggested that a native penchant for truth and morality was all one needed to recognize the viciousness of the war's aims and methods. Very simply, it was "the responsibility of intellectuals to speak the truth and to expose lies." Chomsky made a strong case that the complicity of academic intellectuals such as Arthur M. Schlesinger Jr., Walt Rostow, McGeorge Bundy, Henry Kissinger, and other high-profile academics in government (an elite he dubbed "the new mandarins") in forming and defending American foreign policy was morally disgraceful. The double-talk of American propaganda, which called the war against the rebel National Liberation Front a "democratic" crusade while admitting that the guerrillas had more popular support than the Saigon regime, and even more the cold-blooded discussions of bombing tactics by expert policy analysts, Chomsky argued, showed a striking disregard for the truth, and consequences, of ideas. Having thus betrayed their vocation in the name of "national interests," Chomsky wrote, contemporary intellectuals fostered a profound "moral degeneration" in American life at large.[24] (Chomsky was not the only one to challenge the integrity of the intelligentsia. Conservative scholars Robert Nisbet and Thomas Molnar authored comparable polemics from a distinct point of view, complaining that classical virtues of learning and wisdom, geared toward maintaining traditions, had been lost in a world demanding that all knowledge have a practical use.)[25]

In condemning the social and political associations that shaped the work and status of the new mandarins, however, Chomsky suggested that his criticism issued from a detached standpoint of autonomous reason, an Archimedian point beyond society, and that "truth" served as an abstract standard against the corruptions of power. These rationalistic premises were subject to the same criticism Hymes made of Chomsky's linguistics: political discourse and commitment could hardly be abstracted from the array of social forces shaping action in particular settings. Moreover, the implicit insistence that the life of the mind remain apart from social attachments not only strained against the drift of Chomsky's own time (toward socialization of intellect) but also seemed ill suited to his own involvement in mass protest. Like other dissenters, Chomsky decried the advent of "the scholar-experts [or mandarins] who are replacing the free-floating intellectuals of the past," citing as an alternative model of integrity the critic Randolph Bourne, whose famous essay "War and the Intellectuals" decried the apologia the Progressive intelligentsia gave for Woodrow Wilson's war program in 1917.[26] Bourne became a ubiquitous icon of vocation in the mid-1960s, serving as the principal hero in Lasch's *New Radicalism* and as figurehead in Ronald Radosh and Louis Menashe's account of the Vietnam teach-ins.[27] Yet there was something odd in appeals to his name. A yearning to recreate the "unattached" intellectual tacitly assumed that the end of an extra-institutional intellectual vocation had destroyed social criticism and moral integrity, yet the numbers of academic intellectuals who joined protests through such *organized* means as the teach-in suggested that socialized intellect was not incapable of criticism. The answer to corrupting links with centers of authority lay not in the pursuit of an isolated standpoint of "free-floating" autonomy but with the construction of alternative poles of social power.

The End of Ideology Debate and the New Revolt against Positivism

Four premises governed the doctrine of a new Enlightenment: commitment to social consensus, engineering positivism, the principle of educational primacy, and the hope of maintaining an engaged but apolitical academy. The first two became key elements in the decade-long debate that followed publication in 1960 of Daniel Bell's *The End of Ideology*. In these collected essays, Bell, a leader among postwar sociologists, both welcomed the apparent drift of intellectuals in the 1940s and 1950s away from "extreme" political ideologies, especially those of the Left, and decried the loss of vitality in American political thought. For the rest of the decade, writers in a number of fields from anthropology to philosophy argued whether there had been an "end of ideology" in the West since World War II and whether it was, or would be, a good thing—a mark of progress or of decline, of enlightenment or a lapse in criticism. Misguided in many ways and fraught with misunderstandings, the dispute persisted because the idea of an "end of ideology" became embroiled in both the critique of "consensus" and a new revolt against positivism.[28]

The idea of an "end of ideology" had complicated roots in postwar liberal anticommunism and in existentialist critiques of "totalitarianism." Soon after World War II, writers who had once adhered to left-wing politics, such as Arthur Koestler and Sidney Hook, spokesmen of the new transatlantic organization called the Congress for Cultural Freedom (CCF), urged Western intellectuals to overcome their old ideological differences and unite in opposition to Soviet communism. Meanwhile, Albert Camus decried all political

33

doctrines urging people toward apocalyptic conflict, and Hannah Arendt defined "totalitarianism" largely by its commitment to remake the world in the image of doctrinal ideals. Thus an "end of ideology" suggested the dissolution of sharp political boundaries within Western societies (in fact, the CCF's 1955 meeting in Milan lauded the flexibility of policy making in so-called "welfare states," which rejected a strict divide between free markets and government intervention in the economy) and the declining appeal of "total ideologies" that had once infused violent mass movements with messianic aspirations. The "end of ideology" was a celebration of mixed economies devoted to social welfare as well as an appeal for new ways of thinking about politics and social change.[29]

Coming through these currents of thought, Bell entitled his book *The End of Ideology: On the Exhaustion of Political Ideas in the 1950s,* and the combined title and subtitle, seeming at once to celebrate the achievement of social stability and bemoan the inadequacy of contemporary intellectual life, hinted at his ambivalence. Bell looked forward to a new era in which thinkers approached political life with modesty, skeptical of grand hopes for change and committed to a kind of responsibility that carefully measured the consequences of political actions and regularly revised policy aims accordingly. He believed intellectuals had betrayed their calling in earlier decades by surrendering critical reason to the appeal of mass movements and their transformative ideologies; it was bitter for him to suffer, in turn, the reproach from Dennis Wrong, Henry David Aiken, and others that his strictures on moderation and skepticism kept intellectuals from meeting their responsibility for criticism and visionary ideas. Bell was satisfied enough with American society to think ambitious reforms were possible within it, and as he showed by cofounding the journal *The Public Interest* in 1965, he thought professional scholarship and rational discussion could help solve social problems. But his confidence in a new Enlightenment went only so far, and critics who seized on Bell's *End of Ideology* as a defense of the new Enlightenment's most complacent assumptions—the virtue of the existing social consensus and the promise of positivism—misunderstood.[30] Although he applauded the end of messianic ideologies, Bell also decried trends toward bureaucratic rationality and communal decay that made it difficult to define "the public interest" or achieve the ethical consensus needed to carry out the most important initiatives on its behalf. And rather than revive the positivist dream that unbiased "social science objectivity" could supplant all conflict over policy making, Bell insisted that social problems were profoundly moral in character and that any social science reduced to a kind of value-free technique was part of the problem with modern bureaucratic society, not the solution. The nuances of Bell's work did not register, however, and "the end of ideology" became a metonym for the major issues agitating intellectual life.

The idea of consensus, for instance, had become prominent in many fields since the 1940s but encountered sharp criticism beginning in the late 1950s.

Sociologists who claimed societies rested on "common values" that integrated individuals in a shared sense of expectations and obligations, political scientists who perceived a country's "civic culture" as the bedrock of its political life, and historians who emphasized certain constants of belief as the key to understanding the American past were all working the vein of "consensus." In sociology, the idea was challenged by a small but growing corps of "conflict theorists" such as Lewis Coser, Barrington Moore, and (of a younger generation) Randall Collins, who saw social fractures as more normal and salient in social affairs than harmony. In historiography, John Higham classed Daniel Boorstin, Louis Hartz, Richard Hofstadter, and David Potter together as part of "the cult of the 'American consensus,' " which Higham described as "a massive grading operation to smooth over America's social convulsions."[31] But it did not always clarify matters to propose "conflict" as a foundational principle opposite to "consensus"—both played a part in governing social affairs—or to suggest that consensus always entailed conservative political values of order and stability, for the study of consensus could be motivated also by an intention to criticize the ways and means of maintaining an oppressive order. Few observers doubted, anyway, that a consensus of some sort prevailed in Cold War America. The real contest lay between those who regarded the American consensus as capacious and progressive and those who saw it as a narrow current of permissible political belief confined by dogmatic anticommunism and paeans to corporate business.[32]

The new revolt against positivism had a more wide-ranging impact on American intellectual life and assumed more varied forms than the dispute over consensus. The term "positivism" has had various uses since its origin in the "positive philosophy" of French sociologist Auguste Comte, but when H. Stuart Hughes, writing in 1958, described the "revolt against positivism" that commenced a new trend of modern European thought in the late nineteenth century, he had in mind the general proposition that methods of science could be applied to understanding society just like any other object in nature. The unity of science, or the methodological uniformity of social and natural sciences, has been taken as a standard of positivistic views, generally speaking, as has the principle that science yields positive knowledge by strictly keeping value judgments distinct from the apprehension of "facts." Although many contemporary social scientists were not positivists in the nineteenth-century sense of viewing society just like any other natural object, a "positivist persuasion" prevailed in the 1960s among most academicians. They tended to accept an "engineering model" of science, in which the purpose of "pure research" was to disclose the nature of reality and provide useful knowledge to others interested in practical pursuits, whatever their purposes. Efforts aimed at perfecting mathematical, statistical, and computing techniques in the social sciences signaled the prevalence of the positivist persuasion in the 1960s, but a potent reaction against the hegemony of the engineering model was also brewing in a wide range of fields.[33]

In one dimension of the new revolt against positivism, critics assailed what might be called directionless science—a hegemonic scientific worldview that eschewed, or precluded, any attempt to define meaningful goals for human action. According to George Lichtheim, contemporary confidence in the ability of science to provide the means of modifying the conditions of life made it "the instrument of total reconstruction" but failed to address the question of what purposes science should serve. "In the name of what aims and values?" he asked. "Science as such has no answer to this question. Nor will it ever have one." David Bazelon complained that "science cannot serve as a 'whole view' " of the human condition and that an unthinking celebration of science for its own sake left "the educated class" unable to define general goals to which it could, or should, devote its expertise. In a 1962 essay titled "The Myth of a Value-Free Sociology," Alvin Gouldner warned, "If we today concern ourselves exclusively with the technical proficiency of our students and reject all responsibility for their moral sense, or lack of it, then we may some day be compelled to accept responsibility for having trained a generation willing to serve in a future Auschwitz." Convinced that complacency reigned, Gouldner argued that university and society alike needed if anything "more commitment to politics and ... more diversity of political views" and that old arguments for shielding research from value biases no longer applied. Sociologists, he suggested, should serve as personal exemplars to their students, "expos[ing] them to the whole scientist ... with all his gifts and blindnesses, with all his methods and his *values* as well."[34]

The new revolt against positivism also included a revitalization of religious sentiment in the 1960s, despite the decline of church attendance and the rise of new secular theologies. Works such as Gibson Winter's *The New Creation as Metropolis* (1963), James Pike's *A Time for Christian Candor* (1964), and Harvey Cox's *The Secular City* (1965) urged the reconciliation of religion with the secular world of reason and science and called for jettisoning the mythic elements of Christianity in favor of its practical ethics of service, fellowship, and fulfillment. The worldliness of such authors, not to mention that of the even more naturalistic "death of God" theologians such as Thomas J.J. Altizer and William Hamilton, was intended to revivify religious sentiment by making it ordinary and to uplift the ordinary by infusing it with meaning. Even as these writers counseled revitalization through reconciliation, a countercurrent of contemplative, mystical, and spiritualist sentiment appeared in Thomas Merton's monastic writings, new interest in Eastern religions (particularly Zen Buddhism) starting around 1960, and Jewish attention to cabalistic and Hassidic traditions. The link between the critique of directionless (or dangerous) science and a new pursuit of the sacred became clear in two movies by Stanley Kubrick—*Dr. Strangelove* (1964), with its mad scientist modeled on a composite of physicist Edward Teller, German missile builder Werner von Braun, and strategic theorist Herman Kahn, and *2001: A Space Odyssey* (1968), in which a mystic evocation of human rebirth follows a story of runaway technique.[35]

The fear that science and technology lacked the moral direction that "values" should provide may have missed the point, however, for the problem of positivism arose precisely when the engineering model of science put knowledge to use on behalf of very definite social goals such as weapons development. In the 1960s, several prominent scientists mounted their own critique of science, arguing not that science lacked direction but that it was too much directed by extraneous interests. The term "Big Science" appeared in a 1958 article by physicist Hans Bethe and figured prominently in other writings thereafter by Merle Tuve, Alvin Weinberg, Norbert Wiener, and Paul Zilsel, who claimed that researchers' dependence on expensive machines, large grants, and organized enterprises turned their agenda toward "pursuit of technological goals rather than scientific understanding" or that science in "the megabuck era" had been corrupted by the values of big business and government. In many respects, these critics of "Big Science" resembled the humanists who decried the loss of the independent intellectual. As historians James Capshew and Karen Rader have pointed out, "their criticisms were flavored with a certain nostalgia for an earlier, more innocent age ... [for] the stereotyped lone investigator of the past, working with the proverbial sealing wax and string in a private laboratory." While properly directing attention to the concrete social values guiding research, such critics suggested that ethical science would be revived if left to native values of the independent scholar.[36]

Another current did not hark back to a morally whole independent researcher but challenged the idea that social observers, as scientists, uncovered objective knowledge of the world. Their aim was to promote instead a "phenomenological" or "cultural science" that grasped subjective states of mind among human actors. Anthropologist Clifford Geertz, an influential proponent of "cultural science," fired one of his antipositivist salvos in an essay entitled "Ideology as a Cultural System," in which he argued that it was absurd, or vicious, to decree an end of ideology, for humans, at least of the modern world, could not do without it: "Whatever else ideologies may be ... they are, most distinctively, maps of problematic social reality and matrices for the creation of collective conscience.... [I]t is through the construction of ideologies ... that man makes himself for better or worse a political animal."[37] Humans created and dwelled within "webs of meaning," and Geertz developed a hermeneutic method of "thick description," demonstrated in his renowned essays on Balinese ritual, that explored the deeply layered significance of gestures, acts, routines, and practices. Stress on the meaningful character of social existence, requiring a method of subjective "understanding" rather than causal explanation, challenged what Geertz and his followers regarded as faulty, indeed destructive, attempts to reduce diverse societies and cultures to generalizations about universal, lawlike social processes.[38]

A related critique of objectivity figured in the new style of newspaper writing that appeared around 1962 in articles by Jimmy Breslin of the *New York Herald Tribune* and Gay Talese of the *New York Times:* reportage that was novelistic in tone, capturing the immediacy of lived situations and the subjective experience of the individuals involved. The point was "to be there," said *Tribune* reporter Tom Wolfe, leading propagandist for this "new journalism." Market pressures had led newspapers and magazines to try new kinds of engaging "features," but the antipositivist ethos of the times also helped journalists question traditional standards of objectivity, at least if that meant impersonal observation and an account of "just the facts."[39] The new journalism offered something else: "Personality, energy, drive, bravura ... style, in a word." Indeed, aside from his genuine talents in depicting scenes and personalities, Wolfe delighted in whiz-bang flourishes of offbeat punctuation and onomatopoeic exclamations. But there was also method behind his manic demeanor. Despite the strident antiacademic pose he often affected, he swam in the same stream as scholars of his day, having earned a Ph.D. in American Studies at Yale University in 1957 and imbibed the prevailing "myth-symbol" approach to studying American culture. Wolfe saw himself as a cultural anthropologist, dedicated in Geertzian fashion to plumb the subjective experience of American life through detailed description of gestures, artifacts, and habitual practices.

In Wolfe's view, the old journalistic world dominated by "totem newspapers," each catering to the "outlook on life" prevailing in a distinct social class, was unprepared to understand, say, the déclassé spirit of custom-car design, subject of the title piece in his first book, *The Kandy-Kolored Tangerine-Flake Streamline Baby*. Here was a world unto itself with ethical and aesthetic standards as integral as any other. Combining learned allusion to art history and professed disdain for the caste-bound norms of traditional art criticism, Wolfe declared that "these customized cars *are* art objects"; the leader in the field, George Barris, "pursued the pure flame and its forms with such devotion that he emerged an artist ... like Tiepolo emerging from the studies of Venice where the rounded Grecian haunches of the murals on the Palladian domes hung in the atmosphere like clouds."[40] In fact, the real story in postwar America, Wolfe argued, was the death of "the old idea of a class structure," and he aimed to be chronicler of the new cultural democracy, in which "suddenly classes of people whose styles of life had been practically invisible had the money to build monuments to their own styles."[41] Yet, like earlier cultural critics of "mass society," Wolfe looked at society deprived of class-bound order as a peculiar, invertebrate mass. It dissolved into a multitude of "statuspheres," each a little lifestyle enclave, from surfers to hippies to custom-car aficionados to the elite New York arts crowd, each straining to find a place or standing for itself by means of "sheer ego extension." All about, Wolfe saw "chronic chaos," and his varied portraits—"the pump house gang" of surfers sporting about in burning Watts or Ken Kesey's Merry Pranksters turning manic fun into a coldhearted bad trip—told the same story: a growing "lack of social concern."[42]

Wolfe mocked "intellectuals" anxiously concerned with poverty and war. They hadn't recognized, he said in 1968, that "we're in the middle of a ... Happiness Explosion," a "pandemonium with a big grin on" that promised its own "apocalyptic future" of "ego extension, the politics of pleasure, the self-realization racket, the pharmacology of Overjoy."[43] Actually, Wolfe's work was like a mirror, perceiving rampant egoism all around while celebrating his own. He claimed that the new journalists had achieved "a strange sort of objectivity, an egotistical objectivity but an objectivity of sorts in any case" by disclosing the "real" story of the 1960s in its tumult of "manners and morals."[44] Wolfe's firsthand reports on the scenic lives of the wild and hazy gave his readers some kinds of thrills, but those accounts, based on his own fascination with "style," also helped magnify an extremely partial view of the times—as an overextended pursuit of pleasure—and fixed that as the enduring image of what "the sixties" were all about. Outside Wolfe's specialty, though, it seemed that old standards of objectivity still counted. Dissenters seeking clarity in the face of the government's double-dealing pronouncements on Vietnam, for instance, demanded of their journalistic heroes, such as the skeptic I. F. Stone, something that Wolfe was unprepared to deliver. As one participant in an early antiwar teach-in said of the experience, "Facts were demanded and assumptions were exposed."[45] In so simple a demand, the motives and limits of the new revolt against positivism should have become clear. Although it was essential to challenge the feigned disinterestedness of official knowledge and disclose the actual biases and commitments of conventional wisdom, it was impossible to deny the hope of attaining something one could trust as truth.

Scientific Revolutions and the Social Character of Knowledge

Knowledge and ideology, objectivity and responsibility, facts and values, the preeminence of science and the new revolt against positivism: these were the terms of a long debate concerning the parameters of truth under the new conditions built by the socialization of intellect. The key issues revolved around the tension between principles of disinterestedness and engagement, that is, between an old conception of knowledge claiming objectivity on the grounds of its distance from biases, commitments, or special interests of any kind and the new ways that the production of knowledge was bound up in extra-academic social and political affairs by organizational ties and claims on responsibility. Theoretically, the problem of disinterestedness and engagement came to a head in debates on the history and philosophy of science occasioned by Thomas S. Kuhn's 1962 book *The Structure of Scientific Revolutions*, for if, as Kuhn suggested, the development of science was embedded in social and historical contexts, on what grounds could humans strive to secure truths, or warranted assertions about reality?

Kuhn's intervention came at a time when the reigning doctrine in philosophy of science, logical positivism, was a ripe—or overripe—orthodoxy. Logical positivism began in the 1920s with the Vienna Circle of Moritz Schlick, Herbert Feigl, Otto Neurath, and Rudolf Carnap and was introduced to a broad English-speaking audience by A. J. Ayer in 1946. It defined science as a combination solely of verifiable observations and mathematical logic—both free of any subjective thought—and on this basis sought to provide a sound foundation for its claims to represent sure knowledge. The earliest versions of the doctrine insisted that all laws of science assume a strict logical form and that theoretical terms used in these laws (such as "mass" or "energy") be related to empirical data by precise "correspondence rules." Although introducing some flexibility in these strictures during the 1940s and 1950s, the positivists remained dedicated to the view that science developed "upward" from observation to empirical generalization to the definition of theoretical terms and their disposition in generalizations or "laws," and that scientific knowledge grew cumulatively as theories were applied to wider ranges of phenomena, or as new, more comprehensive theories subsumed older ones of more limited scope. From the early 1950s onward, varied critics such as Willard V. Quine and Karl Popper challenged the way positivists understood the meaning of statements, the nature of logic, and the significance of verification in scientific procedure, but the positivists' views remained influential in many disciplines at the beginning of the 1960s.[46]

Nonetheless, by this time, it was clear that the positivist view established a certain canon that applied at best to only a few sciences. Others, especially "historical" sciences such as Darwinian biology, could not be reduced as the positivists demanded to a logical form resting on elementary observations and basic axioms, and few theorists were willing to excommunicate such commonly recognized scientific fields. Obviously, scientists did a number of things to accumulate knowledge (or reliable generalizations) that did not meet the positivists' abstract prescriptions—and it now appeared that this situation spoke to the inadequacy of the abstractions, not the sciences. The first major attack on the historical adequacy of logical positivism came in a 1962 essay by Paul Feyerabend, an adherent of Popper's school of "critical rationalism." Feyerabend showed that even theoretical physics, the science deemed closest to the positivists' model, could not be said to have developed cumulatively, since key terms and observations of early systems such as Kepler's or Newton's failed to fit neatly as elementary components or deducible findings within Einstein's.[47]

Published the same year as Feyerabend's essay, Kuhn's work became in time the subject of concerted attention for its distinctive notion of the "paradigm," a sort of conceptual framework that determined the questions to be regarded as relevant within a scientific domain and the kinds of answers that could be taken as satisfactory responses to those questions. Given that, Kuhn defined "scientific revolutions" as "those non-cumulative developmental episodes in which an older paradigm is replaced in whole or in part by an incompatible new one."[48] The relation between Einstein's relativity theory and Newtonian mechanics was a case in point. Once the shock of the new subsided, positivists would say, it became clear that relativity marked an improvement in knowledge, not refuting classical mechanics but subsuming it as a limited perspective within a more comprehensive framework. Yet Kuhn argued that relativity and classical mechanics were distinct paradigms and as such were, strictly speaking, incommensurable. For a time in the development of physics, these two paradigms competed, and defenders of each talked past each other, incapable of meeting on common ground or rationally convincing opponents of their theory's superiority.

Resolution of the impasse was in part arbitrary. Kuhn cited Max Planck's remark that "a new scientific truth does not triumph by convincing its opponents and making them see the light, but rather because its opponents eventually die, and a new generation grows up that is familiar with it." To be sure, individual scientists could undergo a kind of conversion, sensing the move from one paradigm to another as a gestalt shift: that is, they might suddenly see the world through a different lens and recognize how effectively the new framework disposed, and made coherent, familiar observations. Particular conditions also served to make such a gestalt shift compelling Kuhn argued there was indeed a "normal" condition of science in which a single paradigm reigned and research was carried on to apply its principles to a steadily widening range of phenomena. For some time, this process enriched and verified the governing paradigm, but research also typically uncovered phenomena that fit ill under that umbrella, and although minor adjustments of the paradigm might account for such "anomalies," there came a time when accommodating revisions, like the addition of further "epicycles" to the cosmos of Ptolemaic astronomy, appeared increasingly forced or fruitless. At such a moment, a new theory—dubbed "extraordinary" rather than "normal science"—might appear that offered a way out of the quandary, with a more elegant way of comprehending precisely those anomalies that the prior age of normal science had divulged but left unorganized.[49]

Kuhn's work excited a very sharp opposition. The suggestion that the development of scientific knowledge was contingent on irrational processes (conviction, conversion, or generational succession) enraged followers of Karl Popper, who made unlimited rational criticism the watchword of scientific method.[50] In fact, a recent survey of the early Kuhn debate concluded that it was Popper's followers, not old positivists, who most objected to *The Structure of Scientific Revolutions,* and that Kuhn actually championed certain standards of the positivist heritage: he upheld not only the unity of science (generally, *one* basic theory reigned at a time in each discipline, in contrast to Feyerabend's argument for the virtue of multiple, competing theories) but also the principle of steady progress at least within the bounds of "normal science." In later formulations of his view, Kuhn also strove to depict historical paradigm shifts in a somewhat more progressive light, at least insofar as new paradigms permit disciplines to address a larger scope of problems, with a greater degree of accuracy.[51] Although it became common in later years to suggest that Kuhn and other historicists "undermined belief in such notions as scientific truth and ... helped to inspire a deep epistemological skepticism," such conclusions stem neither from Kuhn's intentions nor from the substance of his argument.[52]

Kuhn made a compelling case for a more socialized conception of science. Paradigms were artifacts of scientific *communities—shared assumptions* that served both to guide research and to draw practitioners together in communication with one other. Paradigms were the means of "socializing" new practitioners as members of a discipline: one's apprenticeship consisted of "internalizing" the paradigm, learning the "exemplars" or classic experiments that demonstrate the character of relevant questions and appropriate answers and thus the "values ... shared by the scientific community into which [one] seeks admission." All these terms—the social basis of action, the "socialization" of participants, the necessity of consensus (or "common-value integration") for the persistence of a community—show how Kuhn's view was rooted in the sociological perspective, based largely on the work of Emile Durkheim and Max Weber, that held preeminence in the United States after World War II. Thus recent commentators suggest that Kuhn actually stood within the liberal "consensus" school of the early 1960s, aiming to defend the social prestige and self-regulating autonomy of the scientific community and deflect interference from a nervous public or "outside" social authorities.[53] Notwithstanding this criticism, Kuhn's move to recognize the social character and context of knowledge was decisive in breaking new ground. To be sure, despite his historicism, Kuhn made only glancing reference to events or conditions outside the sphere of science itself that affected the development of scientific ideas, and he argued for "internal" accounts that study the history of scientific fields solely in their own terms. In some respects, too, Kuhn's reliance on a conventional sociology of consensus groups introduced another kind of artificial norm into the study of science, but the basic point of his historicism—that it is necessary to flee the abstraction and idealism of the positivist account to grasp the real character of scientific practice—still stands.

Examining the characteristic tension in intellectual debate of the 1960s between expectations of a new Enlightenment and fear that social engagement threatened the integrity of knowledge has shown that each party to the debate stumbled over ambivalent commitments to both social relevance and the pursuit of truth. In fact, the implicit challenge posed by the socialization of intellect in the 1960s was to reconstruct a sense of knowledge that could both recognize how inquiry is embedded in a field of social interests *and* uphold the possibility of achieving warranted assertions about the nature of reality.

Undoubtedly, the social context of inquiry complicates the notion of truth, just as the social mobilization of the postwar university raised appropriate questions about the critical independence of scholarship. Nonetheless, the conclusion drawn by many observers since the 1960s that the discovery of science's social embeddedness marked the onset of a period in which all knowledge is suspect and unstable appears necessary only on the basis of sharply polarized terms of truth and interestedness, objectivity and relativity. By attempting to formulate some sense of improvement in scientific knowledge while acknowledging the social force of guiding theories, Kuhn's work should be recognized as one of those ventures, such as John Dewey's and Max Weber's, intended to supersede such dualistic terms.

Trying to surpass the limits of Kuhn's critique, some recent philosophers have proposed "naturalizing" epistemology, that is, turning the philosophy of science into a science of science, using all the resources of the social, natural, and cognitive sciences to examine what scientists actually do to accumulate what knowledge we have.[54] In studying the social and technical conditions of scientific inquiry, and the social and technical efficacy of its findings, this approach recognizes the warrant behind scientific knowledge, such as it is (avoiding the corrosive skepticism that concludes the social and historical contexts of knowledge deprive it of any truth value), while still permitting a critique of scientific practices (avoiding the tendency for defenses of science to consider the current incarnation of the scientific estate absolute). Just such a balance, promised by a study of science that recognizes both its limits and its promise, is needed to help restore confidence to intellectual pursuits. Intellectual work that matters presupposes the conviction that knowledge (or warranted assertions about reality) is both accessible and socially useful. That conviction gave élan to intellectual life in the 1960s, and it remains too important to surrender.

three

Development and Its Discontents

The kind of ambivalence that troubled intellectuals in assessing the consequences of socializing knowledge—a new Enlightenment or the decline of critical thought—was only one manifestation of a more deep-rooted tension in the thought and culture of the 1960s: the matter of "development" and the coexistence of currents in American thought that either advanced or derided it. Never before in modern Western intellectual history had the voices vaunting social progress and denouncing its pretensions been quite so clear and contentious, so evenly set at loggerheads. To be sure, the ideology of progress and civilization that prevailed in Europe and America since the eighteenth century had always been accompanied by a romantic spirit of rebellion against the modern world, and from the beginning of the twentieth century, there appeared in several social science disciplines, and in the world of letters at large, a vigorous criticism of the assumption that social life evolved in a "linear" fashion. At midcentury, following the catastrophic war of 1914 to 1918, the rise of terrorist states in its wake, and the greater cataclysm of 1939 to 1945, it was not uncommon for writers to assert that "progress" had been stalled, shattered, or reversed; perhaps it was always illusory. Although dramatic postwar economic growth, accompanying the rise of the United States to worldwide hegemony, helped revive evolutionary and progressive ideas by the early 1960s, it still could not eliminate the voice of doubt and opposition. The persistence of the romantic tradition, the recent memory of midcentury disillusionment, and new political forces challenging American power abroad and at home all worked to resist evolutionary confidence.

Ideas about social development, that is, social change as an unfolding process moving in a definite direction, took varied forms in the 1960s, according to the region of the world or the dimension of human experience they considered. Regarding the world abroad, the most prevalent developmental idea was the theory of "modernization," fashioned to explain and assist processes of economic growth and social change that would bring the new so-called Third World of poor, mostly postcolonial countries closer to parity with standards of the Western world. Largely an innovation of postwar social thought, modernization theory peaked in the early 1960s. Later, it met a concerted opposition that attacked on several fronts. Radical "dependency" theories aligned with anti-imperialist movements of the poor countries challenged modernization theory's assumptions about the causes of, and solutions to, underdevelopment, and some scholars reconsidered the theory's model of how the modern West itself had emerged. Regarding the American scene, the most prevalent developmental idea was a generally optimistic discussion of "postindustrial society," considered a new stage in social life only just beginning. This stage was sometimes also called "postmodern," but that name most often applied specifically to the realm of culture, where different critics were looking for signs of another watershed in the arts. Some perceived a new breakthrough, others a calamity; a few imagined even a restoration of premodern forms of experience and expression. All these notions, from modernization to the postmodern, aimed to grasp the course of events in a decade preoccupied by the sweep of social change.

Modernization Theory and Its Critics

As a grand theory entailing a retrospective view of how society had evolved in the West, an anticipation of ongoing social change there, and a prediction of how poor postcolonial countries of the world would develop into societies enjoying economic growth and some form of citizenship, the idea of modernization took off in the late 1950s and early 1960s and, despite sharp criticism starting around 1963, continued to be a significant theme in American social science into the 1970s. Key works marked the theory's heyday: Daniel Lerner's *The Passing of Traditional Society: Modernizing the Middle East* (1958), S. N. Eisenstadt's *Essays on Sociological Aspects of Political and Economic Development* (1961), David Apter's *Ghana in Transition* (1955; revised in 1963), and Marion J. Levy's *Modernization and the Structure of Societies* (1966). The old *Encyclopedia of the Social Sciences* (1930–1935), the great compendium that marked the first blossoming of academic social research in the United States, had no indexed entries for "modernization" (nor for "development" or even "economic growth"), but the revised edition of 1968, the *International Encyclopedia of the Social Sciences*, devoted three long articles to the topic. The reasons for modernization's absence before the mid-1950s and then its sudden boom tell a great deal about the character and meaning of the concept.

The ostensible ultimate aim of modernization—a global equality of nations in which economic productivity, citizen participation, and scientific learning governed all—had hardly been the object of any Great Power in the ages of colonial expansion and modern imperialism, when talk of a "civilizing mission" was a transparent cover for European (or American) domination of the outlying world. The conceptual predecessor of modernization was "Europeanization," but as British scholar George Young pointed out in the old *Encyclopedia of the Social Sciences,* that usually meant "Europeanization by extermination" (pioneered in North America) or "Europeanization [by] exploitation of peoples." The term was losing its utility in any case as recent history forced observers into tongue-tying usages: "The future Europeanization of Asia," Young noted, "will proceed from Asia itself, under the pressure of nationalism and communism, both of which will tend to end its dependence on Europe." Perhaps a new word was needed for this peculiar anti-European "Europeanization." Meanwhile, disciplines of modern social science had come to neglect issues of social change over time. Not since Adam Smith had mainstream economists (except the German school) devoted significant attention to the historical development of economies. Despite their origins in evolutionary theories of development, sociology and anthropology (especially in the United States under Franz Boas's influence) had, by the twentieth century, turned to ahistorical concerns with conditions of social cohesion and the plurality of cultural patterns.[1]

In much of European and American intellectual life, concern with historical change and social development had long been a specialty of socialist and other dissenting, reformist schools of thought. In England, the socialist R. H. Tawney developed the field of economic history, and in Austrian economics, historical or developmental issues were left largely to the Marxists. *The Theory of Economic Development* (1911), by the conservative Joseph Schumpeter, was the exception that proved the rule, an indication of Schumpeter's intellectual sympathy with the theory, if not the politics, of the Left. Indeed, as an émigré at Harvard in the 1930s, Schumpeter found his favorite student in the Marxist Paul Sweezy, who answered his teacher's account of economic growth with his own *Theory of Capitalist Development* (1941).[2] Similarly, one of the few American scholars to study social development in the interwar years, University of Chicago anthropologist Robert Redfield, found his models for "the process of transition [from] folk to urban culture" in Mexican towns reshaped by left-wing forces of the Mexican revolution.[3] When Redfield's circle established the journal *Economic Development and Cultural Change* in 1952, furthermore, it was edited by another Austrian émigré, Bert Hoselitz, who had grown up, intellectually, in Austro-Marxist circles.[4] Some of the earliest uses of the term "modernization" appeared in this journal.

The conditions occasioning the rise of a new theory of modernization after World War II, and particularly from the mid-1950s onward, combine a number of different factors. The organization of the Committee for Economic Development in the 1930s by business leaders friendly to the New Deal, combined with Nelson and David Rockefeller's promotion since 1940 of economic-development aid for poor countries abroad, signaled a new willingness among American elites to undertake limited kinds of planning to promote growth. At the same time, young scholars who had adopted or flirted with Marxism in the 1930s entered the academy after the war, and even if they had fled the far Left, they often maintained old interests in progressive social change and could make common cause with liberal internationalists such as Redfield. When the 1955 Bandung (Indonesia) conference of nonaligned nations and the subsequent decolonization of Africa revealed a new Third World of poor countries, many led by militant nationalists such as Nasser and Nkrumah, their drive for independence and progress appealed to left-liberal scholars as a kind of generic "modernization" freed of "Europeanized" taint. The political scientist David Apter, for instance, was a former Marxist who devoted his energies to studying the independence movement in Ghana and formulating theories of development.[5]

The late 1950s also witnessed a revival of evolutionary concerns in American anthropology at the hands of self-conscious progressives such as Leslie White, his student Marshall Sahlins, and other young scholars such as Eric Wolf and Sidney Mintz. White considered Boasian cultural anthropology "reactionary" for failing to deal with issues of social change, and Sahlins, introducing a collection of essays by White's students, *Evolution and Culture* (1960), asserted that the revival of these concerns stemmed from "a worldwide conflict between older, entrenched social orders and once-lowly and dominated peoples whose awakening has made 'progress' again the slogan of the day."[6] At the same time, however, the rise of the Third World helped make it a battleground in the Cold War as the United States sought to combat the Soviet Union's declared support for "wars of national liberation." Modernization then became a carrot that American policy makers offered the Third World, as in John F. Kennedy's Alliance for Progress, and Kennedy's rhetoric seemed to convince activist liberals that a benevolent and disinterested American program of worldwide development, long a reformist's dream, was possible.[7] The idea of modernization thus grew from a number of contending purposes: bourgeois interests in economic growth, social democratic commitments to equality and progress, Third World nationalism and sympathy for it, and Cold War policy objectives.

Several of these elements came together in Walt W. Rostow's landmark book *The Stages of Economic Growth* (1960). A child of socialist parents, Rostow had adhered to Marxism when he first broached the study of economic history in the 1930s, but Cold War anticommunism triumphed over his youthful radicalism. Now he intended to explain, without relying on the "economic determinism" he ascribed to Marx and Lenin, how different countries reached the point of "take-off into self-sustained growth" and moved ahead, through a "drive to maturity," to the stage of "high mass consumption." In the process, his historical learning backed a carefully honed political apologia and polemic. Having identified the "preconditions" of takeoff as the emergence of a "substantial middle class" and an effective unified state, Rostow failed to explain why these forces arose in some cases but not in others, or to examine what other factors moved an economy along to subsequent stages. Instead, he focused on the undetermined political "choice" facing countries enjoying "high mass consumption," between promoting greater goods production, better welfare services, or military assertiveness. Due to its peculiar "reactive nationalism" (not because of innate imperialist urges of advanced capitalism), Germany had chosen the last of these, precipitating the major wars of the twentieth century, and the Soviet Union's aggressiveness stemmed likewise from its inability to apply its productive energies to domestic, democratic ends. Given his voluntaristic viewpoint, Rostow not only denied that American wealth and power made the United States an imperialist force in world affairs but also reached the happy conclusion that the United States could choose not one but all three options, meeting not only the baby boom's demand for goods and services but also the threat posed by a "missile gap" that left the United States lagging behind Soviet rocketry. Although that gap soon proved illusory, Rostow's views on power and development gained prominence when he became a Kennedy foreign policy aide.[8]

The Cold War invective in Rostow's *Stages* showed how politicized development theory could be. For many proponents, however, the concept of modernization was "less ideological, more interdisciplinary" than Rostow's study of economic growth. It aimed to go beyond the limits of economics to grasp a wide range of social, psychological, and cultural factors involved in the transition to a "modern" way of life. For at least some researchers, modernization even aimed to go beyond the Cold War. Daniel Lerner claimed that the new concept of modernization should supplant old ideas of Europeanization or Westernization precisely in order to comprehend Soviet-style as well as capitalist development, and Harvard researcher Alex Inkeles was confident that schooling in the Peoples Republic of China promoted the same values and personality traits that marked all modern social systems. The apparent ecumenical attitude of the new modernization theory may have encouraged some liberal academics to applaud revolutionary nationalist movements abroad as a species of modernization and even to adopt some of the suspicions those movements bore toward Western, and American, power.[9]

Two main varieties of modernization theory prevailed in American academic life. Based on Robert Redfield's Mexican community studies and legacies of Robert Park and John Dewey, a "Chicago school" studied transitional phenomena on the path to modernity. Just as Redfield saw the newsy *corrido* (topical ballad) of Mexican town life as an intermediate cultural form halfway along the "folk-urban continuum" between traditional folk songs and modern mass culture, so Daniel Lerner looked closely at the role played by the individual who moved between village and city, became familiar with newspapers and radio, and thus achieved "an expansive Self, newly equipped with a functioning empathy, [and capable of perceiving] connections between its private dilemmas and public issues." Modern society was, in Lerner's Deweyan terms, "participant society." The transitional emphasis of the Chicago school encouraged attention to the commingling of tradition and modernity, as in Milton Singer's work on India, *When a Great Tradition Modernizes*, which saw Hinduism adapting to, not resisting, modern practices.[10] On the other hand, a Harvard school, based on Talcott Parsons's formal scheme of "pattern variables," saw sharper disjunctions. The characteristic pattern of modern societies—a tendency to apply the same "universal" standards to all individuals in common circumstances, to assign occupations according to individuals' achievements rather than fixed traits, to circumscribe authority such as "doctor's orders" to specific settings, and to carry out tasks such as a medical examination independently of one's feelings—helped highlight traditional aspects of social life, such as a landlord's "diffuse" authority over a peasant, which needed change before modernization could begin.[11]

Both styles stressed elements of culture and personality. Lerner had made the trait of "empathy" a key to modern society, for the ability to imagine oneself in someone else's shoes opened the door to changing roles, mobility, and participation in political discourse. In the Harvard orbit, social psychologist David McClelland argued that modernizing societies possessed large numbers of individuals who had a psychological "need for achievement," as opposed to a counterproductive "need for power." Above all, however, the common assumption of varied modernization studies was, as political scientist David Apter puts it, that development implied "linear growth [with] ... integrative and pluralistic social and political consequences." Movement from traditional to modern standards was expected to bring societies greater wealth, democracy, equality, and stability. And though modernization theory rested in part on older ideas about the "rise of the West" (particularly Max Weber's work on the spirit of capitalism), the goal of development, given the left-liberal milieu in which many of the young modernization scholars matured, was not always assumed to be capitalism per se but rather, as Apter writes, a social order "approximated in social welfare and social democratic states."[12]

The liberal or "progressive" tenor of modernization theory in the late 1950s and early 1960s also appears in its special attention to the social status of women and the promise of gender equality. At this time, a new historiography of women had commenced with Eleanor Flexner's *Century of Struggle: The Women's Rights Movement in the United States* (1959) and studies in the early 1960s by scholars Anne Firor Scott, Jill Ker Conway, and others of Jane Addams, settlement houses, and the rise of social welfare policy.[13] Gerda Lerner, who shared with Flexner (and journalist Betty Friedan) a background in Popular Front circles of the 1940s interested in women's emancipation, started a radio show called "Forgotten Women in American History" in 1963 while beginning her historical research on women and abolitionism.[14] Also, as Barnard scholar Mirra Komarovsky helped build a sociology of modern women, other researchers in the late 1950s examined such matters as the impact of women's wage earning on their role in family decision making, on child welfare, and on children's ideas about sex roles.[15] Sociologist William J. Goode linked social development with trends toward "sex egalitarianism" and, in his magisterial *World Revolution and Family Patterns,* showed some of the mildly radical sentiments that could be associated with ideas of modernization.

A self-declared adherent of C. Wright Mills's "critical" sociology, Goode surveyed "family changes" in the West, the Middle East, Africa, India, China, and Japan and found all of them converging on the "conjugal family system": a unit of husband, wife, and children relatively independent of larger kin networks. Because this "system" offered greater independence to young people, freedom in choice of a mate, easier divorce, and a greater degree of equality between the sexes (at least in ideology and gradually so in practice), "it appeals to the disadvantaged, to the young, to women, and to the educated," Goode wrote. "It promises freedom and new alternatives as against the rigidities and controls of traditional systems. It is as effective as the appeal of ... land redistribution or an attack on the existing stratification system. It is radical." Its supporters, he found, included the Third World nationalist movements— Nasser's Egypt, the Algerian revolutionary movement, and independent Africa. Goode was not blind to the survival of male dominance in family relations even in "advanced" Western countries and doubted the quick achievement of "full equality to women," but he asserted, "the general position of women will improve greatly." Opposing any nostalgia for traditional values, he argued that changing family patterns were "part of a still more important revolution that is sweeping the world in our time, the aspiration on the part of billions of people ... *to choose* for themselves—an aspiration that has toppled governments, both old and new, and created new societies and social movements."[16]

In some quarters, modernizing talk about evolving societies helped to challenge conservative gender ideals in the United States. In "Equality between the Sexes: An Immodest Proposal" (1963), sociologist Alice Rossi complained that "practically no feminist spark [survived] among American women," but as she relied on egalitarian findings from recent social research to make her argument, she demonstrated a revival was afoot. Stating that "traditional conceptions of masculine and feminine are inappropriate to the kind of world we can live in in the second half of the twentieth century," and that equality was both feasible and functional "at the level our industrial society has now reached," she clearly relied on the rhetoric of modernization to make her case. She called for "a socially androgynous conception of the roles of men and women," and although putting most emphasis on admitting women to full equality in occupational life, she did not neglect the need for changing other aspects of social life (particularly gender roles in housework and child rearing) and issued an early call for something like "coparenting" of children by men and women. Missing was direct attention to relations of power between men and women, though Rossi commented on the injury done to young girls who always saw "men [as] bosses over women" in work life, and she forecast changes in sexual experience, so that men and women might encounter each other as "equal partners, and not as an ascendant male and a submissive female."[17]

Betty Friedan's better-known book *The Feminine Mystique* (1963) was more modest than Rossi's "Proposal." Even as Friedan promoted occupational opportunity for women, she did not emphasize, as Rossi did, the need for a new social network of child care centers, and she downplayed the aim of transforming gender relations in home life. Yet Friedan's argument also offered something new: an implicit *critique* of modernization. Her experience as a successful magazine writer helped her describe vividly the "problem that has no name"—a malaise afflicting modern women that stemmed from the suppression of their talents and energies in lives dominated solely by marriage and motherhood. Indeed, after the book's publication, thousands of women readers wrote to Friedan concurring with her diagnosis and relating their own frustrations with feminine ideals. Building on the work of psychologists Erik Erikson, Abraham Maslow, and Bruno Bettelheim, Friedan demanded for women the chance at human fulfillment that came with creative and professional careers and condemned the middle-class household as a "comfortable concentration camp" that infantilized its women inmates. This telling bit of hyperbole raised familiar doubts, drawn from memory of the Holocaust, about the course of modernity. Moreover, in describing the sexual counterrevolution that had, since the late 1940s, she said, supplanted old feminist goals with a feminine mystique, Friedan saw not progress but regression in sex roles, and a terrible conservatism that endorsed the present as the end point of social development.[18]

Friedan's reservations only hinted at a change in mood. Before long, troubles upsetting the theory of modernization became apparent even to its proponents. Sluggish economic growth and the collapse of several parliamentary Third World regimes into dictatorship led Daniel Lerner to admit in 1964 that "modernization, it now appears, is harder than one supposed." At the same time, S. N. Eisenstadt sought a general explanation for "breakdowns of modernization." All sorts of anomalies appeared. In 1965 economist Carter Goodrich reported that Argentina had seen faster growth in the 30 years before 1930 than since and was now facing economic "strangulation." More significantly, by the mid-1960s, several observers perceived American power and Third World aspirations as antithetical. The Cuban revolution of 1959 boldly asserted that national development could begin only when U.S. domination of the island's social and economic life ended; in Latin America, the Cuban example inspired new guerrilla movements, and in response, the United States implemented counterinsurgency and antirevolutionary policies that overshadowed and undermined the development aid it offered. The argument by some cold warriors that the Saigon regime was effectively "modernizing" South Vietnam, even as American bombs devastated the land and its villages, further disgraced modernization theory. Whereas in 1964 neither Lerner nor Eisenstadt believed their disappointments demanded basic changes in outlook, others in the orbit of development theory prepared to break with the field's liberal establishment.[19]

One response to the frustrations of modernization theory was the development of a *conservative* modernization theory, particularly by the political scientist Samuel Huntington, who argued in the mid-1960s that social order and strong states were more important prerequisites of development than liberalized social relations or widespread political participation.[20] A bolder departure lay in the radical critique of modernization by figures previously affiliated with its left-liberal mainstream, such as the Columbia University sociologist Immanuel Wallerstein. His early book *Africa: The Politics of Independence* (1961), written in sympathy with the new nationalist leaderships of liberated Africa, aimed to show how those nations "are seeking to further the process of modernization" defined in terms of national unity, economic development, and popular political participation—all of which Wallerstein expected in time to foster liberal, pluralistic standards of government. By 1967, when Wallerstein published a book on the pan-African movement, he had concluded that the hoped-for "modernization of African societies" was frustrated, above all, by worldwide conditions of trade favoring the rich countries. From this point, Wallerstein went on to develop a radical analysis of "the capitalist world-system," which became an influential paradigm in the 1970s and led him to regard modernization as a "concept [that] has died."[21]

Meanwhile, Andre Gunder Frank, a German-born economist who worked with Bert Hoselitz at the University of Chicago in the mid-1950s and moved to Latin America after he was radicalized by the Cuban revolution, fashioned a rejoinder to modernization theory focused on the phenomenon of "dependency." In 1967 Frank argued in his first book that "underdevelopment" was due not to primitive social conditions in countries left outside the stream of progress but rather to economic distortions caused by the *integration* of these countries in worldwide economic relations funneling wealth from outlying regions to powerful capitalist metropolises. Frank's work was not unprecedented: the Marxist analysis of Paul Baran's *The Political Economy of Growth* (1957) had already shown how the effects of modern imperialism prevented poor countries from simply repeating the course of Western economic development, and the Argentinean economic reformer Raúl Prebisch had earlier popularized (at least in Latin America) the idea that the Third World was inhibited by unequal trading relations between countries of the "center" and "periphery." Frank even recognized a debt to Hoselitz's brand of economic sociology, and to Redfield's principle that "there are no peasants without the city ... no city without its peasants," that is, wealth and poverty could not be understood apart from each other.[22]

By calling for Third World revolutions to break the bonds of dependency, Frank challenged the gradualism of modernization theory. Similarly, other writers in the 1960s questioned its implicit view of the Western past as a smooth progression toward growing democracy and security. In *The Social Origins of Dictatorship and Democracy* (1966), the iconoclastic scholar Barrington Moore Jr. considered the cases of Nazi Germany and militarist Japan along with Britain and the United States as various "routes to the modern world," all of them marked by sharp class conflicts and founded, even in the most benign case of Western democracy, on a history of violence. In a not unrelated vein, E. P. Thompson's *The Making of the English Working Class* (1963) took issue with a portrait of British modernization by American sociologist Neil Smelser that failed to see how liberal society in Britain was built atop the violent suppression of a vibrant, proletarian people's culture in the early nineteenth century. The American Herbert Gutman applied Thompson's methods of social history to the study of American industrialization and found that some of the most benevolent elements of the modern welfare state stemmed not from the elites who promoted economic growth but from workers who defended "traditional" values of work and community against industrialists. In none of these cases was an undiluted approval of modern development possible.[23]

There was yet another riposte to ideas of modern development, one that inverted the evaluation and saw modernity tending inexorably to unfreedom rather than freedom. Such propositions derived from various sources—a romantic sensibility, still alive in bohemian and avant-garde circles, that set the vital individual against the suffocating routines of organized institutions; the existential classicism of Hannah Arendt, who saw the modern world as a moral desert lacking the rudiments of life-giving civic participation; and descendants of conformity criticism who searched the past for origins of social regimentation. In 1965 Michel Foucault's *Madness and Civilization* appeared in English, arguing that the apparent growth of personal liberty in the modern world only masked the development of refined control over individuals managed by public authorities, epitomized by the asylum, which stigmatized, segregated, and incarcerated people guilty of deviant behavior.

A more widespread view was simply one of impatience with the self-congratulatory assumption of modernization theory that the order of life present in "advanced" countries set the standard for "development" and hence suggested the limit of change. Betty Friedan made this point. Making "occupation housewife" the "model for all women," she wrote, "presupposes that history has reached a final and glorious end in the here and now, as far as women are concerned."[24] A year after Friedan's book appeared, Mario Savio of the Free Speech Movement at Berkeley spoke similarly against the "end to history," insisting that students, like American blacks or workers facing displacement by automation, "will not accept an end to events, this historical plateau, as the point beyond which no change occurs."[25]

The Idea of "Postindustrial" Development

Although the theory of modernization gave a not unfounded impression that it viewed Western development with a contented sense of closure, another potent idea of development, "postindustrial society," emerged in the 1960s to portray the United States not at the end but just the beginning of a new stage in social change. David Riesman wrote of postindustrial society as early as 1958, and Daniel Bell used the term independently in 1959.[26] The idea was well suited to a time when the energies and aspirations of reform revived and reformers imagined modern life moving toward more socialized terms of existence. Indeed, a 1960 essay by Riesman and the young radical historian Staughton Lynd showed how American liberals and radicals together used the idea to understand and perhaps shape the course of change. This collaboration began in the early 1950s when Lynd, a University of Chicago graduate student, helped Riesman prepare a book-length study of Thorstein Veblen, and in a 1960 paperback edition, their coauthored introduction suggested a vision Veblen had missed: "Admiring both the matter-of-fact skepticism he believed industrial man to possess and the amiable unassertive humanity he attributed to pre-industrial man, Veblen was unable ... to bridge the two cultures, or to envisage *a post-industrial world* ... both abundant and fraternal."[27] The two adjectives named the themes of postindustrial discussion: the promise of productivity and the need for more communal forms of economic and political organization.

Varied definitions of postindustrial society appeared. In Riesman's "Leisure and Work in Post-Industrial Society" (1958), the term denoted the aftermath of the industrial revolution, which Riesman deemed complete as popular resistance to factory discipline waned and manufacturing technology won near-unanimous acclaim.[28] Work no longer seemed central to people's lives, but consumption alone provided no meaningful replacement: postindustrial society still needed to cope with the uses of expanding leisure time. With different premises, Daniel Bell defined postindustrial society as "one in which the intellectual is predominant": expansion of the social functions of science, development of computer-based techniques of modeling and simulation, and growth in public and private funding for research and development all served to make intellectual institutions (notably the university) as socially "central" in contemporary society as the business corporation had been since the rise of modern capitalism.[29] These distinct themes of leisure and science came together with an emphasis on social services in the 1964 manifesto "The Triple Revolution," signed by a mix of reformers and radicals including Robert Heilbroner, Irving Howe, Gunnar Myrdal, Bayard Rustin, Tom Hayden, and Todd Gitlin. With automation in mind, they foresaw "a new era of production [whose] principles of organization are as different from those of the industrial era as those of the industrial era were different from the agricultural." The way to cope with vast productivity gains from computer-controlled systems and the mass unemployment they threatened was to sever the link of employment and income maintained by an old industrial society governed by scarcity; a new society beckoned "in which the norm will be either non-employment, in the traditional sense of productive work, or employment on the great variety of socially valuable but 'non-productive' tasks made possible by an economy of abundance," particularly activities, in social service, "that relate people to people rather than people to things."[30]

The young radicals of the "New Left" shared in the idea of postindustrial society. The *Port Huron Statement* assumed a postindustrial posture as it pinned a strategy of student organizing on the premise that the university was a new strategic locus of contemporary society, tied to centers of political power and social action far more intimately than earlier academic institutions had been.[31] Those who sought to define what made the New Left distinct often argued that the opening of a new stage of society rendered the "Old Left" of socialist and communist parties obsolete; thus Massimo Teodori, one of the New Left's first anthologists, remarked that "the American New Left is perhaps the first, embryonic expression of a new force which confronts the problems of postindustrial society."[32] In an interesting New Left book titled *A Disrupted History*, SDS leaders Greg Calvert and Carol Neiman wholly embraced postindustrial language, describing a body of "scientific, technical, and professional workers," needed to "design and run ... automated and cybernated machinery," who displaced the "old working class" and Marx's proletarian strategy. In training for those roles, students could lead a revolution, promoting personal liberation and communal solidarity as they made universities "a living model of the struggle for a new society" beyond work and scarcity.[33]

The early discussion of postindustrial society was, however, riven by empirical disputes and growing political differences. Daniel Bell never accepted the projections of massive productivity gains offered by the "Triple Revolution" manifesto and refused to consider the alleged obsolescence of work a hallmark of postindustrialism. In his 1966 book *The Reforming of General Education*, Bell reasserted that the social and cultural preeminence of "theoretical knowledge" (i.e., basic, rather than applied, science) gave postindustrial society its distinctive principle: an "orientation toward the future" was necessary to provide long-term guidance to the generation of knowledge as a social and economic resource. A society organized to anticipate long-range needs was perforce focused on central, national institutions. Indeed, Bell wrote at a time when the recent civil rights acts lent some plausibility to his claim that American life had entered a new period in which "the conscious direction of social change [is undertaken] by the federal government."[34] Behind this formula of postindustrial society lay an idealized image of the welfare state, fully developed and bringing to fruition the evolutionary trend that enabled a democratic polity to shoulder tasks of social planning.

Others gave postindustrial society a dystopian cast. Without the reforms needed to render the new forces of productivity benign, the "Triple Revolution" writers warned, "we may be allowing an efficient and dehumanized community to emerge by default," turning the potential for a world beyond work into a strictly stratified order in which elites kept an Orwellian eye on a burgeoning underclass of obsolescent hands.[35] In French theorist Alain Touraine's view of postindustrial society, dissent was called for in the hope of preserving a small measure of private space apart from the omnipresent, omnivorous, and intrusive agencies geared to maximizing productive growth as an end in itself.[36] In this context, New Left thinking on the subject was profoundly ambivalent, seeing postindustrial society sometimes as the current condition of life that spawned new aspirations for change, sometimes as a model of the reformed society yet to be achieved, and sometimes as a new oppressive order rebels had to oppose.

For most of the 1960s, however, the optimistic dimension of postindustrial theory predominated. Whether postindustrial prophets foresaw a free postscarcity world liberating impulses of play from the constraints of work or the emergence of a full-fledged welfare state, their visions rested on the prevailing image of the affluent society Galbraith had outlined and particularly on Galbraith's proposition that recent development rendered the problem of social goods and the ineffectuality of the marketplace acute. Riesman's "Leisure and Work in Post-Industrial Society" centered on his claim that prospects of material abundance made cooperative or collective management of social and economic affairs more imperative. "Relatively well-off and well-educated Americans," who had lost not only the old productivist work ethic but even the "zest" for commercial consumption, led the way toward a new ethos:

> The amenities which [they] desire, once their own families are well provided for, are not those which can be bought by individuals acting in isolation from each other. They are rather such social goods as pleasant cities and sprawl-free countrysides.... But it is just at this point that the paucity of our individual goals, when amplified at the general social level, creates the most terrifying problems.... some of our desires have been made highly visible by advertising and market research.... But other desires, which require cooperation to be effective, are often lamely organized and all but invisible.... It is extraordinary how little we have anticipated the problems of the bountiful future.[37]

Similarly, in a 1962 discussion with Daniel Bell on postindustrial society, one participant argued that demands not easily satisfied through market mechanisms emerged once production came to rely on intellectual capacities ("human capital") and services became the growth sector of the economy: "The American public today, a metropolitan public by and large, requires a series of services [in recreation, education, and health] which American private enterprise cannot produce because of barriers to investment and to sale for profit. Therefore, the public cannot secure what it most wants and needs and could afford to pay for."[38]

Generally, postindustrial society appeared to its theorists as one in which social development pressed beyond the logic of markets, beyond an order in which economy was the determining structure and economics the privileged discourse. In one guise or another, the postindustrial idea suggested the obsolescence of the economic. Even Bell, who denied postindustrial society was "posteconomic" in the sense of escaping scarcity, claimed that it was governed by a "sociologizing" mode of decision that surpassed an "economizing" mode—the first mode taking into consideration integral social processes involving public resources and goods such as education and environmental quality, the second demanding only the efficient allocation of discrete inputs to given production processes.[39] The alleged eclipse of economics as system of thought or motive principle figured in Touraine's *The Post-Industrial Society:* Its "most widespread characteristic ... is that economic decisions and struggles no longer possess either the autonomy or the central importance they had in an earlier society which was defined by the effort to accumulate and anticipate profits from directly productive work.... Nowadays, it depends much more directly than ever before on knowledge, and hence on the capacity of society to call forth creativity."[40]

To be sure, the liberal social democratic outlook that spawned the postindustrial imagination betrayed an element of wish fulfillment, for by forecasting the immanent evanescence of the economic principle, it assumed that the forms of capitalism were dropping away and neglected facts about the power of wealth and corporate business in social affairs. Thus, left-wing critics argued, postindustrial theory provided an ideological fig leaf for contemporary capitalism. Nonetheless, the theory also sustained a polemic against market norms of social integration and provided a milieu of hope, one that played some role in fostering the rise of New Left radicalism. The New Left could see the prospect of surpassing capitalist norms as not inherently dubious and find in postindustrial theory a version of older socialist aspirations. To describe a postindustrial order as a "service society" in which the relationship of "people to people" supplants the industrial relationship of "people to things" is to retain the hope of achieving a society beyond reification, where the satisfaction of social needs supplants the economic calculus, and interpersonal service replaces the impersonality of "efficiency." If postindustrial society were regarded as something not yet achieved but only beckoning to us from the other side of a prolonged and troubled transition to a way of life more socialized, more rooted in the generalized experience of learning and applying experimental knowledge, and more open to the creative individuality of each and all persons, it would retain the radical potency it had in the 1960s.

The Avant-Garde's Second Wind and "Postmodern" Culture

As the diagnosis of postindustrial society emerged, other American writers began to use the term "postmodern," usually to describe contemporary culture. The derivation of the two terms was distinct, originating in two different quarters of intellectual debate and discussion, and it was not yet common to suggest, as some writers did in the 1980s, that postmodern culture was the form of sensibility typical to a postindustrial society. But the concepts were alike as attempts to name the dimensions of change and the prospects of the new in the 1960s. In both cases, too, the meanings ascribed to these terms changed considerably in subsequent years, obscuring the sense they initially had. Consequently, retrospective attempts to trace "postmodernism," as it came to be understood in the 1980s, to a profound sea change in culture occurring in the 1960s must be examined with some care and skepticism.

In the late 1950s, several writers claimed that "modernism" or "the avant-garde" had reached its end in the postwar world as the innovative literature and arts of the early twentieth century and the critics who championed them found acceptance in the curricula and at the lecterns of the new universities. For movements predicated on nonconformist experimentation and self-conscious estrangement from popular culture and middle-class opinion, such "success" signaled defeat. Cordial relations between "formerly intractable artist[s] and the no longer hostile bourgeoisie" made new literature intellectually slack, Harry Levin claimed. Leslie Fiedler argued that an avant-garde that once based its creative strategy on "offense" could not thrive when "only a diminishing minority of ever more comical bigots cries out in protest" and a growing college-educated audience greeted every new venture in shock with a bemused tolerance. When Irving Howe remarked that we are at "the end of one of those recurrent periods of cultural unrest, innovation and excitement that we call 'modern,'" it was clear that "postmodern" signaled a kind of "end of ideology" in art. Writers who were called postmodern in this sense included Bernard Malamud, Saul Bellow, and John Updike. Their "neorealism" gave up modernist attempts to jar the reader with disjointed narrative and linguistic play; their protagonists were uncertain that the established social world could provide them with a stable sense of meaning, but they also knew there was no exit from their responsibility of living in that world.[41]

After 1965 the meaning of "postmodern" changed dramatically, and some of the same writers who had mourned the demise of adversarial energy in the arts now recognized a "new sensibility" of opposition afoot. Howe, who was more appalled than cheered by this turn, now discerned "one of those startling shifts in cultural temper" that seemed to leave behind the styles he had described as postmodern in 1959. In 1965 Fiedler likewise described "post-Modernist literature" in terms of a "radical transformation ... of *homo sapiens*,"

58

a move away from standards of rationality, restraint, and order in gender roles, adding up to an offense "we really cannot abide." By 1971, when literature professor Ihab Hassan described "the postmodern spirit," he claimed, "Everywhere, Western art—like science, politics, morality—participates in the renewal of shapes, straining the structures of human life." Since the first diagnoses of the postmodern condition as artistic quiescence, in other words, the avant-garde had got its second wind: adversarial arts resurfaced, in league with the renewal of social protest in the early and mid-1960s.[42]

Calling such currents an avant-garde rests on a distinction drawn by critic Andreas Huyssen: The "historical avant-garde," he writes, consisted of early-twentieth-century movements such as dada, surrealism, and Russian constructivism, which wedded artistic experiment to new technologies, political protest, and revolutionary aspirations and sought to overcome the breach between "life" and "art." On the other hand, "modernism" bore stronger bonds to nineteenth-century romantic notions of a religion of art that set the refined sentiment of the artist against the philistinism of society at large. This distinction is far from hard and fast for early-twentieth-century art movements or for their legacy after World War II. Nonetheless, many features of new art in the early 1960s justify an emphasis on their avant-garde character: their form-breaking and genre-bridging impulses, affiliations with dissenting social and political sentiments, hostility to the arts establishment and skepticism of established modernism, a friendlier attitude toward popular culture, their appreciation of the vitality and mobility of urban life and their desire to bring art into touch with it, and even their confrontation with censorship.[43]

The avant-garde revival appeared in the shift from neorealist fiction to a new style of writing marked by outré fantasy, images of excess both exhilarating and chilling, and bitter parody. William Burroughs's *Naked Lunch* (1959), a disjointed, bewildering depiction of drug addicts that conveys the hellish degradation of their existence while still pouring scorn on "normal" social life, signaled the trend. There was a genuinely antinomian element, committed to untrammeled passion and contempt for convention, in some "underground" writing that surfaced in the 1963 anthology *Writers in Revolt*, edited by the misanthrope and sometime pornographer Alexander Trocchi and others. Yet a more palatable style of dissent appeared in novels such as Joseph Heller's send-up of military organization and authority, *Catch-22* (1960), in which absurdist comedy veils an encounter with horror, and in similar works by Kurt Vonnegut and Ishmael Reed. This writing shared a style of humor developed by liberal political comics (from Mort Sahl to Dick Gregory), by improvisational comedy troupes such as Chicago's Second City, in Lenny Bruce's vulgar and provocative stand-up routines, in screenplays by the satirist Terry Southern, and in the sometimes scurrilous magazine *The Realist*, edited by anarchist-bohemian Paul Krassner. Often self-consciously crude, sophomoric, or aggressively sexual, such humor dealt with both political and private life, mocking constituted authorities and established conventions with varying degrees of bitterness and fury. This approach added a distinctive element to the new fiction. Whereas the parodic novelists revived the fragmented narrative and jaundiced view of social existence that characterized early literary modernism, they often dispensed with the modernist focus on private consciousness and psychological depth. Rather, figures described in simple, even cartoonish, terms flit bewildered through experiences that burlesque conventional society, and while these scenarios had something Kafkaesque about them, their distinctive mood was set by the tone of raucous and derisive laughter.[44]

The new avant-garde took varied forms. Allan Kaprow, an artist and art historian working at Rutgers University, coined the term "Happenings" for quasi-theatrical events intended to leave plenty of room for improvisation and chance occurrences: typically, a small set of players placed in either constructed or natural settings carried out a minimal set of instructions for trivial, absurd, or bizarre acts and sounds (spreading strawberry jam over an auto wreck, for instance, while spectators blow police whistles). "I began wanting to collage the impossible—to paste-up action, to make collages of people and things in motion," Kaprow wrote of his intention to bring art into the world.[45] A related "event-art" movement called Fluxus adopted the revolutionary rhetoric of 1920s Russian constructivism in calling for a new democratic art borrowing "found objects" from the world of mass production and encouraging artistic amateurs to join cooperative performance groups. At about the same time, the new "free jazz" of virtually unbounded collective improvisation practiced by Ornette Coleman, Cecil Taylor, and others, as well as the work of young dance innovators such as Judith Dunn, Ruth Emerson, and Yvonne Rainer, showed that an emphasis on group process and spontaneity figured in the most various avant-garde performance practices.[46]

A number of observers then and since have doubted whether these currents warrant the name "avant-garde," since they rarely had to sustain a prolonged marginal existence. Allan Kaprow's Happenings, for instance, were soon commissioned by art programs at major public universities. To treat the newer arts, however, merely as a faux avant-garde enjoying mainstream acclaim would miss something of their tenor. For a time at least in the early 1960s, experimental arts still faced instances of official repression (particularly censorship of avant-garde film distribution), and the new practices shared the historic dispositions of the avant-garde to bridge the "gap between art and life" and to join forces with political protest and radical advocacy. Julian Beck and Judith Malina, founders of the Living Theatre company, turned toward a more provocative, participatory style of theater event as they joined pacifist campaigns against nuclear weapons in the late 1950s and early 1960s, and the Judson Memorial Church, a prime venue for experimental dance, theater, and poetry in New York's Greenwich Village, saw its art patronage as wedded to its role as a center for civil rights activism.[47]

The rebellious arts of the early 1960s constituted an authentic, albeit latter-day, avant-garde that faced the peculiar circumstances of tilting against an art establishment that already welcomed classic modernism. For this reason, a few writers at the time called the new currents "postmodern." Yet that term, as well as the arts and ideas closely associated with it, really owes its widespread appeal to developments of later years. A self-proclaimed postmodern architecture, for instance, arose in the early 1970s to promote a rapprochement of building design with popular taste. (In some respects, this movement was anticipated in 1966 by Robert Venturi's influential *Complexity and Contradiction in Architecture*, but although his manifesto assailed the rigid prescriptions of "orthodox Modern architecture," Venturi refrained at that time from naming a new style and indeed appealed to the role of complexity and ambiguity in *other* "modern" arts and sciences.) Also in the 1970s, social movements such as cultural feminism, deep ecology, and solidarity with indigenous peoples built a concerted criticism of "modern" notions of social progress. American incorporation of French poststructuralism during the mid- to late-1970s, furthermore, provided academic cultural criticism with a new vocabulary that was opposed to "centered" notions of self and reality and open to the diverse, fragmented, and uncertain qualities of experience. By the early 1980s, postmodernism was typically defined as a sea change in cultural sensibility marked by efforts to dismantle settled patterns of coherence and uniformity in social thought and practice, a leveling of "high art" and popular culture, widespread suspicion of (or loss of faith in) scientific reason and industrial organization, and the assumption that when "reality" as such is beyond our ken, experience is embedded in the unending circulation of meanings that make up "texts" and "textuality." The question remains whether this full-blown, self-conscious ideology of postmodernism can rightly claim to have its origins in the avant-garde arts of the 1960s. Mere continuity over time in use of the same term, given the changing meanings associated with it, does not suffice to justify that claim, and significant differences in sensibility between the 1960s and the 1980s raise further doubts.[48]

The French theorists of poststructuralism, for instance, were part of a radical generation that emerged during the late 1960s and turned against a "modern" French standard (Jean-Paul Sartre's existential philosophy) with an "antihumanist" program derived largely from late writings of conservative German philosopher Martin Heidegger. The poststructuralists built a critique of bourgeois individualism on Heidegger's claim that the "will to will" (the Promethean urges of the self hoping to achieve absolute autonomy) was responsible for the cultural catastrophe of modern life. The antihumanist animus of the French theorists, however, and the privilege they gave to forms of textuality (in place of the humanists' emphasis on individual consciousness) were not really widespread features of the American avant-garde of the 1960s. While the parodic novelists offered a more or less hostile vision of order, regimentation, and authority in modern life, they retained such homely humanist notions as a desire for truth, tenderness, and personal intimacy. One of the absurdists, novelist John Barth, published a 1967 essay showing that much contemporary fiction, notably the dizzying, metaphysical stories of Jorge Luis Borges, dwelled primarily on the ways humans created fictions for themselves; Barth, however, did not mean to suggest that the contemporary artist could do no more than portray the complications of text-making itself. When fiction writers in the 1960s described "the loss of reality and meaning" in the world at large, Barth wrote, they saw it "as a distortion of the human condition," not as the kind of liberation hailed later by postmodernists.[49]

A closer analogue to the ideology of postmodernism (and particularly the critique of self, vision, realism, and homogeneity associated with poststructuralism) can be found in quite a different quarter of American thought and culture in the 1960s, aside from the avant-garde arts: the work of Marshall McLuhan. McLuhan was a relatively obscure Canadian literature professor brought to intellectual celebrity after he published his 1962 book *The Gutenberg Galaxy* at age 51. Although his speculations about the social and cultural transformations initiated by new electronic media seemed akin to some of the visionary prospects suggested by postindustrial theory, his intellectual biography ran in circles quite distant from the social democratic reformism of that school. Studying in England during the 1930s, young McLuhan had associated with the Catholic conservatism of critics G. K. Chesterton and Hilaire Belloc and published articles sympathetic to fascism.[50] Given this questionable past, the mature McLuhan was forced to find new ways of conveying his ideas.

It was difficult in the early 1960s to reach a large reading audience with conservative views. William F. Buckley Jr. had founded the magazine *National Review* in 1955, and Russell Kirk added the scholarly quarterly *Modern Age* in 1957, both devoted to building a community of intellectuals on the Right. The early 1960s witnessed a quickening of this movement: *National Review* columnist Frank Meyer led a concerted effort to heal the breach between libertarian and traditionalistic conservatives, and William Buckley mentored the new Young Americans for Freedom (YAF). Having issued a manifesto denouncing the welfare state and calling for faith in God, patriotism, free markets, and victory over world communism, YAF burgeoned with members devoted to promoting a run for president by the standard-bearer of the Republican Party right wing, Barry Goldwater. Nonetheless, these were at best "years of preparation," as George Nash, historian of the movement, put it. Conservatives still had only a "small foothold" in academic life, and their defense of segregation on "states' rights" grounds (including vicious attacks on civil rights leaders such as Martin Luther King Jr.) helped ensure their marginality in intellectual and cultural life. Few conservatives were inclined, or able, to challenge the prevailing view of American scholars that the United States was defined by a "liberal tradition," and the most articulate, like Buckley, frankly regarded themselves as out of step, committed to a "counterrevolution" against the persistent "collectivism" of the New Deal tradition. One way to break out of the intellectual backwater and convey conservative values in an inhospitable environment, however, was McLuhan's, in which antimodernism paradoxically dwelled under cover of technological euphoria.[51]

According to McLuhan, the electronic media of his time promised to knit the world together in a "global village"—a "single constricted space resonant with tribal drums." The reunification of the world by electronic means brought with it a revolution in senses, dethroning the hegemonic sense of vision (made paramount by the conjoint beginning of "print culture" and Renaissance humanism in the fifteenth and sixteenth centuries) and reinvigorating "audile-tactile" senses so prominent in earlier ages. The perceptions of "primitive man," McLuhan wrote, were open to varied sensual inputs and permitted a more immediate sense of belonging to the natural world, whereas the ideal of visually recording the image of the world around us (mimetic realism), cultivated by print-reading habits, split humans off from the world itself and produced the myth of the "individual ego." New media, particularly television, promised to establish a "unified field of electric all-at-oneness" that reinvented the immediacy of primitive art, with salutary effects: "The 'simultaneous field' of electric information structures, today reconstitutes the conditions and need for dialogue and participation, rather than specialism and private initiative."[52] But McLuhan's echo of the characteristic 1960s emphasis on enrichment of the social sphere did not mean he shared a progressive critique of capitalism. Reflecting his youthful enthusiasms, he lauded the national solidarity of Germany and Japan in the previous war, noting that these peoples, "while far-advanced in literate and analytic technology, retained the core of auditory tribal unity and total togetherness." Lest his critique of modern regimentation suggest any solicitude for personal liberation, he explained that print culture "created national uniformity and government centralism, but also individualism and opposition to government as such." Citizen armies and public schools ("the nation in arms" and "the nation in schools") and equal rights and free speech (unrestricted access to published material was, he sneered, a "consumer attitude to literature") all struck McLuhan as marks of a world governed by hierarchical control *and* ungodly rebellion.[53] His critique of "hierarchy," furthermore, referred only to the modern, bureaucratic sort, not the priestly order that inhered in the "true" spiritual unity of a premodern religious culture. That McLuhan's embrace of contemporary media such as television made him seem a revolutionary, breaking with conservative defenders of "high culture," was one of the great illusions of the 1960s. His thinly disguised antimodernism heralded a new world, to be brought about by a great leap forward into the distant past.

The Relevance and Revision of Development Theory

In the 1960s, confidence in promises of modernization coexisted with a distinctly antimodern criticism of contemporary life. Despite economic growth and social reform after World War II, there remained a deep suspicion, voiced by romantic, radical, and conservative thinkers, that dark forces of power and destruction were endemic to modernity. The tendency to see modern life as a catastrophe only gained strength among social critics as the Vietnam War revealed again (for those who had forgotten) the death-dealing capacity of modern technology. Thus a spirit of historical pessimism and cultural despair persisted in the 1960s even as prosperity, reform, and artistic renewal encouraged grand hopes for wholesale personal and social change.

The contradiction between an overly simple confidence in the beneficence of change and an equally general suspicion of contemporary trends rested in part on problems of definition. Discussions of change and development are typically hobbled by what Andreas Huyssen has called a "holistic notion of modernity," a tendency to presume modernity comprises a particular, coherent set of attributes—prosperity, individualism, and democracy for some observers; power concentration, atomization, and manipulative control for others.[54] Similarly, most talk of development has assumed a linear form, suggesting that change follows one path toward a single conceivable goal. A more supple concept of development that is capable of measuring the detriments, defaults, *and* realizable promises of evolutionary social change might be fashioned if such assumptions of holism and strict linearity are surrendered. Sensitivity to the "combined and uneven" character of social development, for instance, recognizes any society as a hybrid, not a wholly integrated organism. In these terms, the Russian revolutionary Leon Trotsky tried to explain the roots of radical change in seemingly stagnant "backward" or colonized countries. Trotsky recognized in such cases "a drawing together of the different stages of the journey, a combining of separate steps, an amalgam of archaic with more contemporary forms": although prospects for steady progress in the Victorian sense of the term were jammed in some respects, the "more contemporary forms" within those countries also made possible rapid, revolutionary leaps.[55] "Advanced" societies are also hybrids: industrial organization stands alongside postindustrial technologies; capitalist markets combine with social services. Globally, rich countries coexist with poor countries that accommodate many of the displaced functions of industrial production on which the former depend. A tangled, disjointed kind of social order and development prevails for all.

Such an approach avoids simple holism and linearity but presumes a normative concept of stages (on which the judgment of "unevenness" depends) as well as a telos, a goal toward which change tends. Yet concepts of stage and telos can be justified as essential to social understanding and social action. Any attempt to analyze main causes of change in human history would rest on some kind of structural theory that distinguishes basic types of societies—the differences, for instance, between small-scale "stateless" societies, state-organized societies without secularized markets, and mercantile societies lacking widespread labor markets.[56] Moreover, the course of contemporary social change gains meaning as it is situated within some theory of development that imagines the possible ends in sight. This sense of trajectory helps determine a range of feasible actions to take in trying to move trends toward desirable goals; responsible action for change depends on it.[57]

None of these fundamentals necessarily limits the goal of contemporary development to what prior generations have defined as the essence of modernity, to stereotypical features such as the ascendance of science over religion, technical specialization over generalized knowledge, individualism over solidarity, impersonal efficiency over sentimental ties. Modernity might be regarded as a moving target, a possible future based instead, perhaps, on the reinvigoration of synthetic understanding, communal bonds of affection, and facilities of social interaction.[58] Such prospects animated a good deal of the activism that lit up the 1960s. We might still recognize them as evolutionary possibilities, even if only a revolutionary break with the established order of things can bring them to fruition.

four

Authenticity and Artifice

One of the chief paradoxes of the 1960s was the coincidence of devotion to the ideal of authenticity—of discovering, voicing, and exercising a genuine, whole personality freed from the grip of mortifying convention—and fascination with the ways of artifice, with the calculated techniques of image making or "the games people play." Each of these poles posed complex issues and paradoxically merged into the other. Authenticity combined such ideals as personal autonomy and flexibility, free self-expression, determination to pursue truth and "face reality," and a search for well-grounded and meaningful motives to action. Yet the urgent pursuit of truth was not immune to the insidious effects of show—to stylized, illusory ways of being "real." John Schlesinger's 1965 movie *Darling* made the point nicely: the protagonist declares her desire to live freely, refusing obedience to convention in order to meet the variations of experience frankly and fully, only to become entrapped (as a star model) in the industry—fashion advertising—that perfects the arts of mendacity. On the other hand, fascination with artifice was never merely an invitation to things false or meretricious. Pop art, for instance, gravitated to the media of commercial advertising and the impact of the mass-produced image, but in exploring those realms, many pop artists believed they were bringing art into the "real world" of the modern city, where life was surrounded by mediated messages. In many ways, then, aspirations to authenticity and the practice of artifice mingled together. The Velvet Underground, a rock band associated with Andy Warhol's pop art salon, affected a gritty "realism" in songs giving cool, hard depictions of the seamy side of life. Critic Susan Sontag, who hailed the "camp" sensibility for promoting "a new standard [of] artifice as an ideal," also decried critics who emphasized "interpretation" of art and literature because she sought an aesthetic that would help us "experience more immediately what we have" in the world before dulling the senses with an accumulation of layered meanings.[1]

Despite the curious overlap of these terms, the striking appeal of authenticity in the 1960s spurred debate over its social implications. Marshall Berman's eloquent book *The Politics of Authenticity* argued that the Enlightenment (particularly Montesquieu and Rousseau) had "open[ed] up a whole new theoretical perspective": "We can now see how the 'natural' self of man is threatened by his 'social' self; how the spontaneity of 'people as they really are' is repressed by the social roles they are forced to play; how the human variety which nature produces is subverted by the uniformity of character which society demands." But such anti-institutional notions of authenticity, sharply opposed to social conventions of all sorts, made no sense to sociologists who "argued against dualist oppositions of human nature and social order, against individualist conceptions of the self," as Philip Rieff put it in *The Triumph of the Therapeutic* (1966). For Rieff, the cultural crisis of his time was marked by the apparent loss of any compelling reason for an individual's submission to regulation by social institutions, which must be grounded in some kind of belief, faith, or self-subjection to greater meaning shared with others. With no socially significant motivation other than the individual's well-being, Rieff feared, society lost its moorings and began to dissolve.[2] Yet the two sides of this argument need not have been counterposed so bluntly. In the hands of so keen a writer as Erving Goffman (1922–1982), demands for authenticity and the inevitability of artifice were combined in a theory of social interaction that sharply criticized social institutions but also recognized them as the basis of personal integrity.

Expression, Impression, and the Narcissistic Society

"There are too many things we [Americans] do not wish to know about ourselves," James Baldwin wrote in *The Fire Next Time*, his passionately eloquent challenge to white racism, as he appealed to the ethic of authenticity.[3] Baldwin suggested that American whites, so quick to forget their country's record of violent racial oppression as they denounced "black militants," exuded bad faith. African Americans at least saw through the nation's liberal ideology: "That man who is forced each day to snatch his manhood, his identity, out of the fire of human cruelty that rages to destroy it ... achieves his own authority, and that is unshakable ... because, in order to save his life, he is forced to look beneath appearances, to take nothing for granted, to hear the meaning behind the words."[4] As part of the national and personal self-reckoning demanded by struggles for racial justice, the ethic of authenticity echoed in other areas of American thought and culture during the 1960s. Writing of the sexual double standard that imposed a regime of "frustration" and "duplicity" on young women of the 1950s, Janet Malcolm has remarked: "We lied to our parents and we lied to each other and we lied to ourselves, so addicted to deception had we become. We were an uneasy, shifty-eyed generation. Only a few of us could see how it was with us."[5] Breaking through such customary standards to something like a "real self," or "self-expression," Malcolm suggested, helped make confessional poets such as Sylvia Plath and Anne Sexton models of authenticity to young women seeking freedom in the 1960s. Later, the radical feminist publication *Notes from the Second Year* affirmed "authenticity" as its only editorial policy, urging on women the "courage to say what you mean." Tellingly, a 1973 feminist anthology of women's poetry was entitled *No More Masks!*[6]

The impulse to strip away illusion, look behind appearances, and gauge the validity of long-held, oft-professed ideals or norms followed demands for social change; revealing unhappy truths was always a staple of social criticism. As Erving Goffman wrote, citing an account of police brutality, "Recent studies of the police suggest that ... justice is more summary than had been thought."[7] In this sense, authenticity became a kind of social imperative. But it also gathered force as a norm of personal life, especially under the influence of popular strains in philosophy and psychology. Authenticity "comes close to being the one new and absolute virtue in existentialism," wrote Hazel Barnes, and it figured in Jean-Paul Sartre's *Being and Nothingness* as a demand to face the reality of the human condition, to bear the burden of being a free subject responsible for one's own actions, and to resist all temptation to accept the status of an object determined by outside forces.[8] Openness to change also figured prominently in Sartre's account, for he regarded "man" as a creature "who is what he is not and who is not what he is," one who is in a continual process of "becoming," of "making himself."[9] Such authenticity, however, remained an austere and rigorous ethic that made little room for such appealing notions as personal wholeness, uniqueness, and expressive identity; it was anything but an easy achievement.

More popular ideals of authenticity had emerged in new neo-Freudian, "humanistic," and Gestalt therapies. All these currents preached individuation. Erik H. Erikson's neo-Freudian notion of "identity" as the signal achievement of the stage of life he named "youth" (an inner sense of unity, derived from love and work, that was congruent with "one's meaning for others") struck some critics as a recipe for social conformity; nonetheless, it offered the early feminist Betty Friedan a notion of autonomy that put the shortcomings of housewifely dependency in high relief. The humanistic psychologists Gordon Allport, Henry Murray, Carl Rogers, and Abraham Maslow moved even further away from orthodox Freudianism in trying to shift the focus of psychology from neurosis to a phenomenology of "mental health." Maslow described a kind of maximal mental health in the "peak experiences" of "self-actualizing" persons who found autonomy in moments of perceptual acuity and intense creativity. Similarly, the Gestalt therapy of Fritz Perls, Ralph Hefferline, and Paul Goodman promised to help the person to reclaim "his

Wholeness, his Integrity" by a process of "assimilating the novel, by change and growth." Gestalt therapy voiced a sharp distrust of "existing social arrangements [falsely depicted] as immutable laws of man and society" and boldly recommended the surrender of inhibitions, asserting an anarchist confidence in the natural balance to be achieved psychologically and socially by unfettered selves.[10]

As a rule, these therapies placed a value on self-development and self-expression that was at least equal to, if not weightier than, the value of social conventions; the goal of authenticity, for some of its proponents, implied an anti-institutional animus verging on antinomianism. At an early point in his career, Henry Murray, the humanistic psychologist most interested in the role of the unconscious, toyed with Nietzschean ideas that the pursuit of personal wholeness demanded the transgression of conventional morality, the liberation of deep desires that brought the individual "beyond good and evil." Maslow, at least in his private journals, embraced Nietzschean principles more wholeheartedly. For him, the force of "one's true inner nature" was bound to elicit the hostility of society at large. Maslow never conceived that his notion of "self-actualizing" personality would apply to any but a small minority of individuals—"innate superiors"—and he believed his psychology should develop "a doctrine of an elite [and] degrees of humanness" to "make the world safe for superiors." Perls, who may have originated the phrase "Do your own thing" in his antipathy toward conformism, was known for outlandish acts of self-expression, including crawling around on his belly in the midst of one of Maslow's lectures.[11]

Nonetheless, the ideal of authenticity in the 1960s did not entirely lack a social ethic. Perls's collaborator Paul Goodman was a noted communitarian theorist whose best-known book, *Growing Up Absurd* (1960), criticized less the repressiveness of society as such than its failure to provide individuals with viable "work or vocation," that is, the means to combine self-fulfillment and social participation. Although quite different from Goodman, David Riesman likewise imagined the personal ideal of "autonomy" in terms that aimed to adjudicate individualism and sociability: the autonomous personality Riesman described at the end of his landmark book *The Lonely Crowd* was not, as commonly understood, a reinvention of the sturdy, self-willed bourgeois man, but rather an attempt to repudiate the conformist elements of the new, widespread "other-directed" character type while retaining its virtues of emotional sensitivity and capacity for collaboration with others.[12]

In any case, the impulse toward assertive individuality was strong in the culture of the 1960s and became especially potent in new literary trends. The Beat poets, a marginal literary subculture in the mid-1950s, had already cultivated an ethic of self-expression. With long lines intended as verbal analogues of jazz saxophone improvisations, Allen Ginsberg's *Howl* (1955) was designed for oral performance, as a boisterous outpouring of personal sentiment and an agonized lament.[13] The autobiographical and scandalous self-revelatory impulse of the marginal Beats was brought into the mainstream of literary practice with the rise of the "confessional" poets, signaled by Robert Lowell's *Life Studies* (1959) and followed after 1960 by the work of Anne Sexton, some of John Berryman's poems, and, most notoriously, Sylvia Plath's posthumous *Ariel*.[14] Reacting against the dominant strain in American poetry of the 1940s and 1950s, a highly formal and craftlike verse that Lowell (originally one of its leading practitioners) came to feel was unable to "handle much experience," the new writing sought to achieve spontaneity and immediacy in quick, almost improvisatory composition, plain diction, bold images, and "brutally frank self-exposure."[15] In the preference for "experience" over "polish" lay a strong dose of antiformalism, a view that aesthetic conventions were artificial impositions or constraints—"lies" from which one should "break loose," thus "stripping away ... inauthentic coverings" to disclose the truth of "what you really feel."[16]

Plath became something of a martyr to this confessional ethic. In the *Ariel* poems, written rapidly in the last six months before her February 1963 suicide, she found the "voice," it was said, that accompanied her emerging "real self."[17] As critic Elizabeth Hardwick wrote a few years later, the fascination of Plath's poetry stemmed from the impression that there was daring truth in such self-revelation, especially because the self so disclosed was, in many ways, unpleasant: her poetry, Hardwick said, never presented Plath as a "nice person."[18] The images of *Ariel*, particularly her outburst of hatred toward her father, who died when she was eight years old ("Daddy"), and her reflections on her own "resurrection" following a failed suicide attempt ("Lady Lazarus"), were sharp and brutal, drawing on images of Holocaust atrocities to voice violent sentiments. Nonetheless, Paul Breslin has pointed out, while Plath portrayed herself as open to inspection, she could not avoid a measure of self-conscious ambivalence about doing so, expressing resentment at how "The peanut-crunching crowd / Shoves in to see / Them unwrap me hand and foot."[19] Breslin suggests that Plath was not so much exposing her "self" as elaborating a "myth" of a poet struggling toward "uncontaminated authenticity," fleeing from social relationships that inevitably appeared as "snares." The myth was not entirely false, but Plath's private letters and journals also showed another side: her aspirations for success as a writer, her moments of vigor, happiness, hope, and tenderness. Indeed, the immediacy sought by the confessional style was not always best suited to reveal the varied, partly unified entity that is a "self." An ethos of confession mistaking strong feeling for "reality," or urgent impulses for "truth," encouraged a style of emotional extremism as likely to shatter a self as enact it.[20]

Pop art offered a counterpoint to the confessional poets. Artists such as Andy Warhol, Roy Lichtenstein, Claes Oldenburg, James Rosenquist, and Tom Wesselman adopted images and techniques from popular media and commercial milieus, rebelling against a recently established standard—the New York school of painting including Jackson Pollock and others—just as

Lowell cast aside the "crystalline" standard of postwar verse. Whereas the poets sought a more expressive style, however, pop artists rejected expressivism. The "extroverted rather than introverted" pop current showed "disdain for sentiment and even for sensitivity" and embraced the forms of the cartoon, billboard, celebrity photo, and product label. Yet such artifice had its own authenticity. The 1962 show at New York's Sidney Janis Gallery, which first assembled work by these artists, called them "New Realists." The name "pop art" came from the British critic Lawrence Alloway. He had participated in a London circle of young artists trying during the mid-1950s to overthrow old "idealist and absolutist" fine-art traditions hostile to forms of contemporary design and entertainment and disdainful of the modern world as such—a highly artificial stance, to their minds. They proposed "acceptance of science and the city ... in terms of fact condensed in vivid imagery," an art that would draw into painting, collage, and other works "forms available to the spectator through mass media [as] a shared world of references."[21] Likewise, the American pop artists would make art "in the world," an aspiration signaled not only by selection and quotation of commercial and media images but also in more widespread use of materials such as vinyl, Plexiglas, and neon.

Early pop art had an egalitarian, democratic urban esprit. To be sure, it was not "critical" of its environment, and at times, its proponents voiced a happy embrace of commercialism. The British pop artists admired "the American way of life," the "gleaming exotic images and extravagant attitudes which were so heavily propagandized in Europe and which, for us, implied not only an optimistic and classless society, but also that every American had his hot-rod and his surfboard."[22] Consequently, the critic Dore Ashton offered a typical response to pop art in writing: "Far from being an art of social protest, it is an art of capitulation."[23] Other critics have tried to defend the movement by citing—not always convincingly—a satirical or parodic attitude toward popular culture in pop art's appropriation of its images.[24] Yet who would demand that John Coltrane be "critical" of a popular tune such as "My Favorite Things" when he took it as a basis for improvisation? Even without a "critical" agenda, pop art was not merely complacent or jejune. The bold, awkward swaths of jarring color in the yellow hair, turquoise eyelids, and red lips of Andy Warhol's silk-screened image of Marilyn Monroe, when compared to conventional glamour images of her, highlight the modes of generating effect that our immersion in consumer culture makes virtually invisible. Pop offered an aesthetic that sharpened the senses in a particular kind of environment, where impressions large and small are made by calculated use of a color, a pinstripe, a special kind of ambient light.

Pop art was determinedly anti-auratic in its attempt to deprive artworks of the "aura" (as Walter Benjamin described it) that sets art apart in a hallowed realm resonant with meaning. James Rosenquist, who came to pop art with a sensibility shaped in part by his trade as a billboard painter, declared he was "not concerned with symbolism of any kind." It was in this sense that pop art was enamored of the "newly minted, mass-produced" effect of commercial artifacts: they carried no past and thus no memory and no "character" acquired with age, no "mystery," and no indication of the author's "personality" that could distract from the impact of the image itself.[25] In some respects, such notions hint at a democratic desire to develop the potential for popular creativity and sensibility; they suggest the ability of many (rather than a "talented" few possessing the charismatic authority of high art) to make art of the common things in their lives and to appreciate artfulness in their "built environment."

However, the pop ethos of impersonality had its drawbacks. To be sure, despite their principled resistance to disclosing the artist's personal presence in their work, most of the leading pop artists ended up establishing a kind of signature style (Oldenburg's soft sculptures, Lichtenstein's "bendayed" cartoon panels). Andy Warhol, on the other hand, made a style of his signature. By the late 1960s, he relied on his name alone to make commercially valuable artworks out of the mass-produced prints he or his assistants churned out, in a determined mood of nonchalance, from his aptly named salon, the Factory. Warhol's career and persona suggested two principles wedded together: first, a cult of industrial mechanism that demanded a kind of self-effacement indicated in other respects by Warhol's affectation of complete emotional indifference to human events around him; second, a grand apotheosis of celebrity indicated not only by his wish to be seen in the company of beautiful people but also by his renowned declaration that in the new world of mass media, everyone will someday enjoy "15 minutes of fame."[26]

This curious combination of self-effacement and celebrity, like confessional poetry's tendency to magnify and dissolve the self, posed a paradox that piqued the interest of psychologists concerned with "narcissism." The diagnosis of "narcissistic personality disorders" became prominent by the late 1960s, based on work by English Freudians D. W. Winnicott, John Bowlby, and Mary Ainsworth, who examined a child's earliest relations with the mother; on the "revisionist" German-American analyst Ernest Schachtel, who borrowed existential themes to explore the child's active and inquisitive encounter with the world; and on the more "orthodox" Freudian theory of Heinz Kohut at the University of Chicago. Kohut tied this new kind of psychological disturbance to malfunctions in a child's early interactions with a nurturer. John Bowlby's *Attachment* (1969) also recognized a common "blockage in the capacity to make deep relationships, such as is present in affectionless and psychopathic personalities." In a more popular vein, the existentialist psychologist Rollo May, in *Love and Will* (1969), described the chief clinical problem of his day as the inability to "experience genuine feelings," being "out of touch [and] avoiding close relationships."[27] With its concern for the troubled dynamics of human attachment and connection, narcissism theory, rather than therapies of identity and self-actualization, might be the decade's most telling innovation in psychology.

All these writers intended to break down assumptions of a strict distinction between the individual and society, ego and outer reality. In their focus on early sensations of dependence and the gradual process of individuation, these analysts emphasized the role played by empathy and mutuality, the fluid interaction of personalities between parent and child that shaped a child's transition to ego independence, and the residues of that transition that left healthy individuals with a sense of vital connection between self and the world—the basic element in lifelong capacities for play, imagination, aesthetic experience, and creative activity. In Kohut's cogent analysis, a parent's empathic response to a child's needs permits the emerging individual to build an integrated self while moving away from a primordial sense of undifferentiated unity with the world at large. These are the balanced achievements the pathological "narcissist" lacks: the personality disorder is not a matter of "self-love" but rather the absence of a viable self. As part of a disordered internal life, raging impulses confront an unduly punitive "superego"; the narcissist oscillates between a grandiose inflation of self-importance and abject dependence on the approval of superiors, remaining fixated on bodily pleasures that are strangely divorced from any resonant emotion.[28] Narcissism is thus a syndrome combining magnification and dissolution of the self (like Warhol's cult of empty celebrity); it is marked by an inability to distinguish the self from the world, and the absence of vital links to others.

The psychology of authenticity and the critical analysis of narcissism both arose in conditions of rapid social change. The ideal of authenticity came not only from a conviction, stoked by the black freedom struggle, women's movements, and other forces, that oppressive social conventions ought to be unmasked, but also from a broader feeling that the obsolescence of an old social order rendered all established roles radically artificial—things a vital self might shed. Rollo May noted that "ours is an era of radical transition," and that problems of emptiness, apathy, and disconnection might stem from the fact that "cultural values by which people had gotten their sense of identity had been wiped away."[29] Identifying those moribund values with "Horatio Alger values of work and success," May hinted that the "radical transition" of his day lay in the post-bourgeois implications of affluent society. At its base, May's interpretation echoed the basic proposition of Philip Rieff's *Triumph of the Therapeutic*: the loss of a compelling sense that overarching standards of meaning and commitment (a faith or dogma) governed one's action left society an enervated mass guided by nothing but a dumb, manipulable urge for enjoyment. Whether loss of cultural ballast was a good or bad thing, demanding movement to something new or recovery of something old, remained debatable. In any case, a critique of narcissistic society, formless and reduced to a mass of passionless, self-absorbed atoms, carried great weight in the 1960s.

An early evocation of this critique was Walker Percy's 1961 novel *The Moviegoer*. Jack (Binx) Bolling, son of a deceased surgeon from an old, elite New Orleans family and a nurse from the backcountry, has been "adopted" by his upper-class aunt, who wants him to attend medical school and to help safeguard her stepdaughter, Kate, a suicidal young woman demanding of love and attention who cannot get through the day without being "told what to do." As his 30th birthday approaches, Binx, who works as a stockbroker, feels oppressed by "ordinariness" and intimations of death. He carries himself with extreme apathy, claiming to care for nothing but watching movies and dallying in romance, usually with his secretaries, though he also persists in a vaguely defined "search"; occasionally he registers, in moments of déjà vu associated with remembered movie scenes, an odd, bracing sense of "reality." One day, without warning, Binx takes Kate, who is near despair, with him on a business trip to Chicago. Later, decrying his "irresponsibility," his aunt prepares to break relations and defends her own sense of class distinction as a bulwark of moral order. She is "not ashamed to use the word class" and claim that "people belonging to my class [are] better than other people." "We're better because we do not shirk our obligations.... We do not whine. We do not organize a minority group and blackmail the government." Binx cannot muster such ardent traditionalism, but his lament bears a conservative regret about the loss of anything but dumb desire in the modern world:

> Now is the thirty-first year of my dark pilgrimage on this earth and knowing less than I ever knew before, having learned only to recognize merde when I see it ... living in fact in the very century of merde, the great shithouse of scientific humanism where needs are satisfied, everyone becomes an anyone, a warm and creative person, and prospers like a dung beetle, and one hundred percent of people are humanists and ninety-eight percent believe in God, and men are dead, dead, dead; and the malaise has settled like a fallout and what people really fear is not that the bomb will fall but that the bomb will not fall—on this my thirtieth birthday, I know nothing and there is nothing to do but fall prey to desire.... Nothing remains but desire, and desire comes howling down Elysian Fields like a mistral. My search has been abandoned; it is no match for my aunt, her rightness and her despair.... Whenever I take leave of my aunt after one of her serious talks, I have to find a girl.[30]

Often, in the critique of narcissistic society, there emerged a conservative element ready to judge the leveling of social distinction, and popular aspirations for gratification, as marking the onset of social dissolution and self-absorption. In a related fashion, a dynamic intellectual current of conservatism led by political philosopher Leo Strauss and students such as Walter Berns, Martin Diamond, and Harry Jaffa reasserted the role of "virtue" in political life and rejected the modern liberal emphasis on "rights" as a purely individualistic doctrine eroding the integrity of the national community. The argument, furthermore, that the welfare state, based on rights and entitlements, exercised a corrupting influence and encouraged an epidemic of personal license figured in the rhetoric of Barry Goldwater's 1964 campaign, to which Jaffa, a political scientist at the Claremont colleges, contributed as a speechwriter.[31] Yet the moral critique was far from limited to tradition-minded political conservatives. It often appeared as part of a sophisticated liberal plaint and echoed through popular movies and plays, such as *Alfie* (1965), which ends with the libertine protagonist confessing his emptiness while wistfully listening to church bells, or *Who's Afraid of Virginia Woolf?* (1964), in which George and Martha likewise confront their own moral exhaustion as Sunday dawns. The claim that moral standards and social order were unraveling was a well-established part of American thought and culture in the 1960s, well before the usual suspects (such as a popular "counterculture" or radical feminism) appeared on the scene. It is in any case a peculiar notion of the 1980s and 1990s that "the sixties" can be blamed for promoting corrosive individualism and moral decline, since the potent desire for human connection that founded a critique of narcissism was itself such a prominent feature of American thought in the 1960s.

The Social Self in the Work of Erving Goffman

"One of the greatest writers alive today," declared Marshall Berman in 1972, "is a man whom our culture hardly knows, the sociologist Erving Goffman." A modest University of Pennsylvania professor, Goffman had published *The Presentation of Self in Everyday Life* (1959), *Asylums: Essays on the Social Situation of Mental Patients and Other Inmates* (1961), and other books leading up to *Relations in Public: Microstudies of the Public Order* (1971). Berman hailed Goffman as an avatar of authenticity. His arch depiction of pretension in the performance of social roles and his exposure of the harsh impress that organized institutions made on human behavior suggested a deep suspicion of convention—even an anti-institutional mood of revolt. Indeed, his analysis of norms in everyday social interaction resonated with young radicals. They, Berman wrote, knew "the importance of *form*":

> They understood how a culture's system of manners, of decorum, its rules of civility, propriety, order, could crush human life as effectively as any column of tanks. They hoped to tear down the walls of our structures of "deference and demeanor," to rip off our social masks, to create new forms through which people could express what they really felt, and confront each other directly, free and equal, face to face.[32]

But Goffman could be interpreted as a theorist of artifice, too. Alvin Gouldner called Goffman an apologist for consumer capitalism and its ethos of image making and impression management; more recently, historian Kenneth Cmiel placed Goffman among conventional sociologists who complacently accept the fragmentation of personality in diverse social roles, denying the possibility of a genuine, "whole" person. Goffman himself surprised some admirers when he introduced *Relations in Public* with caustic remarks about current trends toward the "unsettling" of social "ground rules," which left individuals vulnerable to "social molestation."[33] From this, Berman concluded that Goffman had retracted his earlier attacks on convention, but it would be better to see that Goffman's subtle social perspective on personhood rendered antithetical interpretations of his work equally one-sided and pushed beyond both authenticity and artifice.

Born in Alberta, Canada, Goffman graduated from the University of Toronto and began graduate studies at the University of Chicago in 1945.[34] A number of Chicago traditions converged in his training—the "interactionism" of George Herbert Mead, which examined the social construction of the self in the exchange of cues and gestures between actors; the hard-boiled urban research founded by Robert Park and carried on by Everett Hughes; and the ethnography of social classes promoted by W. Lloyd Warner. An extra-academic intellectual current of the late 1940s also played a crucial role in forming Goffman's disposition. A kind of radical personalism, which broadly characterized the anarcho-pacifists of Dwight Macdonald's *politics* magazine, the existentialists in Liberation France, the philosophers of the Frankfurt school, and the critique of "totalitarianism" by Hannah Arendt and George Orwell, found echoes in Goffman's earliest work. Fearing the uses of instrumental reason that gave the modern state the capacity to organize and manipulate masses of people, this new style of postwar radicalism insisted that the person be regarded as an end in itself, never a mere *means*, and hoped to find a defense against organized social control in the haven of small-group intimacy.[35] Reflecting these ideas, Goffman's doctoral dissertation, intended first as an anatomy of social classes in a small Shetland Island town, became a study of face-to-face communication that set the stage for all his subsequent work.

The microscopic dissection of everyday conversation in Goffman's dissertation supported an argument over sociological method. Language, Goffman pointed out, could be understood in either "instrumental" or "expressive" terms (neighbors in the island town he named "Dixon" might exchange information about the current price of wool, but in so doing, they aimed also at an emotional effect, that is, to appear neighborly). Most sociological studies of interaction had too strong a bias toward language's instrumental capacity. "The implication [has been] that we take into consideration the actions of others (the better to achieve our personal ends, whatever these may be) and not so much that we give consideration to other persons. By 'consideration' we have tended to mean calculation, not considerateness."[36] Social conversation ought to be examined, Goffman wrote, as a form of *ritual* in Emile Durkheim's sense, whereby persons are endowed with "sacred qualities" and regarded as "delicate objects which must be treated with care, with ceremonial offerings and propitiations."[37] In the unremarked practices of acknowledging a neighbor, engaging an acquaintance in conversation but delicately approaching a stranger, showing full involvement with others even if only as a show, Goffman discerned forms of ritual recognition of the person, not as a means to purposive ends but as an end in itself.[38] Terms of common sociability constructed the sphere of the person, for within the homely rituals of face-to-face interaction, the person as such was honored.

Such premises provided the foundation for social criticism in Goffman's later book *Asylums*. He described mental hospitals, along with other "total institutions" (prisons and army camps), as places marked off by more or less impermeable boundaries from what he called "civil" or "civilian society" at large: in such institutions, all aspects of an individual's life are subject to a particular regimen. Within hospital walls, a set of practices—denial of privacy to patients always under surveillance, subjection to kinds of direct authority usually reserved for children, talking about patients in the third person while they are present, and so on—failed to grant an ordinary degree of respect to persons and created instead interaction norms that compelled patients to act as nonpersons. A patient's noncommunicative indifference to surroundings, self-absorption, and surrender of "normal" bodily self-control, then, were less manifestations of an organic or psychic pathology than they were a social product of the institution. Goffman's argument seemed to be a perverse demonstration of social psychology's proposition that personality emerges out of a set of behaviors determined by the demands of routine interaction with others—perverse because social interaction in these cases yielded not the integration but disintegration of personality. Furthermore, there remained in *Asylums* the disturbing suggestion that the practices characterizing such "total institutions" were not exceptions but analogues to the "normal" world of "civilian society." Indeed, Goffman's next book, *Behavior in Public Places* (1963), described the fine grain of regulations governing ordinary social interaction as an onerous imposition on persons, casting society as a kind of totalitarian engine of discipline. The number of petty acts and gestures that are demanded of people involved in social situations demonstrates "the *thoroughness with which our lives are pressed into the service* of society." Furthermore, "The ultimate penalty for breaking the rules is harsh. Just as we fill our jails with those who transgress the legal order, so we partly fill our asylums with those who act unsuitably."[39]

Remarks such as these, as well as the intellectual company he kept in the 1960s, helped give Goffman his reputation as an anti-institutional critic. His critique of asylums and medical definitions of mental illness resembled the "labeling theory" of deviance developed in the early 1960s by Goffman's graduate school associate Howard S. Becker and others. They insisted that behaviors "variously called crime, vice, nonconformity, aberration, eccentricity, or madness" could only be understood properly in the context of relations between the alleged perpetrators and other more powerful forces ("police, courts, physicians, school officials, and parents") who control "how people define the world, its components, and its possibilities." The issue was the social power to "label" suspect behavior "deviant" rather than the intrinsic character of the behavior itself.[40] The so-called antipsychiatry writers Thomas Szasz and R. D. Laing likewise aimed to cast doubt on ontological definitions of what is normal and abnormal. "In the context of our present pervasive madness that we call normality, sanity, freedom," Laing wrote, "all our frames of reference are ambiguous and equivocal. A man who prefers to be dead rather than Red is normal. A man who says he has lost his soul is mad. A man who says that men are machines may be a great scientist. A man who says he *is* a machine is 'depersonalized' in psychiatric jargon."[41] In this context, judgments of health and illness are arbitrary, and modern psychiatry, Szasz argued, became a mechanism of social control capable of draping coercion of nonconformists with a "self-flattering rhetoric" of "help."[42]

Strictly speaking, however, Goffman should not be classed with these currents. The anti-institutional animus of the antipsychiatrists, in particular, stemmed from existential, and highly individualistic, assumptions that posed the self against society. Goffman, on the other hand, began his career aiming to find a home for the self *in* society, and later *The Presentation of Self in Everyday Life* mounted a broadside against ideas of authenticity. In this book, Goffman's idiom was "dramaturgical": in social life, he suggested, there are "front regions" where persons aim to "give off" impressions sustaining the roles they assume (e.g., gestures of authority that are customary in delivering a lecture, supported by a kind of professional collusion, or "teamwork," in which a colleague testifies to the lecturer's credentials)—and "back regions" where they get into costume, share tricks of the trade, and let down their guard. Notwithstanding the oscillation individuals undergo between front regions and back regions, however, Goffman denied that in privacy there is any "real" person apart from the artificiality of social roles. Rather, the self is a theatrical effect: "A correctly staged and performed scene leads the audience to impute a self to a performed character, but this imputation—this self—is a *product* of a scene that comes off, and is *not a cause of it.*"[43]

Thus Goffman denied that a free, integral subject, in any simple sense, resided within or behind the practices of social enactment. Whatever entity it was that donned and doffed the masks of social life was neither substantial nor definable. Yet Goffman did not mean that individuals are mere creatures of their roles or have no reality apart from the social practices molding their action: just as common as the expert enactment of roles is the phenomenon of "role distance," a need people feel to separate themselves from character, to demonstrate they are something other than their masks. An individual in a role "uses whatever means are at hand to introduce a margin of freedom and maneuverability, or pointed disidentification, between himself and the self virtually available for him in the situation." Still, this gave no ground for a hidden dimension of authenticity. The common view that roles are profane and "the real person" sacred, Goffman insisted, was "a vulgar tendency in social thought," a "touching tendency to keep a part of the world safe from sociology." Goffman had *sociological* explanations for the seemingly antisociological phenomenon of role distance. Social actors, he suggested, must occasionally break out of role just to attain the ends their role demands (like a surgeon making jokes to sustain the morale of his operating team). Furthermore, the very variety of roles each person enacts in modern society requires granting official status to something called "the person" that has rights beyond all particular role attributes.[44]

Goffman wanted to build an ethical defense for the integrity and autonomy of the person without relying on any kind of metaphysical individualism or personal essentialism that departed from the sphere of sociology. For him, personhood could be sustained only *in* society. Despite the rhetoric he sometimes used to castigate the harshness of a disciplinary society, Goffman never intended to obscure the difference between total institutions and civil society. Unlike the antipsychiatrists, he respected the terms of sociability and avoided any temptation to valorize the anomie of the mad, for although the demands on the individual to evince a suitable degree of involvement in social occasions might be onerous, they are integral parts of a social ritual that grants the participant a measure of dignity and personal security. The alternative is a kind of extreme self-involvement that seems free until the attendant lack of order reveals the utter absence of personal security—a point made with chilling effect by Goffman's story of witnessing the rape of an elderly asylum inmate by a younger one in the midst of a crowded ward of indifferent isolates.[45] On the other hand, Goffman never believed that the absence of "authentic" personal substance behind social roles in any way rendered the person defenseless. Goffman's mentor Emile Durkheim had taught that "the sacred" was defined solely by the prohibitions on profane contact that surround it, not by any particular attributes it possesses, and likewise for Goffman, the person was an "empty" category whose boundaries are constructed by the gingerly dance of social observances.

Goffman's use of theatrical imagery in *The Presentation of Self in Everyday Life* was less a cynical enterprise in unmasking socialized deceit than an argument for the profoundly social (or interactive) character of personality, one that admires the performative capacity of individuals to take part in social action by assuming roles.[46] Yet inevitably the dramaturgical perspective also served to undercut social conventions, for performances often *are* "deceptions," and in certain social situations, we are able to discredit the performances of others, particularly their status claims of respectability or distinction.[47] The performative character of social life paradoxically asserts the inherently socialized character of the person while it renders social roles themselves contingent, accidental, or artificial. In Goffman's view of social life, there is a delicate balance to be struck between the need to preserve appearances—for the sake of social interaction and security of the person—and the need to puncture them.[48]

Goffman's work, moreover, upheld a moral democracy of persons; it showed a willingness to criticize all forms of social practice that violate the principles of ordinary interaction, that degrade or desecrate the person. He routinely punctured the pretensions of class, doubting, for instance, that either refined performative capacities for social interaction (poise, grace, sangfroid) or lapses in etiquette, on the other hand, were exclusive attributes of particular classes, high and low; he insisted that social hierarchies rested on no unique *personal* qualities of the individuals involved.[49] He also analyzed the "stigma" of race and the humiliations of gender hierarchy.[50] But if it was possible to mount a critique of these and other oppressions (in asylums and prisons), that critique need not rest on abstraction of the self *from* society or hostility to institutional regulation per se. Goffman remained convinced that humans had to live with the profound fragility of the social fabric and had reason to cherish the norms of social interaction that maintain that fabric as the preserve of the person. In this way, Goffman's paradox—the need to preserve appearances and puncture them—signaled one of the decade's great intellectual feats. He demanded respect for the individual without setting him or her apart from society and criticized society without imagining a standpoint of absolute personal truth outside society.

The Gay and Lesbian Presence in 1960s Culture

In 1966 composer Steve Reich premiered his piece of electronic music *Come Out* at a benefit for the Harlem 6, young black men beaten by police and framed for the murder of a white storekeeper. The phrase "Come out to show 'em" was drawn from a defendant's tape-recorded statement, suggesting a felt need to reveal the pain and anger of Harlem youth beset by brutal cops. Recycled on a tape loop and doubled on itself to make two voices, now in unison, now out of phase, the phrase was repeated at varying speeds to create a rush of rhythmic sound.[51] Three years later, *Come Out!* was the publication of the Gay Liberation Front, the main left-wing organization of activists to follow the "Stonewall rebellion," when patrons of a Greenwich Village gay bar, the Stonewall Inn, fought back against a police raid.[52] For this movement, "come out" meant leaving secretive ways behind and asserting one's identity in public. The two uses of the phrase in 1966 and 1969 had no direct relation with each other except that both evoked the impulse to authenticity, and the conjunction between them suggests the dependence of the emerging gay and lesbian movement on the example set by agitation for black freedom. But even as the call to "come out" appealed to authenticity, to "be oneself in the world" despite social convention, gay and lesbian experience also entailed acute attention to matters of appearance and artifice—in the role playing that guided social life in the subculture of gay and lesbian bars, in the aesthetics of camp, which brought a homosexual sensibility to avant-garde and popular arts, and in a keen understanding of manners and masks that came with the challenge of living differently in the face of rigid standards.

Although Stonewall symbolically marks the birth of a militant movement of self-assertion, a trend had begun some years earlier for gay and lesbian communities, writers, artists, and modes of expression to assume a greater presence in the broader culture. The harsh repression of homosexuals that accompanied anticommunist hysteria in the early 1950s had not disappeared: in June 1963, the State Department announced it had terminated or denied employment to more than 200 "security risks," almost half described as "sex deviates."[53] Gay men and lesbians faced a common threat of unprovoked assault, police harassment, imprisonment, or public disgrace. "Enlightened" opinion viewed homosexuality no longer as a crime or sin but as a "sickness." By the early 1960s, the medical profession declared that the pathology was not congenital, as once believed, but developed in children primarily owing to dysfunctional family dynamics—an idea that only confirmed the view that homosexuals could and should be cured. As historians have recently pointed out, however, all this coincided with the growth of gay and lesbian communities focused in certain urban residential districts and gathering spots, and thus with a gradual countermovement toward the legitimation of their own different sexuality.[54] A 1963 *New York Times* story headlined "Growth of Overt Homosexuality in City Provokes Wide Concern" upheld the "sickness" view but found psychiatrists worried that by "achiev[ing] social acceptance," homosexuals would turn away from "seeking and obtaining treatment." Six months later, a new survey found homosexuals "have gone beyond the plane of defensiveness and now argue that their deviancy is 'a desirable, noble, preferable way of life.' "[55]

New kinds of self-affirmation and protest stirred in the main "homophile" organizations, the largely male Mattachine Society and the lesbian Daughters of Bilitis (DOB). In the 1950s, these groups modestly hoped only to encourage "understanding" of homosexuals (often relying on help from medical authorities who still considered them sick) and insisted their members avoid any public show of nonconformity. Starting in 1961, however, Frank Kameny of the Washington, D.C., Mattachines challenged federal job discrimination and by 1965 led picket lines at the White House demanding "Equality for Homosexuals." In the mid-1960s, Barbara Gittings, editor of the DOB journal *The Ladder,* adopted the line that "homosexuality is not a sickness," and Craig Rodwell, who had picketed the New York City draft board in 1962 to protest antigay discrimination by the military, hung posters declaring "Gay Is Good" in the Oscar Wilde Memorial Bookshop he opened in 1967. Angry street demonstrations followed police raids on bars in Los Angeles and San Francisco in 1966 and 1967. Cracks appeared at the same time in professional opinion: a few prominent psychologists and psychiatrists such as Evelyn Hooker, Hendrik Ruitenbeek, and Judd Marmor rejected the "sickness" interpretation; advocates of labeling theory explained how nonconformity became stigmatized as "deviance"; Thomas Szasz's critique of psychiatry suggested that "helping" homosexuals with a "cure" was a form of coercion; and most legal scholars backed efforts to decriminalize consensual homosexual activity.[56]

A growing gay and lesbian presence in literature, theater, and popular arts took many forms in these years. The celebration of gay desire by Allen Ginsberg and James Baldwin, the prevalence of homosexuality in William Burroughs's phantasmagoric *Naked Lunch*, and the blunt but lyrical portrait of a homosexual underground in the newly translated writing of Jean Genet were all well known. John Rechy's sad, gentle *City of Night* (1963) and May Sarton's openly lesbian novel *Mrs. Stevens Hears the Mermaids Singing* (1965) also won considerable attention. The avant-garde of the early and mid-1960s featured a gay presence: Joe Cino, the leader of the new theater ensemble Caffè Cino, told his troupe, "Let's bring the gay thing out into the open!" and showcased the play *The Madness of Lady Bright*, about a "screaming preening queen," by gay playwright Lanford Wilson. In other works not predominantly about homosexuals, gay and lesbian figures nonetheless played significant roles, such as the charismatic Lakey in Mary McCarthy's novel *The Group* (1964). Thus, although the number of lesbian pulp novels had skyrocketed from the late 1950s to mid-1960s, it now appeared that the mainstreaming of homosexual themes would short-circuit the development of "a separate lesbian literature." Gay themes or a gay sensibility might also appear in veiled or "coded" forms, as in the 1961 movie version of Truman Capote's *Breakfast at Tiffany's*, which showed young people in the city tormented by their need to appear as what they are not.[57]

The weight of gay and lesbian themes in contemporary literature sparked a good deal of comment in the mid-1960s. In April 1963, New York theater critic Howard Taubman complained about the profusion of veiled homosexual allusions onstage and cried out, "If only we could recover our lost innocence and could believe that people on the stage are what they are supposed to be!"[58] By then, it had already become a pastime among clever theatergoers to speculate about the gay meanings of Edward Albee's plays. Taubman's complaint was echoed by others, including the theater critic turned film reviewer Stanley Kaufmann and the novelist Philip Roth (who denounced Albee for writing "pansy prose"). Such criticism led Benjamin DeMott, in the inaugural issue of *New American Review* (1967), to insist that rather than making a special kind of gay art, writers such as W. H. Auden and Jean Genet struck a vein of generic human truth in examining homosexual experience. Other critics argued in various ways that a specifically gay sensibility had shaped key elements of contemporary culture at large. Leslie Fiedler found a "homosexual revolt" to be a prominent part of the "revolution in sensibility" he described in his 1965 essay "The New Mutants"; and Susan Sontag, in her famous "Notes on 'Camp' " (1964), argued that one of the "two pioneering forces of modern sensibility" was "homosexual aestheticism and irony" (the other being "Jewish moral seriousness").[59]

Sontag defined "camp" as "the love of the exaggerated ... of things-being-what-they-are-not." Manifested in a taste for old glamorous fashions or highly stylized movies that invite parody, camp is "the furthest extension in sensibility, of the metaphor of life as theater," introducing "a new standard: artifice as an ideal." Sontag recognized some similarities between camp and pop art, but pop art, she claimed, was too "serious." Camp by contrast fostered a "comic" view of the world that "neutralizes moral indignation, sponsors playfulness." Throughout most of her essay, Sontag downplayed the direct connection of camp to gay and lesbian sensibility, but she indicated the bond clearly enough by emphasizing the salience in the camp canon of androgynous and "epicene" (both masculine and feminine) figures and its sensitivity to "a double sense in which some things can be taken," suggesting the coded means gays relied on in public for mutual recognition and communication. Subsequent writers have argued, furthermore, that the demands placed on gays and lesbians to keep up appearances, and their acute understanding of how standard ways of asserting gender identity pointedly exaggerate certain sexual traits, have made "theatricality" a central element of modern gay and lesbian experience, indicated especially in the role of "female impersonator" or drag queen.[60]

The claim that camp reflects a common gay and lesbian sensibility, however, must be assessed carefully. Modern gay and lesbian life has always been differentiated into special communities defined not merely by gender but by social class and color as well. Above all, gay male and lesbian experiences have diverged in key respects, especially in the late 1960s as lesbian identities and organizations emerged more closely tied to the women's liberation movement than to the old homophile movement. Whereas camp performance appealed most clearly to men, several feminist and lesbian feminist leaders attacked the heritage of gendered role playing among homosexuals, which distinguished "butch" from "femme" and "real men" from "queers," as a manifestation of sexism (or in the case of drag queens, misogyny). A preference for authenticity over artifice appeared among gay men, too, as the movement for frank self-avowal called for them to cast off "the agony of the mask," and countercultural ideals of sexual freedom and "natural" ways encouraged younger gay activists to seek "egalitarian relationships free from role playing."[61] On the other hand, a delight in the artfulness of self-presentation had long been part of a gay world. (In *City of Night*, the drag queen Miss Destiny recalls a party with a sense of personal triumph: "Everyone thought I was Real!") After Stonewall, where drag queens led the fight, it was hard to say one could not "authentically" enjoy role playing.[62] One street fighter, Sylvia Ray Rivera, said he was "really" a man who liked dressing as a woman. Thus gay and lesbian experience helped highlight how hard it is to disentangle authenticity and artifice. Amid the comedy and anguish of life, perhaps, the relish of self-presentation is not always incompatible with self-knowledge or with a need for social acceptance, however the self is fashioned.

Authenticity in Popular Music

It would seem authenticity could hardly flourish in the business of popular music. Pop music in the early and mid-1960s shared with pop art a fondness for what art critic Lucy Lippard called "the jazzy, blaring, glaring, hectically 'fun' urban environment"—the mood Richard Lester created in his movie with the Beatles, *A Hard Day's Night* (1964).[63] As the "British invasion" hit the United States, rock 'n' roll was frankly associated with commerce and fashion. Leading players such as John Lennon and Brian Jones, veterans of Britain's art schools, were keenly attuned to matters of style; male rock stars and leading models paired off; and fans followed the mode of new fashion houses catering to working-class youth.[64] This milieu was both hyped and excoriated in the movie *Blow-Up* (1966) by Michaelangelo Antonioni: there, in a world of artifice, reality had become so remote and inaccessible that a hip fashion photographer immersed in London's rock scene cannot convey to anyone else what he knows about the murder he witnessed in a park. Yet it also seemed that performers and audiences of popular music achieved a kind of empathic communication and, through that bond, experienced something genuine and profound. Main forms of popular music—jazz, folk, blues, and rock 'n' roll—all conveyed an ethos of authenticity, resting on the idea that musicians expressed feelings deeply rooted in themselves and on the audience's conviction that artists spoke truly, having wrested creative autonomy from the image machine of the music business. So strong was this sensibility that when black vocal groups from the Motown label toured Britain in 1965, their highly choreographed acts fell flat and crowds stayed away, even though the Motown sound of the Temptations and Smokey Robinson offered some of the best songwriting and most compelling dance music of the time.

As the 1960s opened, jazz was turning in new directions. Once (as "swing") a popular music with a mass audience, jazz had become a music for musicians, connoisseurs, and coteries of devoted fans with the advent of bebop in the 1940s, when small ensembles premiered a style of rapid, fluid improvisations at odds with the formality of big-band arrangements. The 1950s brought a style of lush sophistication called "cool," but by the end of the decade, a rougher, faster, driving sound resurfaced in the "hard bop" played by Sonny Rollins, Max Roach, and Miles Davis's new bands. Some of these players, reacting against the view common among white music critics that jazz was an "American" classical music, began to insist that jazz was a distinctly black form of musical expression rooted in African traditions. By 1961 some observers noted the rise of "a New Black Music" marked by a rebellious spirit (as early as 1960, bassist Charles Mingus and drummer Max Roach bolted the established Newport Jazz Festival to found the New York Jazz Artists Guild, an autonomous showcase for innovative musicians), an interest in African drumming rhythms and other non-Western forms of music, and a style of unstructured improvisation that some older critics considered chaotic or even "anti-jazz."[65]

The best-known of the new players, North Carolina–born saxophonist John Coltrane, had played with luminaries such as bebop pioneer Dizzy Gillespie and Miles Davis. Having broken a heroin addiction and experienced a religious awakening in 1957, Coltrane began leading his own ensembles and moving beyond "hard bop" practices of basing melodic improvisation on ever faster, more complicated chord changes. He studied incessantly in search of new tonal qualities and compositional techniques adaptable to tenor and soprano saxophones. His album *My Favorite Things* (1961) showcased a modal method in which improvisation worked not through conventional Western harmonies but in scales borrowed from Indian and Arab music. Above all, his long, stretched-out solos emphasized the expressive element in jazz performance, and his use of nondiatonic sounds (snorts, screeches) added to the intense and passionate color of his playing. Coltrane described his music as "talking, laughing, and crying" through his horn, and audiences recognized it as "music coming directly from the man ... not the horn." In later records of 1965 and 1966, *A Love Supreme, Ascension,* and *Meditations,* his performances were "rawly emotional, visceral enough" to put off some earlier fans, but that only confirmed his reputation for "uncompromising honesty, total devotion to the creation of beauty as he, the artist perceived it, regardless of the cost in terms of lost popularity."[66] By July 1967, when he died from late-discovered liver cancer, Coltrane was a hero of authenticity.

Bob Dylan provides a different case. His career began amid the folk revival of the late 1950s and early 1960s. The music's appeal hinged on authenticity—"the kind of self-expression of a quality music that was home crafted, homemade, self-developed, free, radical," as *New York Times* writer Robert Shelton put it—yet the folk music community was divided between those who admired refined renditions of traditional songs ("high folk") and those who aimed to preserve the rough, rude manner of presentation that common people (nonprofessional musicians) originally gave old tunes ("low folk"). Just below the surface lay a clear recognition among folk devotees that music always remained a "part of theater," replete with "gimmicks," and even Woody Guthrie, the patron saint of the new folk music, warned against putting too much faith in the "pose of simpleness."[67]

Indeed, Bob Dylan was a mythmaker, a middle-class Jewish boy from Hibbing, Minnesota, who told his Greenwich Village acquaintances of his Oklahoma birth, his unsettled life in foster homes and carnival camps, his times hobnobbing with old masters of traditional music. Despite such artifice, he had learned folk and blues styles deeply and quickly made his name as a distinctive performer in the "low folk" mode. He shared principles of authenticity, dedicated to the value of creative independence and the unmediated truth of experience. The answer to questions asked in his famous song about deferred justice and peace "is blowing in the wind," he said, because "it ain't in no book or movie or T.V. show or discussion group." Still, his career moved quickly from one phase to another, as each claim he made to authenticity proved in time artificial, demanding a new start. By the end of 1963, he found "protest songs" to be "a lot of hypocrisy," too distant from the depths of human feeling. Later, as he turned—with the hit single "Like a Rolling Stone" and the album *Highway 61 Revisited*—to rock music, his songs persisted in voicing a contempt for social conventions that blinded people both to themselves and to the realities before them. "There's something happening here, and you don't know what it is," he sang scornfully of a "respectable" man, "Do you, Mr. Jones?" Then, after a near-fatal motorcycle accident and a two-year retreat from the public, his somber and Bible-haunted *John Wesley Harding* seemed to dismiss the bitter surrealistic imagery of his rock records as another illusion, of shameless egoism.[68]

Dylan's first biographer, Anthony Scaduto, noted in Dylan's career an oscillation between a desire for fame and fear of it, a reliance on the press for exposure and hatred of it for boxing him in, an urge to do what was needed to "make it" and his retreat from fans who thought he was something he was not. Dylan proved to be a rare rock star who recognized the artificiality of the image, "Bob Dylan," he had helped create, and with his recurrent attempts to set things right, he self-consciously struggled through the dialectic of authenticity and artifice. He disappointed fans and critics at the end of the 1960s when he sought to demystify his earlier work and talked "as a Cole Porter or Irving Berlin might have talked about their songs." There was some truth here, for Dylan achieved the finest songwriting of his time. But what he had done was to transmute the skills of a Porter or Berlin to an oeuvre that has, among its constant features, a religious sense of humility bound to a staunch solidarity with the downtrodden, a contempt for social pretensions, and a refusal to accept the idea that "life is but a joke." There lies a kind of authenticity that should not be scorned.[69]

The folk revival was followed by a swelling interest in blues music, focused first on acoustic country blues and later on urban, electrified blues associated with the Chicago tradition of Muddy Waters. When Janis Joplin, an aspiring singer from Port Arthur, Texas, went to California in the mid-1960s, she quit folksinging to adopt the blues, which she thought provided a relatively uncrowded field for a woman. By the time she appeared with the band Big Brother and the Holding Company as star of the June 1967 Monterey Pop Festival, she sang with furious passion, giving listeners intimations of deep-seated longings and a spirit of abandon. Her renditions of songs earlier performed by black women, such as "Ball and Chain" and "Piece of My Heart," gave vent to an anguish born of her hometown ostracism as a homely, "unfeminine" girl with bohemian tastes. Joplin even took to modeling herself after Bessie Smith, blues singer of the 1920s and 1930s; Joplin dressed in satin and feathers, cultivating the image of a hard-living woman who flaunted her desire and a handy bottle of Southern Comfort. With its stylistic imitation, extravagance, and theatricality, Joplin's performance might have been camp had it not been so earnest and finally tragic. However much she hyped her image of spontaneity, raw passion, and sexual hunger in complicity with an audience that delighted in wild display, her self-presentation was always a mixture of exaggeration with real wants, disappointments, and drives beyond her control, as well as a mix of expression with professional craft.

Ironically, Joplin was "*merchandised* for her *realness*," one biographer wrote, which is not to say her passionate singing was ungenuine or listeners were not actually moved. But although Joplin thought, almost triumphantly, that she was being paid "to be herself," critic Ellen Willis points out, a kind of image making went on that was not all her own. "Men are used to playing roles and projecting images in order to compete and succeed," Willis wrote, but women like Joplin found that "the acceptable masks represent men's fantasies, not her own." Joplin might protest against her image, insisting, "I've never been any one thing in my whole life," but she ran too far as the hard-living woman unwilling or unable to control her passion and anguish, and she died of a heroin overdose on October 4, 1970. Joplin sang with power and distinction; she howled, like Allen Ginsberg, and his "lament for the lamb in America" could have been for her as well as anyone.[70]

New democracy: Septima Clark, organizer of the Southern Christian Leadership Conference's literacy campaign, at one of the citizenship schools she helped establish, Johns Island, South Carolina, 1958. The schools, set up in homes or shops, were staffed by neighbor-teachers, relying on the expertise of common people to help generate a new spirit of self-determination by the black poor of the South. *Courtesy of the photographer, Ida Berman.*

Art for a new mass public: The New York Philharmonic Orchestra playing its first free summer concert in Central Park, New York, August 10, 1965. With 70,000 attending— a turnout that seemed surprisingly large to officials of the orchestra and the city—the event suggested that art would reach a genuinely mass, democratic audience in the "affluent society." *Courtesy of New York Times Pictures.*

Big Science: The Astron, a device for experiments in controlled thermonuclear reaction, was put into operation in 1964 at the Lawrence Livermore Laboratory (University of California–Berkeley) on behalf of the Atomic Energy Commission. Massive expenditures on physical research, dependent largely on the government's "defense establishment" (Department of Defense, Atomic Energy Commission, and National Aeronautics and Space Administration), represented one side of the new institutions of mass education and organized research coming of age in the 1960s. *Courtesy of Lawrence Livermore National Laboratory/U.S. Department of Energy.*

The passion of amoral science: Peter Sellers as the title character in Stanley Kubrick's 1964 movie *Dr. Strangelove, or How I Learned to Stop Worrying and Love the Bomb*. The crippled Strangelove, coldly calculating survival rates in the wake of thermonuclear world destruction, has risen from his wheelchair at a stirring moment in the War Room. *Courtesy of Museum of Modern Art Film Stills Archive.*

FLUXMANIFESTO ON FLUXAMUSEMENT -VAUDEVILLE - ART ? TO ESTABLISH ARTIST S NONPROFESSIONAL ,NONPARASITIC,NONELITE STATUS IN SOCIETY, HE MUST DEMONSTRATE OWN DISPENSABILITY, HE MUST DEMONSTRATE SELFSUFFICIENCY OF THE AUDIENCE, HE MUST DEMONSTRATE THAT ANYTHING CAN SUBSTITUTE ART AND ANYONE CAN DO IT. THEREFORE THIS SUBSTITUTE ART-AMUSEMENT MUST BE SIMPLE, AMUSING, CONCERNED WITH INSIGNIFICANCES,HAVE NO COMMODITY OR INSTITUTIONAL VALUE. IT MUST BE UNLIMITED, OBTAINABLE BY ALL AND EVENTUALLY PRODUCED BY ALL. THE ARTIST DOING ART MEANWHILE, TO JUSTIFY HIS INCOME, MUST DEMONSTRATE THAT ONLY HE CAN DO ART. ART THEREFORE MUST APPEAR TO BE COMPLEX,INTELLECTUAL,EXCLUSIVE,INDISPENSABLE,INSPIRED. TO RAISE ITS COMMODITY VALUE IT IS MADE TO BE RARE, LIMITED IN QUANTITY AND THEREFORE ACCESSIBLE NOT TO THE MASSES BUT TO THE SOCIAL ELITE.

Return of the avant-garde: Fluxus Manifesto, 1965, by Fluxus art group leader George Maciunas, and Yoko Ono's *Air Dispenser* (1965), a "substitute art-amusement" that mocked the commodity values of art for "the social elite." *Courtesy of The Gilbert and Lila Silverman Fluxus Collection, Detroit.*

Hope for development in the new states: Moses Lawaragu, Akosombo, Ghana, 1963, photographed by Paul Strand at the construction site of the Volta Dam. A veteran of left-wing film and photography circles in the 1930s, Strand was welcomed by President Kwame Nkrumah to tour independent Ghana in the early 1960s, when "modernization" was the common aspiration of Third World nationalists and First World liberals and radicals. *©1976, Aperture Foundation Inc., Paul Strand Archive.*

The realist photographer: World's Fair, New York City, 1964, by Garry Winogrand. Known for his "snapshot aesthetic," Winogrand's craft relied on the most careful composition, suggesting a sharp tension between authenticity and artifice. © *Estate of Garry Winogrand, courtesy Fraenkel Gallery, San Francisco.*

Death and life of great American cities: Jane Jacobs's declaration of a new urban spirit of neighborhood revival was spurred by the grandiose demolition and "urban renewal" projects that began in the 1940s. This photograph by Danny Lyon, from his book *The Destruction of Lower Manhattan*, shows a doomed 1926 building at 100 Gold Street, viewed from the ruins of another structure in the same 60-acre tract, which was leveled in 1967. *Danny Lyon/Magnum Photos.*

An independent art: A leader of the Black Arts movement, Larry Neal teaches a class on Martinican poet and advocate of "Negritude" Aimé Césaire (b. 1913). Neal was recruited as an instructor of literature to the Afro-American Studies program founded at Yale University in 1969 after agitation by Yale's Black Student Alliance. *Photographs and Prints Division, Schomburg Center for Research in Black Culture, The New York Public Library, Astor, Lenox and Tilden Foundations.*

The systematic control of sound: Shown in the Columbia-Princeton Electronic Music Center around 1960, composer and professor of music Milton Babbitt believed that computerized synthesizers offered one of the best means to explore "alternatives to what were once regarded as musical absolutes." *Courtesy of Milton Babbitt.*

93

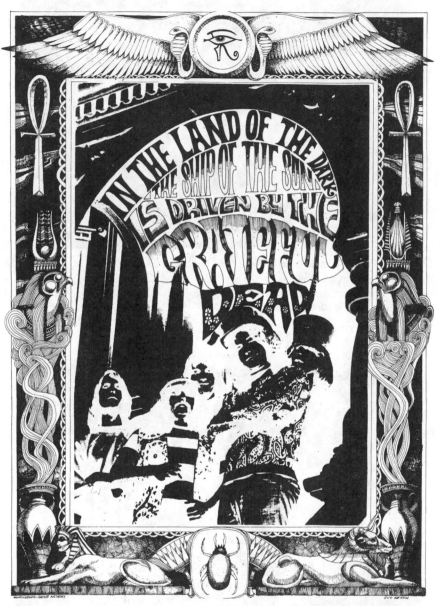

In the land of the dark: The Manichaean vision of the emerging "counterculture," setting a culture of Life against the culture of Death, was revealed in this February 1966 graphic. *From San Francisco* Oracle, *Art by Rick Griffin, Photo by Gene Anthony, Design* Oracle *Staff.*

Q: And Babies? A: And Babies: Antiwar poster, starkly portraying the massacre by U.S. soldiers at the Vietnamese hamlet My Lai, created by the Art Workers' Coalition of New York and distributed worldwide.   _The Artists' Poster Committee of the Art Workers' Coalition, Fraser Dougherty, Jon Hendricks, and Irving Petlin, 1969–70._

The meaning of struggle: Following a police charge to clear an occupied administration building of student protesters, student strike leaders at Harvard University, spring 1969, distributed T-shirts marked with the rationale for continuing the struggle. *Courtesy of Harvard University Archives.*

"Here at Columbia, we have suffered a disaster whose precise dimensions it is impossible to state": Defending the idea of the university as an institution at least partially shielded from the political conflicts of society at large, historian Richard Hofstadter, shown here in 1965, gave a mournful commencement Address, June 4, 1968, following the student protests and strike at Columbia University that spring. *Sam Falk, New York Times Pictures.*

$1.50
PDC

Notes From The Second Year:
WOMEN'S LIBERATION
Major Writings of the Radical Feminists

Love
The Politics of Housework
The Left Debate
Consumerism
Man-Hating
Consciousness Raising
The Myth of the Vaginal Orgasm

Notes from the Second Year: In this collection of articles, edited by Shulamith Firestone and Anne Koedt, 1970, a self-conscious current of "radical feminism" made itself known and initiated a new stage in the ideology of the women's liberation movement. *Courtesy of Shulamith Firestone and Anne Koedt.*

five

Community and Mass Society

At midcentury, it was widely believed that under conditions of modernity, impersonal structures of society supplanted intimate bonds of community. It is clear why this notion took hold. In the United States, postwar periods of the 1920s and 1950s were marked by economic booms characterized by vast expansion of new communications media and widening distribution of mass-produced goods and services. Coming after wartime mobilization, which entailed great migrations and the propagandistic molding of national senti-ment, boom times drew attention to the large-scale reconstruction of Ameri-can life; social thought grew preoccupied with an emerging "mass society" and "mass culture" and with the decline of community or purely local experi-ence. It is remarkable, then, that in the 1960s, "community" was rediscovered as a fact of life or an end to be achieved—something that still counted in peo-ple's lives, to be maintained, salvaged, cultivated, or restored. The rhetoric of community was ubiquitous. Martin Luther King Jr., fresh from the Mont-gomery bus boycott, defined the goal of nonviolent resistance as "creation of the beloved community," where bonds of goodwill supplanted hatred, vio-lence, and oppression. Lyndon Johnson's "Great Society" was to serve "not only the needs of the body ... but the desire for beauty and the hunger for community." After the reform-minded Second Vatican Council, Catholic doc-trine defined the church as "a new brotherly community" founded on princi-ples of "mutual service," which ought to prevail in a broad political commu-nity as well.[1]

The new sense of community took many forms, from a revival of neighbor-hood organizing to the movement of youth nonconformity called "the coun-terculture." Yet the concept of community remained vaguely defined. It appealed to a desire for place (a geographically rooted sense of home) and for

fellowship, posing an alternative to alienation. But community also had traditionalistic implications, suggesting something bounded, homogeneous, and
exclusive—implications that turned up both in conservative movements of
white backlash and in rigid notions of racial authenticity and unanimity that
marred cultural movements of the oppressed. No amount of communitarian
rhetoric could deny the social forces that continued to render community (as
settled, enduring, and coherent localities) unstable, insecure, and in some
respects irrelevant to the solution of genuinely social problems such as
poverty. Nonetheless, demands for meaningful forms of collective action and
experience posed a significant challenge to inherited conceptions of modernity
and raised hopes for a new kind of modern life that would make it feasible,
even amid flux and diversity, to create places for face-to-face interaction, emotional contact, and collaboration in public endeavors.

The Revival of Community

In many respects, the ideal of community was revived by eminently practical
local concerns. By the end of the 1950s, the large-scale urban redevelopment
projects of the postwar economic boom, devoted to highway building, slum
clearance, middle-class housing projects, concentrated commercial districts,
and grand cultural centers, sparked neighborhood protest movements in
places such as New York's Greenwich Village, Chicago's Near West Side, and
Boston's West End. The last, an unsuccessful campaign against plans to raze a
vibrant Italian American working-class district, introduced sociologist Herbert Gans to what he called, in a book that helped promote the rediscovery of
community, "urban villagers." Another kind of community protest, geared to
meeting the bread-and-butter needs of poor city dwellers, emerged in groups
such as the Woodlawn Organization (TWO), founded in a largely black area
of south-side Chicago in 1961 to pressure landlords and indifferent city officials in ways pioneered 20 years before by gadfly Saul Alinsky in Chicago's
Back-of-the-Yards district. A different kind of organizing had continued
unabated through the 1940s and 1950s in many parts of northern cities: efforts
to defend white enclaves from racial integration. Nonetheless, the more liberal example of Alinsky-style organizing helped convince reformers battling
poverty and young agitators intent on building a radical mass movement that
community feeling was a key to winning their ends.[2]

In Greenwich Village, a community mobilization that defeated plans for a
major thoroughfare bisecting Washington Square Park was, an observer said,
a "revolt of the urbs, ... of the pedestrian against the automobile; the community against the project; the home against the soulless multiple dwelling; the
neighborhood against the wrecking crew." Another writer, an editor of the
prestigious *Architectural Forum* and an organizer in the Washington Square
campaign, elaborated these themes in a book that became the watchword of a

new urbanism. According to Jane Jacobs in *The Death and Life of Great American Cities* (1961), the older urban theorists, whether they called for streamlined traffic or greenbelts around cities, exaggerated the rational efficiency of large-scale planning and missed the real source of urban vitality—human hubbub in the streets. Seeking to understand "the intimate and casual life of cities," Jacobs scrutinized the character of sidewalks, parks, and storefronts. With places such as Greenwich Village and San Francisco's North Beach in mind, she outlined conditions of a vital neighborhood: short blocks, a relatively high population density, new and old buildings with varying rents, and a mixture of residences and small businesses encouraging people to "stay put by choice over time." Such places featured "a most intricate and close-grained diversity of uses that give each other constant mutual support"; where efficiency-minded planners saw chaos, Jacobs saw "the real order that is struggling to exist and to be served."[3]

Jacobs's urban vitalism had a definite appeal in its time, offering a human-scaled urban ideal, a critique of overweening planners and of ruthless "urban renewal," and a democratic insistence that improvement of slums lay with "slum dwellers" themselves, regarded as "people capable of understanding and acting upon their own self-interests." Nonetheless, in terms of the kind of communities she took as models of urban health, and in the scope of urban problems she examined, Jacobs's perspective was extremely narrow. In New York, she neglected relatively stable working-class and middle-class districts in Brooklyn and the Bronx, which had thrived for some time despite the segregation of long apartment blocks and separate shopping streets. The Bronx, before the notorious decline during the 1960s and 1970s of its southern section, was already a "wasteland" to Jacobs, who noted its lack of "interesting restaurants." Her references to "eating places and clothing shops," a "whole gamut" of book, coin, jewelry, and art supply sellers indicating a lively neighborhood, suggested the tastes of a special buying public; at times, "diversity" in her account seemed merely a matter of choosing between a Chinese or Italian dinner, and deciding whether to walk or take a cab (subways are rarely mentioned). Jacobs neglected the larger forces that shape the fate of cities and its neighborhoods—matters of wealth, industrial development, and employment; indeed, her narrow focus on the street-level ecology of neighborhoods helped keep such matters out of sight.[4]

Jacobs's approach to urban life showed the kind of realism that gained ground in the 1960s—a desire for direct experience, spurning abstract theory. Mocking "theoretical city planning" that considered statistics on housing density more meaningful than the tenor of street life in poor neighborhoods, Jacobs wrote, "in this book we shall start [by] adventuring in the real world, ourselves." At the time, the redoubtable urban historian and theorist Lewis Mumford mocked what he called "Mother Jacobs' Home Remedies" for the very limited scope of her empirical vision, though the convictions he shared with Jacobs—the need to restore community feeling, and hostility to overdevelopment—helped give his own writings on urban life a greater audience in the 1960s than at any time since his career began more than 40 years before.[5]

Jacobs's realism was countered by another impulse of the time, a utopian element well represented by the 1960 reissue of *Communitas*, by Paul and Percival Goodman. The brothers, philosopher and architect in turn, shared Jacobs's scorn for big development schemes but warned against a dismissal of "planning" per se, for " 'no plan' always means in fact some inherited and frequently bad plan.... a gridiron laid out for speculation a century ago."[6] Their approach to community sought to fuse philosophical speculation about the proper ends of social life with practical outlines of various possible "means of livelihood." Practical visionaries, they offered a number of abstract diagrams of futuristic cities laid out in concentric rings or weblike hexagons. The brothers preferred a decentralized city, where people settled in small collective units (each built around a common plaza) that combined workplaces and residences, remained close to agricultural settlements just outside city lines, and balanced a degree of regional self-sufficiency with participation in world trade. Attending to such material matters, these utopians were more realistic in some respects than the realist Jacobs.

Besides the competing pulls of realism and utopianism, two enduring intellectual traditions figured in many forms of the community ideal. One was philosophical, rooted in classical political theory and an ideal vision of the Greek polis, which emphasized participation, civic consciousness, and holism. This "civic republicanism" survived in John Dewey's idea of democracy as a way of life and led, circuitously, to the "participatory democracy" of Students for a Democratic Society (SDS). This ideal also influenced the utopian speculation of Paul Goodman, whose communitarian anarchism was informed in part by his studies with Richard McKeon, the University of Chicago teacher who combined the spirit of Dewey's pragmatism and classical philosophy. The other strain was the "Chicago school" of urban sociology developed by Robert E. Park in the 1920s. Park's approach combined a laissez-faire disposition (accepting conflict among groups as a natural process of mutual adjustment and suspecting bureaucratic government initiatives) with a frank, democratic sympathy for common people of the city. Despite his conservative leanings, Park had an impact in the 1930s on left-wing authors and activists from James Farrell and Richard Wright to Saul Alinsky. A long-term echo appeared in Jacobs's urbanism. Furthermore, Park's students' reports on rebellious youth and petty crime on city streets bequeathed to a later generation ideas about "deviance" and the sources of social cohesion.[7]

This heritage helped shape government antipoverty policy. According to Richard Cloward and Lloyd Ohlin's 1960 book *Delinquency and Opportunity*, poor neighborhoods suffered from a lack of legitimate means to normal American goals of wealth and success and from a "deviant subculture" of crime, gangs, and defeatism fed by frustration. Ending juvenile delinquency meant opening legitimate avenues of opportunity (in schooling and employment) and restoring an achievement ethic—a prescription Cloward and Ohlin began applying to New York's Lower East Side in a foundation-backed program called Mobilization for Youth. Ohlin later headed a Kennedy administration antidelinquency task force along with a Chicago-school veteran, Leonard Cottrell, whose admiration for "old ethnic neighborhoods" such as Boston's North End inspired a desire to "re-establish community life in the otherwise large, impersonal and bureaucratic ... city." The key lay in teaching people "how to speak, how to use the law, how to approach city hall," and thus, by nurturing what he called "community competence," giving the poor a sense of control over their neighborhoods and their wayward young. When Lyndon Johnson started planning a well-publicized War on Poverty in 1964, the antidelinquency team was already in place with a model for reform, possessing academic prestige and some practical experience.[8] They had learned that city agencies were not inclined to improve schools, housing, and welfare services for the poor unless they were pushed, and the poor themselves were the ones most likely to apply pressure. Self-assertion of this sort met Cottrell's standard of "competence" and added another ingredient to the recipe for community uplift. The War on Poverty's Community Action Program (CAP) begun in 1964 thus called for the "maximum feasible participation" by community residents themselves in local efforts to improve services.

Within the rationale for "community action" was an awkward compromise between a quasi-structural explanation of poverty stressing the absence of jobs and (in talk of a "deviant subculture" and need for competence) a psychocultural theory stressing the inadequacy of the poor themselves.[9] Postwar liberal reformers concerned with racial inequality typically fused these arguments, citing psychological "damage" caused by white racism as reason to offer African American communities special aid. Hoping in this manner to build sympathy for a job-creation program in black ghettos, Daniel Patrick Moynihan drafted his 1965 Labor Department report *The Negro Family: The Case for National Action*, locating a "tangle of pathology" in a tradition of mother-headed families that deprived young black men of values needed for work-related achievement and social mobility out of poverty. By this time, however, the rhetorical formula joining joblessness and damage was losing its cachet. Rising black pride rejected Moynihan's conventional analysis of family and motivation as a racist canard "blaming the victim" of oppression rather than oppression itself.[10] To be sure, the attack on Moynihan's report was misguided in some ways: after all, leaders of the Montgomery bus boycott also believed racism caused some psychological "damage," by fostering a degree of apathy they had to combat. Moynihan's report, however, came at a time when figures on the Right, such as Ernest van den Haag, writing in the *National Review*, were also citing a "culturally deprived home environment" and the alleged motivational deficits of young black men as the reason government aid of the sort Moynihan advocated would fail. Furthermore, Moynihan himself belonged to the intellectual circle associated with *The Public Interest*, a journal originally devoted to liberal reform but also pointedly skeptical of reform strategies that aimed to address poverty by means of neighborhood "empowerment." Given this bias, and the echoes of his arguments that appeared on the Right, Moynihan seemed to hold a conservative position in public-policy debates.[11]

Liberal critics recoiled from the damage arguments of the Moynihan report and applauded instead CAP's attempt to "build on ... positive traditions" of assertive action by the poor, overlooking the social psychological assumptions shared by Moynihan and CAP alike.[12] Cloward's Mobilization for Youth, now backed by CAP funds, was helping residents to organize rent strikes and school boycotts, and such efforts "to redistribute power, if only on the local level," won for CAP an exaggerated reputation as a radical initiative. In substance, however, "community action" avoided a radical attack on poverty. The best means of fighting poverty, according to the National Association of Social Workers in 1964, was a national program providing a guaranteed minimum income to all citizens, and a few others noted that "problems of poverty are only in limited instances localized in character."[13] Federal policy makers had rejected any kind of direct action to redistribute national income and preferred instead CAP's emphasis on providing "opportunity" and nurturing "competence"—essentially conservative ideas about individual advancement and positive motivation.[14] By combining these ideas with somewhat more daring notions about the value of collective action by the poor, CAP rested on profoundly ambiguous foundations.

Started in summer 1963, the SDS venture in community organizing, the Economic Research and Action Project (ERAP), bore some similarity to the notion of community action espoused by Jacobs, Alinsky, and Cloward but was distinguished by its origins in a radical program seeking not merely to uplift but to transform society as a whole. Inspired by the grassroots style of southern voter registration drives led by SNCC, SDS activists thought that a campaign in poor city neighborhoods around problems of the unemployed could spark "an interracial movement of the poor" challenging the structure of wealth, power, and public policy in the United States. In many neighborhoods that became ERAP sites, the effort soon shifted from job-related issues toward campaigns to improve local social services, but the program remained wedded to SDS principles: the goal of making a new egalitarian and participatory society, and the use of political means that prefigured that end in genuinely democratic forms of protest. SNCC veteran Casey Hayden wrote of ERAP, "People need institutions that belong to them, that they can experiment with and shape. In that process it's possible to develop new forms for activity which can provide new models for how people can work together so participants can think radically about how society could operate."[15]

By combining an emphasis on immediate issues with the classical ideal of participatory politics, ERAP merged Jacobs's realism and the Goodmans' utopianism. ERAP was afflicted by many drawbacks—unseasoned activists unfamiliar with the neighborhoods they settled in, extreme antibureaucratic attitudes that made it hard for activists to reach decisions, self-doubts about the radical impact of improving social services. Among the unintended consequences of ERAP, however, was a new self-confidence among young SDS women adept at neighborhood organizing and impatient with the domineering attitudes of their male comrades. These women formed an activist contingent moving toward a revived feminism by a route distinct from earlier advocates of women's rights such as Rossi and Friedan. Furthermore, in some places, ERAP successfully helped poor residents hone their organizational skills and win concrete benefits such as the public distribution of surplus food or tenant-union contracts with landlords. When Mothers for Adequate Welfare, a Boston ERAP offshoot, joined with activists from Mobilization for Youth to help found the National Welfare Rights Organization (NWRO) in 1967, community organizing surpassed its own limits. In demanding among other things a guaranteed minimum income for all, NWRO addressed social and economic policy on the broadest plane.[16]

Black Power as a Reassertion of Community

When the slogan "Black Power" emerged in the mid-1960s, it seemed to mark a basic shift in the character of the black freedom struggle: a move away from a goal of racial integration and its principles of color-blind equality toward a program of black separatism emphasizing racial differences and urging people to identify with a particular community rather than a universal ideal. What truth this generalization holds must be qualified. Ideas and sentiments akin to Black Power were present in the tradition and practice of African American activism well before the slogan was publicized in 1966, and the Black Power idea also profited from the general appeal of "community" in American culture of the 1960s. And although Black Power faced troubling questions about how to draw the boundaries of its community, the assertion of black pride and autonomy was never strictly particularistic but appealed to universal values as well.

Basic elements of Black Power appeared in the black nationalism propounded by Malcolm X, the leading orator of the separatist Nation of Islam who broke with that group and its leader, Elijah Muhammad, in March 1964 and led a short-lived campaign for militant black struggle until his assassination on February 21, 1965. Black nationalism—broadly defined as a doctrine resting its hope for freedom and advancement in America on the solidarity and autonomy of blacks themselves, confident in their possession of a unique and coherent culture drawn at least in part from African roots—had long been part of black politics in the United States, but outside of a few left-wing circles, this current languished in obscurity during the mid–twentieth century until Malcolm X helped revive it.[17] He defined black nationalism as a program of self-help, self-determination, and community control by residents of northern black ghettos, but he was encouraged by his travels in the new states of Africa to add an international dimension that identified African American struggles with a worldwide movement by people of color for freedom from colonial domination. Indeed, sympathy with independent Africa, particularly radical nationalists and pan-Africanists such as Kwame Nkrumah of Ghana, Sekou Toure of Guinea, and the fallen Patrice Lumumba of Congo (plus solidarity with the South African antiapartheid struggle) played a major role in black consciousness of the 1960s. In addition, as his posthumous autobiography explained, Malcolm X's experience of the Muslim pilgrimage to Mecca helped convince him that "racial" identity per se was a fiction fostered by the peculiar American obsession with differences of skin color. Odd as it seemed for a black nationalist, Malcolm X declared near the end of his life, "The Negro revolution is not a *racial* revolt."[18]

Such remarks did not suggest a conversion to liberal ideals of integration. Although he repudiated the antiwhite racialism of Elijah Muhammad's black Muslims and declared the ultimate goal to be "a society in which people can live like human beings on the basis of equality," Malcolm X remained committed to tactical separatism—that blacks maintain their own all-black organizations to promote their struggle for freedom. He merged an emphasis on community, in the sense of local self-determination and African American ethnic solidarity, with a broad view of its significance in the wider world of anticolonial struggles; and by intertwining particular identities and universal ideals, he avoided both a hardened sense of national separatism and wholly abstract visions of human unity. He showed as well a degree of social psychological realism in recognizing the tensions that were bound to roil contemporary movements for racial equality: "If we [blacks and whites] are going to work together, the blacks must take the lead in their own fight.... This phase will be full of rebellion and hostility. Blacks will fight whites for the right to make decisions that affect the struggle in order to arrive at their manhood and self-respect.... The hostility is good. It's been bottled up too long. When we stop always saying yes to Mr. Charlie and turning the hate against ourselves, we will begin to be free."[19] To fashion and maintain alliances in the face of such tensions would have taxed the fortitude of the most seasoned protest leaders and militants.

The spirit of black self-assertion and solidarity gaining ground in the wake of Malcolm X's martyrdom had not sprung from nothing. In one sense, the southern civil rights movement, based on the mobilization of black communities for causes such as the Montgomery bus boycott, had always been a movement of black power; and its goals, as historian Richard H. King has pointed out, always included, besides formal equality before the law, a new black self-respect that was "understood as necessarily collective and both political and cultural."[20] Well before Stokely Carmichael of SNCC led chants for "black power!" at Greenwood, Mississippi, in 1966, the theme had appeared in the impatience and frustration expressed by earlier SNCC leaders. The speech that SNCC leader John Lewis was dissuaded, at the last minute, from giving at the 1963 civil rights march on Washington, D.C., seethed with resentment against liberal government officials who had withheld the support they had promised for SNCC's southern voting-rights campaign: "We will not wait ... but we will *take matters into our hands and create a source of power,* outside of any national structure, that could and would assure us victory."[21]

Nonetheless, the years at mid-decade marked a crucial watershed in the black freedom struggle. Passage of the Civil Rights and Voting Rights Acts in 1964 and 1965 formalized at least the legal goals of the southern movement, and the spotlight turned to the social distress of poor black city dwellers in the North. Nationalists cast a contemptuous sneer at the dream of integration when poverty, poor schooling, and decayed housing demanded immediate response: "Who wants to sit next to a cracker anyway?" Veteran black organizer and social democrat Bayard Rustin unintentionally echoed such sentiments in his 1965 broadside "From Protest to Politics": "What is the value of winning access to public accommodations for those who lack money to use them?" Rustin too thought the civil rights movement had to turn in more radical directions, moving "beyond race relations to economic relations." "The Negro's struggle for equality in America is essentially revolutionary ... [for] their quest cannot ... be satisfied within the framework of existing political and economic relations." To meet public needs in employment, housing, and education and concretely advance the status of African Americans required a massive program of "refashioning our political economy" to permit greater public planning and public services.[22]

The means to these ends, Rustin insisted, was an alliance for social reform welding blacks together with liberal and labor forces within the Democratic Party, an alliance that the new spirit of separatism and nationalism threatened to abort. Young black militants, mistrusting the Democrats, rejected coalition building as SNCC moved to act on the aspirations for independent power John Lewis had suggested. SNCC attempts in 1966 to build a black political party in Lowndes County, Alabama, became a model for the strategy advanced by Stokely Carmichael and political scientist Charles V. Hamilton in their 1967 book *Black Power.*[23] Despite its critique of integration and a few gibes at American capitalism, the book offered a conventional doctrine of political pluralism, suggesting that blacks act as other ethnic minorities did in forging a potent, unified voting bloc of their own. The real edge in the argument lay first in the authors' exposure of "institutionalized racism" woven into the fabric of American life in ways far more tenacious than the de jure segregation that had just been overturned, and second in their rejection of Rustin's coalitionism. Surely, Rustin overestimated the Democratic Party's potential as an agent of radical social reform and underestimated the force of white resistance to black progress; on the other hand, the ethnic pluralism of *Black Power* disregarded Rustin's argument that the interests of the black masses lay in working-class demands that could be shared by a revived and militant labor movement. Neither side fully grasped how race and class were intertwined in American society and politics.

By the late 1960s, ideas of Black Power mingled with a rhetoric of black rage. As one writer put it, Black Power entailed a "sense of being separate" and a "sense of being at 'war,' " sentiments that could be voiced more or less literally.[24] One Black Power advocate called for "organizing two separate and distinct races of people," a marked regression from Malcolm X's mature vision of 1965. "War" might stand for uncompromising struggle or appear in ugly invocations of physical violence, such as the loose talk of "stab[ing] a Jew" in poems by Nikki Giovanni and LeRoi Jones.[25] Antiwhite sentiment was common in Black Power and in many ways not hard to understand (it was, Harold Cruse wrote, a matter of blacks "telling all white people exactly what they think of them as oppressors").[26] But focusing on egregious rhetorical excesses diverts attention from the real substance of Black Power as an effort to revitalize black urban communities, especially in the North. That this effort occurred under the most adverse conditions—as well-paid industrial jobs drained out of cities and white resistance to black social and political advances grew—accounts for the movement's asperity and anger.

A movement of community-based arts promoting racial identity accompanied the rise of Black Power. Writers' and artists' workshops and new ventures in publishing, music, theater, and dance emerged in this milieu with a doctrine emphasizing the proximity of the arts to the life of the streets and the unique resources of African American culture. Newspapers and literary journals named *Black Truth, Black Case, Black World* (originally *Negro Digest*), *Black Liberator, Black Dialogue,* and *Journal of Black Poetry* were joined by black-run radio stations such as Chicago's WVON (Voice of the Negro) and New York's WBLS (Black Liberation Station). The Inter-City Cultural Center of Los Angeles and the Afro-American Festival of the Arts in Newark, New Jersey, were showcases for a new black renaissance. The short-lived Black Arts Repertory Theater School, founded in Harlem in 1965 by playwright LeRoi Jones and poet-critic Larry Neal, set an example for much of this activity throughout the rest of the decade. Intent on fashioning a distinct black aesthetic that would embrace African traditions of communalism and spiritualism in struggle against a debased white or Western culture, Black Arts adopted a kind of romantic racialism and promoted styles that were populistic, didactic, and explosively expressive. Works in this vein were given at times to exuberant celebration of black identity and at others to the cathartic release of rage. In 1968, compiling a large body of essays, plays, short stories, and above all poetry, Jones (soon to be known as Amiri Baraka) and Neal issued the anthology *Black Fire.*[27]

In this context, Harold Cruse's polemical *The Crisis of the Negro Intellectual* (1967) cut a distinctive figure. A separatist, Cruse imagined black communities remade as autarkic cooperative economic enclaves within American society, but he pointedly denied there was a racial or African essence to black experience. Active in black cultural life since joining a Harlem YMCA theater group in 1940, with much of that time spent as an uncomfortable member of the Communist Party, Cruse had lost faith in class-centered strategies of liberation and opted for a politics of ethnic pluralism learned, in part, from Randolph Bourne's 1916 essay "Transnational America." Upholding the idea of a cultural democracy based on a multiplicity of communities within the United States (of which an autonomous black culture would be one), Cruse assailed a WASP establishment that presided over desiccated high arts and "the stultifying blight" of mass culture. He also attacked black intellectuals who followed the chimera of an integrated "intellectual life" and lacked close ties to the black community. Cruse saw Jones and Neal's Black Arts Theater as a promising effort to create an independent art, but as young black writers adopted a strident rhetoric of racial identity, Cruse warned, they misguidedly sought to sever all ties with whites and pretended their culture was essentially defined by its African roots. Opposed to "Garveyism," Cruse insisted that "Afro-American Nationalism is ... a black reflection of the unsolved American nationality question" and that black intellectuals should serve a separate black community that nonetheless remained part of the American scene.[28]

Cruse's judgments were often stilted and exaggerated. His broad attack on *Freedomways*, a left-wing black journal founded in 1961 by Shirley Graham, wife of W. E. B. Du Bois, and featuring such accomplished writers as John Henrik Clarke and John O. Killens, suggested an inability to credit anyone but himself with insight into black nationalism and the black experience. But Cruse's sense of "crisis" captured the dilemmas involved in defining the place and the boundaries of an autonomous black American art. Those dilemmas were poignantly realized in the case of poet Melvin Tolson, whose major work, the book-length poem *Harlem Gallery*, appeared to considerable acclaim in 1965 but was soon afterward almost entirely forgotten. Tolson's career dated to the end of the Harlem Renaissance in the 1930s, when he published poetry in V. F. Calverton's independent Marxist journal *Modern Monthly* and other reviews. A professor at all-black colleges, first Wiley College in Marshall, Texas (where he was the adored English teacher of CORE founder James Farmer), and later Langston University in Oklahoma, Tolson gained wider attention with the 1953 publication of his dauntingly allusive and abstruse *Libretto for the Republic of Liberia*, a high-modernist paean, in a style like T. S. Eliot's, to the soul force of a resurgent Africa.[29] Tolson worked for another 13 years on *Harlem Gallery*, which won the annual poetry award granted by the American Academy of Arts and Letters shortly before his death due to cancer. Although not quite as arcane as the *Libretto*, *Harlem Gallery* remained an arduous work of high-flown poetics, apparently oceans apart from the proudly polemical and didactic poems of black solidarity fostered by the Black Arts movement. Virulently denounced as an artistic Uncle Tom, Tolson hardly appeared at all as a significant figure in the surge of black literary publication following 1965. The charge of aping white aesthetics, however, was an unfortunate one.[30] *Harlem Gallery* was wholly absorbed in portraying black life in a black community. The poem evoked a distinctive African American intellectual tradition of vitality and achievement, inquiring delicately into the matter of cultural identity and the relation between black expression and the dominant Euro-American culture.

In the poem, a group of various figures meeting at a Harlem tavern, the Zulu Club, argue race and aesthetics relentlessly: a self-proclaimed People's Poet named Hideho Heights; the "Race Man," Shadrach Martial Kilroy; an African émigré and scholar, Dr. Nkomo; and the Curator (speaking for Tolson himself), who keeps an apartment gallery of "burnt-in portraits [that] enmesh Negroid diversity." Although Hideho mocks the Curator for "rattl[ing] Eliotic bones," the Curator knows Hideho secretly writes poetry "in the modern idiom." The Curator in turn sometimes admires the streetwise poetics of Hideho's public verse: "The poet is no Crusoe in the Zulu Club." The Curator's roots lie firmly in African American tradition, for "Metaphors and symbols in Spirituals and Blues / have been the Negro's manna in the Great White World," but he denies an impassable divide between modernism and black culture, dubbing "Paul Cezanne, / the father of modern Art, / a Toussaint L'Ouverture of Esthetics" and a "Zulu of the Brush." The Curator rejects Mr. Kilroy's ontological distinction of *Homo caucasicus* and *Homo aethiopicus* (his comrade Dr. Nkomo describes Negroes as "a people in whose veins / poly-breeds / and / plural strains / mingle and run"). The Curator both embraces a consciousness of color *and* insists on broader bounds of affiliation. His aims are particular, for his gallery shows "paintings that chronicle / a people's New World odyssey / from chattel to Esquire," but he bemoans a racialized environment that "shoved the Negro Artist into / the white and not-white dichotomy."[31]

Another artist of Tolson's generation, painter Romare Bearden (1912–1988), negotiated the transition to the era of Black Power more successfully. As a young man in the 1930s, Bearden rejected the demand too often posed by white patrons for work with a recognizable "racial identity" (which he took to be an affected primitivism), but as a son of Harlem and acolyte of the "social realism" current in WPA arts programs, he was also uncomfortable with the formalism and the intensely private, withdrawn mood that came to dominate the postwar school of abstract expressionism. Bearden was nonetheless drawn to the techniques of dripped, layered, and encrusted paint on large canvases, and his work of the late 1950s seemed to fit in the hegemonic New York school until events of the civil rights movement led him in 1963 to reassemble a group in Harlem devoted to understanding "the plight of the Black American artist in America." In 1964, in a sudden aesthetic break, Bearden adopted collage and photomontage to create symbolically dense compositions that depicted black history and community in cotton fields and railway stations of the South, the streets and industrial districts of northern cities, riverside baptisms, and the ways of conjurers and musicians. He sought to "establish a world through art in which the validity of my Negro experience would live and make its own logic." In 1966 Bearden organized an event not seen in Harlem since the 1930s, a large group show called "Contemporary Art of the American Negro," and later helped establish new community-based art centers such as the Studio Museum in Harlem and the Cinque Gallery for young African American artists.[32]

The assertion of identity and reaffirmation of community that characterized Black Power clearly played a large part in Bearden's new art, giving it, he felt, a new authenticity:

> One must be very careful about the matter of racial identity and evaluating it. The difficulty is when [the artist] denies himself, or assumes other identities. As a Negro, I do not need to go looking for "happenings," the absurd, or the surreal, because I have seen things that neither Dali, Beckett, Ionesco, nor any of the others could have thought possible; and to see these things I did not need to do more than look out of my studio window above the Apollo theater on 125th Street.

But the particular ethnic perspective realized in Bearden's paintings never reversed the emphasis that he had always placed on human universals. Largely a self-taught artist, he had drawn from the world history of art a wide range of technical and stylistic elements that appeared in his collages, echoing not only West African sculptural traditions but also the mosaic structure of Gothic stained glass, the surfaces of Italian Renaissance painters Giotto and Duccio, and the compositional poise of Dutch genre and Chinese landscape paintings.[33]

As a cultural movement, Black Power can be understood as a prolonged meditation on the problems of "double consciousness" that W. E. B. Du Bois first broached in his 1903 book *The Souls of Black Folk.* For Du Bois, double consciousness suggested the agony of self-alienation that American racism imposed on blacks, compelling them to view themselves "through the eyes of another," the dominant white man; but it also celebrated a people whose estranged life within America bestowed on them "second sight" and permitted them a unique breadth of cultural reach best expressed in Du Bois's practice of pairing a quotation from European romantic authors and the Negro spirituals, or "sorrow songs," at the head of each chapter in his book.[34] Black Power was fueled by the drive to end double consciousness in the first sense by posing the demand that African Americans be able to define themselves in their own terms, by their own voice, and to wring from whites respect for the primacy of *those* definitions. The rightful urge to achieve self-determination in this sense lay behind the anger a number of militant black writers voiced in 1967 against the white novelist William Styron for his portrait of a black rebel hero in the novel *The Confessions of Nat Turner.*[35] It surfaced in many other ways as well: in Cassius Clay's adoption of the name Muhammad Ali; in the appearance of black jazz critics, such as LeRoi Jones and A. B. Spellman, contesting the journalistic prerogative previously claimed by white writers judging black music; and in everyday resentment of the bigoted outsider's image of black ghetto life that white-run media provided to the nation (a sentiment captured vividly in a scene of Haskell Wexler's 1969 movie *Medium Cool*, in which young black men in a ghetto apartment, acting tough to intimidate a white reporter, demand their own spot on television). To be sure, this very insistence on achieving an independent voice, veering at times into strident claims about unbridgeable or essential differences between blacks and whites, often overshadowed or even repudiated the second side of Du Bois's double consciousness, which proposed the transcendence of any particular identity. Still, the impulse behind Black Power did not lack the capacity to move beyond narrow definitions of ethnic identity.

Larry Neal (1937–1981), who came to New York from Philadelphia the same year Bearden began his black-identified collages, offered some of the most eloquent arguments for a black art in terms that demanded for blacks their own exclusive aesthetic terrain ("a place, ritually, symbolically ... where whites don't go") but also ached with a palpable sense of broad human sympathy. A literature student at Lincoln University, where he focused on Joyce and Eliot, Neal first encountered life in Harlem at a time when the politics of civil rights, anticolonial solidarity with independent Africa, and the sounds of street corner speakers for black nationalism and of John Coltrane's, Albert Ayler's, and Sun Ra's jazz bands all conspired to encourage a new sense of art. An art committed to the black freedom struggle, it would reach contemporary popular audiences and find roots in African tradition at the same time, cultivating the element of "orality" in poetry and drama intended to be read and performed in open public places. The English-language publication of Frantz Fanon's *Wretched of the Earth* also played a part, encouraging a preoccupation with violence against the oppressor as a cleansing force that enabled the oppressed to speak and act for themselves. Much of Neal's mid-1960s poetry and plays brimmed with images of violence, of "stone-cold killers bursting with revenge," brandishing guns or knives to thrust "into the beast-heart" of the enemy, but ambivalence ran through it all. "We were ready for violence," he wrote later. "And everybody knew that violence was wrong."[36]

Neal's violence was figurative. "The first violence will be internal," he wrote in 1968 at the end of *Black Fire*, to "destroy the double consciousness" that prevented African Americans from achieving "a more perfect self." Moreover, he repeatedly posed black musical expression as an analogue and alternative to violence. In a long poem about saxophonist Lester Young, Neal wrote:

> So we pick up our axes [horns] and prepare
> to blast the white dream;
> we pick up our axes

> re-create ourselves and the universe,
> sounds splintering the deepest regions
> of spiritual space
> crisp and moaning voices
> leaping in the horns of destruction,
> blowing death and doom to all who have no use
>   for the spirit.[37]

Neal's wish for a literature fostering a sense of existential power for blacks rested on a nonviolent sentiment, a hope that art itself, rather than physical violence, could do the work of creative destruction, freeing self-expression and opening broader vistas beyond. By 1970 Neal began turning away from his most separatist rhetoric of the mid-1960s and stressed the role of black artists as "synthesizers," building on "the specific, as well as general, ingredients" of "an African culture in America." The particular and the universal merged in his musings on jazz innovators: "You could make your own instrument. And if you can sing through that instrument, you can impose your voice on the world in a heretofore-unthought-of manner. In short, you can create another world view, another cosmology springing from your own specific grounds, but transcending them as your new world realizes itself."[38] Neal's black art imagined a poetry in, but not of, the streets, conversant enough with young people's (mainly young men's) feelings of desperation and rage to share their language, but looking to liberation by aesthetic creation.[39]

Black women writers were familiar with this dialectic of violence and expression. "Talk yuh talk," one character says to the bold, outspoken Barbadian woman, Silla, in Paule Marshall's 1959 novel *Brown Girl, Brownstones*. "Be-Jees, in this white-man world you got to take yuh mouth and make a gun."[40] All the ambiguities of community appear in sharp relief in this coming-of-age novel set in a Brooklyn, New York, neighborhood slated for urban renewal. The Barbadian immigrants who settled in the old brownstones near Fulton Park are bound together by both racial pride and a petit bourgeois hunger for real estate. The community's money-minded conformity drives away Silla's daughter Selina, a young woman who struggles throughout the story for her own sense of place. For Selina, the heart of the neighborhood resides in the community of women, and she admires those, like her hard, unyielding mother of the poor Barbadian hills, who "seemed to use [their] beauty not to attract but to stave off all that might lessen their strength." With that image in mind, Selina finally chooses to resettle in Barbados. Before she goes, however, she visits the site where uniform housing projects rise over the razed brownstones of her youth, and she tosses onto the site two silver bangles she wears on her wrist. Memorializing a community in ruins while seeking a new one by returning alone to ancestral ground, Selina's stance signals the yearnings *and* discontents of community more sharply than most stories of the time.

There was a tendency in the male-dominated Black Power milieu to identify communal welfare with the power of assertive black men, and there are some signs that black women, who had played a paramount role in the postwar freedom struggle, rebelled against a masculine vision of racial community that obscured the conflicts residing within it. This was one of the messages in Toni Cade's 1970 literary anthology *The Black Woman*. Toni Morrison's first novel, *The Bluest Eye*, revealed a disabused perspective on community from a woman's point of view. There is little comfort in this story of a black girl, victim of paternal rape, who desperately wants blue eyes and falls into madness as she seeks satisfaction. Started in 1962 and written mostly in the years after 1965, *The Bluest Eye* was a merciless study of self-loathing. The novel was motivated, Morrison later wrote, by "the reclamation of racial beauty in the sixties" and shared Black Power's insistence on combating the debilitating effects of double consciousness, on fighting "the damaging internalization of assumptions of immutable inferiority originating in an outside gaze." But amid the violence the girl sees and suffers in her home, the trickery of a fortune-teller who leads her to the verge of madness, the pity and final indifference offered her by the adults and other children of the town, there is no sign of a nurturing community. Morrison described her novel as one about "secrets" (of self-hate and the absence of effective community) that are "withheld from us by ourselves and by the world outside." Still, by voicing the hottest ire against the American tradition of race, in terms intended to be "indisputably black," Morrison upheld an elusive ideal of community based on a dawning appreciation of beauty in black experience.[41]

This ambiguity based on the combined repudiation of racism and the assertion of racial identity formed the sensibility of Black Power, and critics of the movement have not sufficiently acknowledged it. The image of community promoted by Black Power advocates often appeared in a form too idealized, too exclusive and separatist, but it would be a mistake to take all separatist rhetoric of the 1960s at face value. Back in the 1920s, when composer and bandleader Duke Ellington proposed renaming jazz "Negro music," he was not attributing a racial property to it. Indeed, he objected that the name "jazz" segregated him: there was only music—good music or bad music—and jazz happened to be the music American Negroes made.[42] Similarly, claims to black distinctiveness in the 1960s did not deny human solidarity. At times, the assertion of a special, particular identity, by resisting and rebutting an oppressor's attempts to dehumanize, helps vindicate universal values of human being.

Counterculture and the Renewal of Affection in Social Life

The term "counterculture" has come into common use as the name for one of the decade's most celebrated phenomena: the assumption of defiantly nonconformist attitudes, uninhibited behavior, and generalized dissent by large numbers of young people joined together by their shared enthusiasm for the new popular music of the time. To start, "the counterculture" might be defined as the meeting of an old, hitherto elite or marginal, romantic-bohemian critique of modern life—one that aimed to free libidinal energy and expand consciousness—with a large constituency shaped by mass culture; and that mass-culture base was built around a market-mediated form of popular expression (rock music) inflected with the rebellious sentiments of the working class and oppressed peoples, particularly African Americans. This sketchy formula, of commerce and community, race and class, love and rebellion, only begins to suggest the complexity of the phenomenon. Above all, it is urgent not to reify "the counterculture," to assume the name denotes a single, very definite thing, for the ideas, practices, and symbols that flourished within the arena of youth nonconformity were always diverse, bound together at best in syncretic ways. Indeed, this milieu changed its shape and form considerably in the course of a decade. Although the term "counterculture" was not attached to it until the very late 1960s, some kind of oppositional subculture had been germinating for some time. The first task in analyzing this inchoate object is to historicize it.

The first stage in the emergence of a counterculture dates from 1955 to 1963, when the alienated ethos identified with the Beat generation of writers enjoyed growing influence in urban areas of youth settlement. Beat writers such as Allen Ginsberg and Jack Kerouac resurrected many elements of the protest against the iron cage of modernity that figured in early-nineteenth-century romanticism and thrived in bohemian quarters for decades afterward. The Beat complaint against acquisitive materialism, rigid social roles, and psychic repression—answered by the search for a fullness of personal experience that broke the bounds of convention and lifted one above the mundane—was hardly new. It echoed Schiller, who denounced the "clockwork" of modern society that glorified habit before genius; Blake, who wished to clean "the doors of perception"; and the American transcendentalists Emerson and Thoreau, who celebrated nonconformity.[43] Beyond those ancestors, the Beats appealed to traditions of artistic rebellion identified with the poet Rimbaud, the dadaists, and interwar American exiles at home and abroad; furthermore, their sensibility as ethnic outsiders—Ginsberg's Jewishness was always present, and Kerouac came from New England's French Canadian working class—melded into a sympathy for the racially oppressed of America, signaled by the Beats' embrace of the jazz idiom. As Ginsberg's open avowal of homosexuality suggested as well, the Beats declared their "outlaw" status more brazenly than earlier generations of dissenting esthetes.

In the years around 1960, the Beats' transcendentalism was complemented by the growing appeal of Eastern religion, fostered by the work of D. T. Suzuki, a Japanese lecturer at Columbia University in the 1940s and 1950s and the best-known Buddhist scholar-apostle in the West, and writings by

Anglo-American Zen advocate Alan Watts.[44] The Beat demand for an uninhibited pursuit of experience meanwhile echoed in special city districts often
nestled near universities—New York's Greenwich Village and the upstart
East Village, San Francisco's North Beach and later Haight-Ashbury, Dinky-
town in Minneapolis, Ann Arbor, Collegetown in Ithaca—where cheap apart-
ments, offbeat coffeehouses and bars, and local color attracted young seekers
after sensation and moral truth. Thomas Pynchon's 1963 novel *V.* portrayed
this milieu in the gritty flats, languorous parties, and madcap escapades of a
band of roommates and hangers-on called "the whole sick crew." By 1964 the
scene was described as a "new bohemia," in which experimental arts ("underground" cinema and Happenings) shared the stage with popular music and
the "frenetic, exultant, near-tribal dance catharsis" (the Frug, the Jerk) that
accompanied it. Reporter John Gruen noted that this bohemia differed from
the old "in seeking more to enlist than to exclude": although this community
was still led by self-conscious groups of artists, the expressive, irreverent,
erotic conduct of life they endorsed seemed available to many.[45]

This milieu had nurtured the folk and blues music revival, which in turn
bore unmistakable signs of moral and political affiliation with the civil rights
struggle of that time. By 1963, however, the same kind of disenchantment that
was turning civil rights activists toward Black Power encouraged some of the
discontented young to withdraw from politics per se and opt for a more intensive and alienated cultivation of self and sensibility. Bob Dylan's repertoire,
shifting from the "protest" mode of *The Times They Are A-Changin'* to intro-
spective, elusive, even mystical songs such as "My Back Pages" and "Mr. Tam-
bourine Man," provided a bellwether of this change.[46] Also in 1963 and 1964,
Timothy Leary and Richard Alpert, recently dismissed from their positions as
experimental psychologists at Harvard University and resettled at an estate in
Millbrook, New York, began a concerted effort to explore and promote the
liberating psychic benefits of hallucinogens. A new drug evangelism filtered
into the "underground" of estranged youth.[47]

These early developments set the stage for the first signs of a self-conscious
"movement." Beginning in September 1966, the San Francisco *Oracle*, from
Haight-Ashbury (followed the next March by a Los Angeles edition), welcomed a "new consciousness" or "new subculture" evolving within Western
industrial civilization. Fashioning a syncretistic ideology, *Oracle* writers acclaimed
Abraham Maslow's ideal of self-actualization while celebrating the psychedelic
experience and mystical doctrines that promised to dissolve the ego. Free love
melded with religious quests ("find a sacrament," one article advised, "which
returns you to the Temple of God, your own body"). Nature worship, in rituals marking the seasonal cycle of equinox and solstice, accompanied a simplistic embrace of Native American cultures and Asian cosmologies. News of
communes (called "Tribes") founded on libertarian, anarchist principles
and a prevailing ethic of nonviolence filled out the pages.[48] Despite the
modern individualism and pharmacology of this milieu, its overriding tone

was critical of advanced technology and professedly hostile to "Western" metaphysics. Lawrence Lipton, an early chronicler of the Beats, wrote in the *Oracle* that the Chinese *Book of Changes* (or *I Ching*) "envisages unresting changes and unpredictable chance as the nature of the universe and provides a tool of cognition and a system of procedures by which man may not conquer nature, as Western man has striven to do in his science, but learn how to live with ... chance events of nature instead of being destroyed by them."[49] The antirationalist spirit was evident also in its stress on pure sensation and the utter uniqueness of individual perception. "If 6 turned out to be 9," Jimi Hendrix sang, "I don't mind ... 'cos I got my own world to look through, and I ain't gonna copy you."

This "new consciousness" was not yet a "counterculture." By 1968 the antiwar movement helped partly reverse the turn within that had begun in 1963, and cross-fertilizing between the new subculture's anti-Western metaphysic and the political radicalism of the New Left gave birth to a counterculture that tended to see itself as a generalized opposition, a movement sui generis that promised to challenge totally the social, political, and cultural status quo.[50] In 1968 the young historian Theodore Roszak may have been first to apply the term "counter culture"—a generational force of "youthful disaffiliation" from a status quo governed by scientific-technological momentum (a "technocracy") and "the only effective radical opposition" in modern society. Not "merely a political movement" of the "traditional left," the counterculture worked "at the non-intellective level of the personality from which these political and social forms issue ... seeking to transform our deepest sense of the self, the other, the environment."[51]

As a counterculture, the youth opposition defined itself by what it stood against, that is, as a culture of life against a culture of death. This Manichaean vision appeared in Beat veteran Gary Snyder's poem "A Curse on the Men in Washington, Pentagon," combining opposition to war, radical disaffiliation, and an identification with Indian ritual: "I kill the white man, / the 'American' / in me / And dance out the Ghost Dance.... This magic I work, this loving I give / That my children may flourish / And yours won't live." In 1968 the Austin, Texas, SDS asserted, "Protest must be affirmative, creative. It is not enough to scream 'no.' ... We must do a love thing: show that there are alternatives to the death we are asked to be a part of. We affirm life."[52] The sensed struggle of life against death gave the counterculture an apocalyptic tone, belying the impression of childlike innocence some of the "hippies" and their observers tried to convey. It is telling that the San Francisco pop renaissance, led by Jefferson Airplane, Big Brother and the Holding Company, and the Grateful Dead, leaned heavily on the most common musical language of the period, electric blues, and its sense of pain. Indeed, countercultural hedonism bespoke desperation, a feeling that life under the umbrella of the arms race might be too short or that life within the mainstream was doomed by deadening, mechanistic routine. As Grace Slick of Jefferson Airplane sang, "When the truth is found to be lies, and all the joy within you dies, you better find somebody to love."

It was primarily an expressive, rather than acquisitive, individualism that flourished in the counterculture. Naturally, in a commercial society where lifelines of communication (particularly rock music) ran through market channels, the counterculture had an entrepreneurial dimension, ranging from small ventures of handicrafts and head shops to larger operations such as the Fillmore auditoriums and *Rolling Stone* magazine. But much of the counterculture's ideology evoked an old tradition of romantic anticapitalism, wherein the forces of life strove against the mortifying effects of money and machinery and yearned for fulfillment in uncommodified human intimacy. Calling for a "Love-In" on the occasion of the vernal equinox, Frederick Adams wrote, "To get the beat, we must blow on the First Big Note of Nature, and move in harmony with greater tides than those that govern rents, interest rates, and payment plans."[53] Charging Haight-Ashbury's small businesspeople with promoting a doctrine of self-satisfied mysticism for commercial reasons, the district's domestic critics, a group of artist-activists called the Diggers, declared property an illusion and distributed free food and health care, showing the countereconomic impulses of the movement and setting an example of communal services followed by other groups such as Ann Arbor's Rainbow People and Oakland's Black Panthers.

From the mid-1960s onward, however, writers and intellectuals looked at the multifarious cultural dissent of the time and fashioned reified images of it that have polarized discussion of the counterculture ever since. Roszak's suggestion that the counterculture was a new opposition destined in time to explode Western civilization from within helped foster an exaggerated sense of the unified force wielded by alienated youth. (If read closely, however, his portrait proved more cautious, and more wary of youth culture's antinomian elements, than that of enthusiasts such as Charles Reich, whose *Greening of America* described a libertarian and pacifistic ethos as the coming wave of the future.) Several liberal sociologists, including Philip Slater, Kenneth Keniston, and Amitai Etzioni, also identified youth as the leading edge of an emergent "new culture"—a value shift in modern society stressing personal autonomy, intimacy, equality, cooperation, and pleasure.[54]

On the other side, some writers described the counterculture as no less a concerted force, but one eroding the cultural ballast of society as such. Joan Didion's famous essay about her visit to Haight-Ashbury, "Slouching towards Bethlehem," has remained a powerful portrait of counterculture as sheer social breakdown. After describing her days drifting with ragged 17 and 18 year olds looking for a kick, Didion wrote, "We were seeing the desperate attempt of a handful of pathetically unequipped children to create a community in a social vacuum. Once we had seen these children, we could no longer ... pretend that the society's atomization could be reversed.... These were children who grew up cut loose from the web of cousins and great-aunts and family doctors and lifelong neighbors who had traditionally suggested and enforced the society's values.... They are less in rebellion against the society than ignorant of it." And then, on the basis of a San Francisco psychiatrist's judgment that the "itch for the transcendental" in a "romantic" movement such as this "lends itself to authoritarianism," she concluded, "They are sixteen, fifteen, fourteen years old, younger all the time, an army of children waiting to be given the words."[55] Surely Didion was carried away by the mass-society theory on the origins of fascism, for these late-1960s castoffs lacked any heroic or militaristic ideal, sought pleasure amid a society not wracked by class conflict but flush with wealth, and professed a gentle ideal of peace and love. Yet Didion spoke for other critics who recognized an unsettling normlessness among these young people and ascribed it to the moral drift of modern society; in a consumerist culture, these observers claimed, the self-indulgent counterculture was more a mirror of the mainstream than an opposition to it.

Yet neither image, admiring or disparaging, suffices for a counterculture so varied and internally contradictory. The hedonism of this milieu cannot be wholly separated from the movement's equally strong emphases on spirituality, communalism, and service, and even the hedonic element of the counterculture can be recognized as having more than one meaning. Only partly due to consumer individualism, it was also a protest against "depersonalized" society, an attempt to democratize the pursuit of happiness, *and* a sign of desperation born of personal distress. Young people's impatience with any settled definition of social roles—an anti-institutional mood expressed in diffuse hostility toward "society"—signaled both the disturbing normlessness Didion found in the breakdown of traditional community *and* the more hopeful sense that marks any moment in history when the prospect of profound social change makes old roles appear profoundly contingent and revisable. Amid the promise of abundance, Walter Lippmann once noted, "the compulsions [of settled social life] are painful, and as it were accidental, unnecessary, wanton and full of mockery."[56]

Whereas Didion saw only "a social vacuum," Talcott Parsons—an observer not usually considered sympathetic to radical currents—suggested that both the new feminism and the "radical youth culture" promoting an ethic of "love" pointed to something profoundly new: the creation of "networks of solidarity on much more highly universalistic bases than kinship and the older sort of friendship, yet at levels which tap the kind of motivational complexes which have been central to them." That is, the counterculture hinted at new kinds of community, beyond clan and enclave, far more appropriate to a mobile, urban modern society—a "new set of associational structures" that people enter voluntarily, different from both traditional families and the impersonal world of economic and political action, permitting bonds of affection to work on a social plane. "The obvious direction of change," said Parsons of the new feminism, "has been the extension of familial-type affectional relations to wider groups, forming something like universalistic 'sisterhoods,' which could eventually include men" as they developed their expressive, emotional capacities. In these trends, Parsons saw "a certain redressing of balance" in the structure of modern societies, which had long emphasized instrumental rationality and "neutralization of the feminine component" of motivation.[57] At the time, radical feminists committed to an androgynous model of human personality might have objected to Parsons's essentialist definition of a "feminine" value dimension but generally shared the collectivist orientation of his analysis.

Thus the counterculture can best be understood in a developmental or transitional perspective. Present in the experience of nonconforming youth in the 1960s were both new, emergent social and cultural forms and signs of social distress marking the obsolescence of old social norms. Cracks in an old order of industrial and familial discipline based in the nineteenth-century heyday of bourgeois society were bound to release furious energies, some of it spent in unbridled individualism.[58] Along with the cheap mysticism, the cult of irrationalism, and the ill-informed embrace of the iconic American Indian, young people in the counterculture often showed a lack of moral judgment, unable to determine clearly where "doing your own thing" threatened to violate their own values of nonviolence and community. The notion of community itself was ill defined within the counterculture, based on a simple ideal of *communitas* as "the nonstructured, nonhierarchical I Thou" relationship of intimacy, when demands of the time called instead for new forms of society, new kinds of organization and association devoted to meeting human needs.[59] Still, the anticommercial and service ventures in the counterculture signaled a growing awareness of the potential promised by a society of abundance, the corresponding need to cultivate a rich field in social relationships of mutual aid, and the possibility, as Parsons suggested, of restoring to modern society the bonds of affection. The resurrection in subsequent years of a deep conservative spirit, devoted to an idyll of nineteenth-century bourgeois order, has sought to ignore these aspects of those times and managed to demonize the transitional elements of the counterculture as simply antisocial.

The Limits of Community and the Integrity of Society

The problematic character of community in mass society became clear in the 1960s even as the ideal of community was revived. The localism that narrowed the focus of the new urban theory and diffused the energy of social reformers, the urge toward exclusivity and unanimity that marred some expressions of Black Power, and the shallow, uncomplicated sense of *communitas* that became a countercultural ideal all signaled faults in the concept of community. Nevertheless, community meant much more than a simple desire to "turn inward," away from a broad, inclusive public life, as some critics have suggested; for these observers, the common note among the "ethnic" move-ments of the late 1960s was an urge to find "a known place among people like oneself," an exclusive kind of group consciousness that helped promote the "fragmentation" of American life.[60] Movements of the oppressed such as Black Power, however, managed despite their limitations to transcend the par-ticularism of ethnic community in their visions of a liberated future. The cul-tural nationalism that urged oppressed peoples to adopt distinctive identities often proved to be more sensitive to the problematic character of community in mass society than its formal ideologies suggested.

The new literatures growing out of the American Indian and Chicano movements in the late 1960s demonstrate this sensitivity. In both these move-ments, protest assumed the militant form of "nationalist" self-assertion, seek-ing liberation by calling on ethnic solidarity and pride, building a community of color on the basis of the group's unique history and cultural heritage.[61] To be sure, each of these "communities" was (and is) internally diverse, and there is a history of sharp rivalries between them, but they may be compared with each other as indigenous or mestizo peoples long inhabiting this continent, possessing traditions under acute pressure from the dominant culture of the United States. The militant movements of protest arose in the 1960s from the tension these peoples experienced between their forced draft into the main-stream culture beginning in the 1940s and the continued discrimination and deprivation they suffered in the wider society they encountered. In the works of two novelists, N. Scott Momaday and Rudolfo Anaya, this experience found imaginative expression in lyrical stories of exile and return, divided loy-alties, and the search for home and identity.

Between the 1930s, when Indian intellectual D'Arcy McNickle published his novel *The Surrounded*, and the late 1960s, when a renaissance of American Indian literature began, few works of fiction, poetry, and drama were pub-lished by Indian authors. McNickle remained a scholar and activist, having cofounded in 1944 the National Congress of American Indians (NCAI), the first major attempt to foster common action by a broad alliance of Indians and the main organization involved in fighting the federal "termination" policy that broke up tribal governments in the 1950s. By the early 1960s, signs appeared of a renewed struggle. Delegates of 90 tribes at a Chicago conference in June 1961 issued the *Declaration of Indian Purpose*, showing their determina-tion "to hold to identity and survival." The National Indian Youth Council (NIYC) was also formed that year, and protests began in defense of Indian fishing rights. McNickle continued to write about the endurance of tribal cul-tures, and by the end of the decade, he was joined by Vine Deloria Jr., a for-mer NIYC activist and NCAI official, whose book *Custer Died for Your Sins* advocated Indian self-determination, a program combining pan-Indian nationalism and an appreciation of specific tribal traditions.[62] More militant protest was to come in the form of the "Red Power" ideology of the American

Indian Movement founded in 1968, the 19-month Indian occupation of Alcatraz island starting in 1969, and the Trail of Broken Treaties protest in 1973. In the meantime, more and more sympathetic writing about Indians appeared throughout the decade by outsiders such as the poet and ritual expert Jerome Rothenberg, novelists Frank Waters and Thomas Berger, and historian Dee Brown. An outpouring of new literature by Indians themselves began in earnest around 1968 with work by Momaday, James Welch, Wendy Rose, Gerald Vizenor, and Duane Niatum.

The Chicano movement also flourished in the late 1960s. After World War II, during which great numbers of Mexican American men were drafted into military service, campaigns for Mexican American civil rights rested on a claim of belonging, and suggested a strategy of assimilation, to a generic American identity. Of course, particular loyalties were not absent, and community organizing for better social services in the barrios persisted throughout the 1950s and early 1960s. Work in these neighborhood campaigns of the Alinsky-styled Community Service Organization (CSO) provided basic training for Cesar Chavez, who later cofounded the United Farmworkers (UFW) with Dolores Huerta. In 1965 the long, arduous grape pickers' strike that began in Delano, California, marked a watershed. UFW appeals to a common Mexican heritage boosted solidarity among field laborers and helped promote the idea of the "Chicano," a term once used to disparage poor, unassimilated Mexicans but now adopted with pride. In campaigns elsewhere—for reclaiming communal land rights in New Mexico, demanding respect for Mexican culture and history in Texas public schools, building a movement of university students, and protesting the Vietnam War in the Chicano Moratorium of 1970—a broad sense of Chicano unity across the Southwest (renamed Aztlán, the fabled homeland of the Aztecs) grew among young people embracing a separate identity. In the writings of radical Chicano scholars such as Rodolfo Acuña and Mario Barrera, Chicanos were described as exploited subjects in an American "internal colony" established by conquest in the 1840s.[63]

The imaginative literature that flowed from the new conviction in communal identity demonstrated, however, how elusive the meaning of community was. In N. Scott Momaday's Pulitzer Prize–winning 1968 novel *House Made of Dawn*, a young Pueblo man named Abel returns twice to his home in the Southwest, a town whose life remains composed of both Catholic Church observance and indigenous ritual practices of the kiva. The first is his return from war in 1945, when his tense sojourn culminates in estrangement from his grandfather, a brief love affair with a wealthy white woman, and a fight that ends with Abel killing a mysterious albino man. The second return, seven years later, comes after Abel's imprisonment and painfully difficult years on probation in Los Angeles among other city Indians. Now, attending his grandfather's last days, Abel runs in the fields as the sun rises, reenacting the ritual races he joined as a boy, and finding transcendence in the "house made of dawn," the land become recognizable as a home.

In the best-known literary work of the Chicano movement, the long poem *Yo Soy Joaquín* (1967), by Denver activist Rodolfo "Corky" Gonzalez, the estranged sense of being Chicano, "lost in a world of confusion / caught up in a whirl of an Anglo society," was portrayed in anger. In more subdued, lyrical tones, Anaya's *Bless Me, Ultima* (1972) gave a compelling impression of Chicano experience, always "betwixt and between."[64] The time frame and place of the novel (New Mexico) is comparable to that of Momaday's. Antonio Marez, a young boy left with his parents and sisters when his older brothers went off to war in the Pacific, recognizes the tensions facing him: the division between his mother's agrarian religiosity and his father's restless vaquero past, between his English-language schooling and his Spanish-speaking home, between the small town and the wider postwar world that his older brothers eagerly embrace—and especially between the Catholic catechism and the pagan traditions practiced by the old woman curer, Ultima, who comes to stay with his family and nurture Antonio's own spiritual gifts before she dies. In the end, it is Ultima's simple faith in "the magical strength that resides in the human heart" that wins his commitment.[65]

In both novels, the death of an old one leads to a victory, in a troubled and divided heart, for the spiritual principles of an indigenous, non-European tradition. But that return is not a final or conclusive one. The old community portrayed in these novels was never one of simple unanimity, and its bounds had been breached by far-flung forces of the dominant culture, to which the heroes are also inevitably tied. Amid the trials posed by the social world abroad, the sustenance of faith depends on embracing the force of tradition, but no settled community of old ways can be restored in practice, and the heart calls instead on the memory of a person or a sacred place.

The idea of community tugged at the awakened sensibility of the 1960s but never achieved a clear, compelling definition. The idea of gemeinschaft, a network of face-to-face relationships in a settled locale, either exaggerated the stability of traditional communities or neglected the limits and constraints of small settlements and traditional dogmas. Appeals to community overlooked the benefits of society as such. As Rose Laub Coser points out in her book *In Defense of Modernity,* not community traditionally defined but the modern experience of multiple roles in varied social settings best fosters an unalienated sense of "individual autonomy, intellectual flexibility, and creativity."[66] And, Coser writes, the greatest enemies of personal development—poverty and powerlessness—cannot be vanquished on the grounds of community but must be answered primarily on the *societal* plane of economic and political change. Clearly, these concerns do not signal the end of community but call instead for innovations that will move beyond old definitions of both community and society. Community, understood as a robust sense of communication, belonging, and security, still requires redefinition on a plane suited to a society of broad-based mobility and interaction. At the same time, "society" might be redefined in ways that move beyond its foundation in either industrial metaphors of functional organization or models of unitary nation-states, toward a more flexible notion: a relation among communities that overlap and interact with each other, a combination that defines membership in very general terms and thus provides an umbrella for varied affiliations of identity, a common life that discovers a kind of ecological unity in the ongoing, practical work of reproducing itself.[67]

six

Systems and the Distrust of Order

By the late 1960s, students in American universities and colleges easily grasped the concept of a "system." The term appeared widely in the natural and applied sciences, denoting the orderly processes at work in any complex array of multiple, interacting variables, be it a living organism, an environmental milieu, or a computing machine. Indeed, the broad application of the concept was itself cause for admiration, hope, or horror. A general theory of systems and its close cousin, cybernetics (the science of communications and control), were not new to the 1960s, but they reached maturity then. To some of their proponents, they provided a basis for the unity of all sciences, an old positivist dream; to others, they suggested a holistic method of interpretation challenging the reductive and analytical traditions of scientific method. To some advocates, the understanding of complexity promised by systems theory and cybernetics opened prospects for social reform; to critics, they suggested only the refinement of coercive constraints. In 1965 Daniel Bell remarked that the keynote to new trends of thought was "the idea of 'Control,' the growing awareness and knowledge of processes which allow us to regulate the wide variety of 'systems' which are operative in the world: machine systems, economic systems, social systems, and eventually perhaps, political systems." Earlier, Beat writer William Burroughs had scoffed, "You see control can never be a means to any practical end.... It can never be a means to anything but more control.... Like junk."[1] Here was another tension of the decade, for if "systems theory" was a watchword of the 1960s, so too was a deep-seated distrust of order.

"The system" also referred to the social and political order challenged by a growing number of critics and young radicals, but in this sense, the *concept* of a system was to be embraced, not spurned. It enabled opponents to draw "connections" among diverse social problems; it indicated that the flaws in society were fundamental, endemic—not incidental. However obnoxious in its given form, systematic order was a fixture of reality. In another range of critical thought, however, the intellectual imperative to discern order in terms of systems was itself suspect; emphasis fell instead on the irreducible disorderliness of reality. A special solicitude for the undisciplined impulse, for giving free rein to a wild spirit, liberating play from the spirit of work, emerged as a Dionysian element of the time, helping forge a countercultural sensibility. Contradiction between systems and the distrust of order echoed in further reaches of intellectual and cultural life, too: in competing currents of modern music, and in the writing of Thomas Pynchon, who speculated whether systematic order was a fact or fiction of our experience.

Systems and the Modalities of Control

The general idea of systems emerged after World War II from studies that perceived connections between the nature of mechanisms and the nature of life. The careers of two figures indicate this convergence: Ludwig von Bertalanffy, who fashioned a "general systems theory" and began promoting it in the late 1950s, was a biologist interested in mathematical formulations of organic processes; Norbert Wiener, the inventor of cybernetics, was a mathematician whose work on complex machine processes interested him in the nature of organisms.[2] Within biology itself, the theory aimed to heal the old breach between camps of "mechanists" and "vitalists," as Anatol Rapoport, Bertalanffy's student and leading advocate in the 1960s, explained: it borrowed from the vitalists their emphasis on the whole of an organism as something greater than the sum of its parts, as well as their objection to explanations that reduce biological processes to simpler chemical and physical events, but it denied (with the mechanists) that these processes were sui generis. Organisms merely operated as "open" (not "isolated") systems whose input-output relations with an environment occasioned changes of state called growth.[3] The conjunction of machines and organisms in the "systems" imagination, however, fostered ambiguity. Although the theory was attacked for reducing life to the deadened routines of technical efficiency, many systems theorists sought to enrich the understanding of natural and physical processes by investing them with attributes of vitality and meaning.

For decades, biologists had described the systematic character of organismic processes—responses to stimuli that restored and maintained an internal equilibrium—particularly since French physiologist Claude Bernard's 1878 study of the body's "internal milieu" and the continuing work on "homeostasis" by Harvard scientists Walter B. Cannon and L. J. Henderson in the 1920s and 1930s. Wiener knew their work, and when during World War II he began applying the notion of homeostatic controls to the problem of designing self-correcting machine processes (specifically, automatic means of aiming artillery based on radar information about moving targets), he settled on the keystone of his new science: the phenomenon of "feedback loops," in which information about the consequences of a certain operation returns to check or guide the operation toward a desired effect. In his projected "cybernetic" studies of information, communication, purpose, and the control of action, Wiener saw a general science capable of addressing patterns of human life, the design of computing machines, and problems that arose in the interaction between the two. For Wiener, life and mechanism came together as comparable ways of using information to maintain and create order in a physical world that otherwise diffused energy (or increased entropy): "It is my thesis that the physical functioning of the living individual and the operation of some of the newer communication machines are precisely parallel in their analogous attempts to control entropy through feedback."[4]

By the 1960s, references to systems, systems analysis, and control appeared promiscuously throughout elite culture. "To information-processing specialists, corporation managers, engineers, and military experts," the critic Robert Boguslaw tartly observed in 1965, "using the word system is to be *au courant* about the latest in technical fashion and good taste."[5] Furthermore, because they had been closely associated with weapons development (in Wiener's work on targeting, for instance, or in Defense Department sponsorship of computer science), systems theory and cybernetics gained a reputation as peculiarly militaristic and technocratic sciences. No figure fostered this notion more than Defense Secretary Robert McNamara, who brought systems analysis (only a distant cousin to Bertalanffy's and Wiener's grand theories) to the Kennedy administration, where McNamara hoped to use complex accounting and simulation methods to achieve rational control first over the nuclear arms race and then over Vietnam War strategy.[6] Even before the horrors of Vietnam helped disgrace such cold-blooded rationalistic hubris, systems theory was attacked for bearing antihumanist implications. Boguslaw's *The New Utopians* (1965) argued that contemporary engineers and managers, pursuing the mirage of total system efficiency, overestimated the capacity of reason to account for all contingencies in human affairs. They promoted an ideal of "frictionless" systems that excluded a normal degree of human conflict and fostered a fatalist mood, as "human beings [go] in search of systems within which they can assume their roles as operating units." Wiener's unitary science of men and machines appalled Boguslaw. "Just as it is possible to make automatic equipment caricatures of human beings," he wrote, "it is possible to make human beings into caricatures of robots."[7]

The idea of systems, however, enjoyed a wider range of influence beyond the world of weapons development and military strategy, with moral and political implications more varied than simply a technocratic interest in efficiency.[8] Out of Norbert Wiener's "cybernetics circle" of scholars convened at MIT in the late 1940s and early 1950s came the "game theory" of mathematician John von Neumann, later adopted and subsidized by the Defense Department as a way of simulating Cold War antagonisms and plotting ways to win. At about the same time, however, the systems theorist Anatol Rapoport and his University of Michigan colleague Kenneth Boulding founded the *Journal of Conflict Resolution,* in which the ideas of unified science, the pursuit of patterns in human behavior, and the emphasis on interrelatedness spawned an interdisciplinary field of inquiry dedicated to world peace. "It is clear as we look over the human experience," the editors wrote in their inaugural issue of 1957, "that there are some conflicts which are fruitful and some which are not—some conflict processes which lead to resolution and integration, some which lead to disintegration and disaster."[9] Systems theory also helped shape the new "cognitive sciences" that "picked up steam" in the 1960s, owing to such different figures as Herbert A. Simon, whose work on the relationship between human problem solving and computer processing helped found the field of artificial intelligence, and linguist Noam Chomsky, who viewed grammar as a kind of system for generating sentences.[10]

Thinking in systems found one of its most potent uses in the emerging field of ecology and environmental politics, where the idea of "ecosystem" captured the delicate interrelatedness of natural milieus and the dangers of upsetting their intricate balance. Oxford botanist A. G. Tansley coined the term in 1935, building on Charles Elton's pathbreaking *Animal Ecology* (1927), which first described "food chains" and defined the idea of an environmental "niche" as a specialized location in the functional order of natural interaction. Because Tansley's ideas were borrowed by American agronomists to quantify the energy efficiency achieved by different farming techniques, the environmental historian Donald Worster has argued that the concept of an ecosystem sustained the "industrial view of nature as a storehouse of exploitable material resources," in contrast to the "organicist" philosophy of the new environmentalists, who recognized a vital spirit, holistic interdependence, and moral significance in nature.[11]

Worster overstated his case, however. Indeed, a new environmentalism arising in the 1960s departed from older traditions of conservation that treated nature as a repository of resources to be rationally managed. In many respects, that tradition of resource management, having reached its peak in the 1930s with the Tennessee Valley Authority (TVA) and the hydroelectric and river control aims of the great dams, was discredited by the 1960s as agencies such as the TVA became known as promoters of environmentally destructive development. The Sierra Club, long dedicated to preserving wilderness rather than conserving resources, was reinvigorated in the 1960s by its executive director David Brower and won a major victory in stopping plans for two new dams in the Grand Canyon. The new environmentalism, however, grew from a widespread popular concern not only in preserving wilderness but also in addressing the many signs of pollution affecting the human habitat. As historian Jim O'Brien put it, this new emphasis brought concerns once identified with public health (pioneered by women reformers in sanitation and worker health and safety such as Ellen Swallow and Alice Hamilton) together with ideas solicitous of nature. The 1962 book on the ravages of the pesticide DDT, *Silent Spring*, by the award-winning science writer Rachel Carson, was most emblematic of this perspective (accompanied by the less well known book by the anarchist Murray Bookchin, *Our Synthetic Environment*, published under a pseudonym, also in 1962). The new environmentalism, therefore, was more "nature centered" than the old conservation movement and more "human centered" than the old preservationism. Furthermore, environmentalism emerged and developed through the 1960s as the product of many diverse concerns and movements. The scandal in 1962 over birth defects caused by the fertility drug Thalidomide, concern about nuclear radiation, the antiwar movement's condemnation of American military technology in Vietnam, the new revolt against positivism and the emerging critique of "modernization," the consumer safety movement associated with Ralph Nader after 1966, countercultural nature worship, and labor struggles such as the 1969 West Virginia mine workers' strike over black lung disease all contributed to public concern—and protest—about synthetic chemicals, destructive technology, industrial hazards, and health.[12]

That some people amid these diverse currents advocated mystical and transcendentalist ideas about nature illustrates Worster's argument that a distinctive moral and organicist view of environment came into being. But even though Rachel Carson manifested the influence of Henry David Thoreau and clearly saw "poetry" in nature, it is hard to imagine her building the argument against DDT without the concepts of the food chain and the means of quantifying levels of chemical absorption that derived from work by Elton, Tansley, and the American agronomists. There lay the basis for Carson's demonstration that pesticides accumulated in a pyramidal manner until reaching massive and deadly concentrations in birds and their predators. She relied on recent developments in the study of ecosystems, and despite furious attacks on her and her book by the spokesmen and scientists of the chemical industry, Carson's work proved in the main to be scientifically accurate. Meanwhile, ecologists such as David M. Gates insisted that "the word 'ecosystem' ... recognized the essentiality of a holistic approach towards ecology." Moreover, Carson's career as a popular writer with professional scientific training, her concern that the polemics against her showed how scientific expertise could be "bought" by industry, and her commitment to making science "part of the reality of living" indicated some of the admirable impulses in the 1960s to socialize and democratize science.[13]

The work of botanist Barry Commoner is also telling. He was well versed in the recent evolution of systems theory and clearly cited it in a book that became one of the most influential manifestos of the new environmentalism, *The Closing Circle* (1971). Commoner's route to environmental activism began in the campaign by peace activists in the late 1950s to publicize the public health dangers of radioactive fallout from nuclear test explosions. Carson herself had recognized pesticides and fallout as "interrelated, combining to render our environment progressively less fit to live in." (In some respects, they were anticipated by Alice Hamilton's concern in 1928 about the effects of radium on women workers who painted it on watch faces.) In the mid-1960s, Commoner analyzed the natural and social consequences of nuclear war, in polemics that relied on the system notion of "complex feedback relations" to demonstrate that government "civil defense" programs offered only a dangerous illusion of security. Later, in *The Closing Circle*, the concept of ecosystem remained central to his arguments about the destructive folly of human meddling in nature. Commoner cited Wiener's cybernetics as essential to grasping the idea of "an ecosystem consist[ing] of multiple interconnected parts, which act on one another" in successive "cycles of events." From such basics, Commoner drew simple ecological "laws": "everything is connected to everything else," and "nature knows best." His reliance on the language of systems, leading to his assertion that "any major man-made change in a natural system is likely to be detrimental" and his call for "human harmony with nature," suggests the ecumenical function of the "ecosystem" in the new environmentalism of the late 1960s.[14]

Systems theory may be faulted for slighting the sheer contingency of historical change and for exaggerating the degree of orderliness ascribed to milieus of either society or nature, which are never in fact so neatly bounded and integrated as the theory suggests. But the dismissal of systems theory, by its critics in the 1960s and since, as a technocratic ideology remains far too simple. Nothing demonstrates this better than a close look at Norbert Wiener himself. Wiener's views were influenced at an early point by his father's Tolstoyan ideals, and while working as a young Boston reporter before 1920, Wiener felt a great deal of sympathy for the industrial workers he observed striking against the Lawrence textile mills. Even in the early 1950s, he wrote as a critic of the prevailing conservative mood in the country. "It is becoming more and more perilous for a resident of the United States to question" the dogma that "a thing is valuable as a commodity for what it will bring in the open market." The primary object of his theoretical concern, information, was neither a commodity to be traded for a price, he insisted, nor a piece of materiel to be hoarded in state arsenals. Alluding to the Rosenberg spy case, Wiener mocked the idea that a scientific "secret" could be "stolen," and he ridiculed the arms race. "The dissemination of any scientific secret whatever is merely a matter of time ... [and] there is no distinction between arming ourselves and arming our enemies."[15]

Wiener's cybernetics anticipated the critics of technocracy. Democracy, he wrote, requires "two-way communication," something shown no respect by such "worshipers of efficiency" as a laboratory chief "who assigns each subordinate a particular problem, and begrudges him the privilege of thinking for himself so that he can move beyond his immediate problem and perceive its general relevance." By the early 1960s, Wiener criticized "Big Science" bound to military imperatives, noting that "the whole arrangement of a military research laboratory is along lines hostile to our own optimum use and development of information." He warned against fitting individuals "not in their full right as responsible human beings, but as cogs and levers and rods" to either mechanical or bureaucratic routines. Instead, he insisted that "to be alive is to participate in a continuous stream of influences from the outer world and acts on the outer world.... Variety and possibility are inherent in the human sensorium and are indeed the key to man's most noble flights." The game theory of his erstwhile collaborator John von Neumann appalled Wiener, for it imagined human relationships in the antagonistic form of two players eager to hide information or distort its transmission. "The integrity of the channels of internal communication is essential to the welfare of society," Wiener wrote, for he associated communication with the making of relations, patterns, and organic form—that is, life. "Organism is opposed to chaos, to disintegration, to death, as message is to noise."[16]

Wiener's cybernetics did not seek, in a conservative vein, to fix a preexisting order, rigid organization, or rule-bound hierarchy on human affairs. It was, nonetheless, an attitude that sought order in things as the promise of meaning and the preservation of life. Here in Wiener's approach might be recognized an Apollonian element—linking together harmony, form, reason, and understanding—in the culture of the 1960s. Wiener began his introduction to cybernetics with a discussion of entropy, the tendency in physical nature toward the dissipation of energy and the breakdown of differentiation in structure. In the book, he seemed haunted by the idea of entropy, perhaps as a metaphor for the grave threats he already recognized were posed by military violence and environmental degradation. In response, at not a few moments in *The Human Uses of Human Beings*, he wrote in an elegiac tone: "Life is an island here and now in a dying world."[17]

Among Wiener's disciples in the 1960s was anthropologist Gregory Bateson, a participant in the early cybernetics circle. He claimed to have reached a synthetic understanding of culture, consciousness, nature, and science, which offered "a new and perhaps more human outlook, a means of changing our philosophy of control and ... of seeing our own follies in wider perspective."[18] Although Bateson used the concept of feedback to understand "social systems" in the 1950s, he claimed that the whole import of cybernetic theory did not gel for him until a breakthrough paper of 1969 called "Form, Substance, and Difference." Reality, he asserted, consists of the "differences" that formally distinguish one phenomenon from another and the processes we have of registering, or communicating, those differences. These processes of recognizing and mapping distinctions are themselves the locus of "mind" in a broad sense, one that surpasses a conventional dualism of mind and body: Bateson regarded mind not as something enclosed within the perceiving brain of the human individual but as something extending beyond the body, immanent in systems of interaction—such as the unified field linking a tree, an ax, the arm and the brain of a tree cutter, or the walking stick that makes the sidewalk part of a blind person's sensorium. Bateson's method stressed patterns, or gestalten, that "interconnected" particular events and signals, denying fixed boundaries to isolated entities.[19]

In this sense, Bateson promoted a kind of structuralism. As he did so, in the late 1960s, a new generation of American scholars influenced in part by the structuralism of French anthropologist Claude Lévi-Strauss, including Wendy Doniger O'Flaherty, Jacob Neusner, and Jonathan Z. Smith, sought to elucidate the "system" that inhered in different bodies of religious tradition.[20] These were arcane intellectual exercises, whereas Bateson's structuralism gained some popular appeal. Speaking to scholarly societies or student groups, Bateson claimed that the cybernetic view of mind broke down, in principle, the sharp distinction between the ego and the world, much as LSD did in hallucinogenic practice, and that only such a holistic connection with the world could reverse the environmental destruction that stemmed from the scientific view of nature as an exploitable object. Bateson brought systems theory full circle, from a positivist vision of unified science to mysticism: "The individual mind is immanent but not only in the body. It is immanent also in pathways and messages outside the body; and there is a larger Mind of which the individual mind is only a subsystem.... What I am saying expands mind outwards.... A certain humility becomes appropriate, tempered by the dignity or joy of being part of something much bigger. A part—if you will—of God."[21] Bertalanffy also claimed to have experienced a sense of "great unity and liberation from ego boundaries" as "moments of scientific discovery [gave him] an intuitive insight into a grand design."[22] The mystical turn of systems theory revealed another dimension of the Apollonian spirit.

Varieties of Antisystemic Sentiment

The diversified field of systems theory met a no less vigorous and varied opposition in the 1960s among those who found reason to distrust or despise the signs of order in contemporary life. "System" and "control" assumed sinister meaning for a number of radicals who recognized an order to the different kinds of abuse they challenged, in matters of race, poverty, and empire, and who, unlike liberals of past and present, saw in the administration of public affairs not the promise of reform but the practice of domination. In this sense, though, one still needed a concept of "system" to fight a system. This was nowhere more clearly expressed than in an April 1965 speech by SDS president Paul Potter at one of the first mass protests against American military escalation in Vietnam. Here Potter revealed the distinctly radical import of systemic consciousness by repeating the term in conjunction with several counts of a sharp political indictment:

What kind of system is it that justifies the United States or any country seizing the destinies of the Vietnamese people and using them callously for its own purpose? What kind of system is it that disenfranchises people in the South, leaves millions upon millions of people throughout the country impoverished and excluded from the mainstream and promise of American society, that creates faceless and terrible bureaucracies and makes those the place where people spend their lives and do their work, that consistently puts material values before human values—and still persists in calling itself free and ... fit to police the world? ... We must name that system. We must name it, describe it, analyze it, understand it and change it.[23]

For Potter, recognizing a "system" implied a breakthrough to radical analysis, a necessary step in knitting together the varied faults in American life into a pattern, one that gave coherence to the phenomena of social life and, in turn, elicited demands for change that had to be fundamental, or "radical"—for only by transforming or toppling a whole structure of things could any particular problems, now seen as symptoms, be remedied.

Besides rooting diverse evils in a flawed fundamental structure, however, the new radicals also criticized American society for *being* systematized, running under a regime so effective in controlling affairs that a rigid stability was ensured. The very idea of "control" had once been a goal reformers and radicals sought: "social control" meant subjecting the modern economy to guidance by the state or by moral values, to put order in what had seemed like the dangerously atomistic or conflict-ridden or even asocial form of life that reformers more or less clearly identified with capitalism. (These values remained intact for a moderate social democrat such as Daniel Bell, for whom the idea of controlling a complex system through limited interventions vindicated a modest notion of social and economic planning.) Now, however, many critics generally spurned "social control" as a vision of coercive restraint and discipline, as the manipulative management of human behavior, intended to ensure order for its own sake and power for the few. This mutation in the meaning of "control" had begun with the discovery of totalitarianism in the late 1930s and Max Weber's critique of bureaucratized society that became familiar in American life after the war. For radicals of the New Left, historical writing in particular helped foster a critique of systematic order. From Madison, Wisconsin, the historian William Appleman Williams criticized the organized "syndicates" of power that grew to dominate modern, centralized American life. The Wisconsin-trained Gabriel Kolko argued in 1963 that Progressive Era regulatory reform was promoted by business itself and represented not a popular victory but the "triumph of conservatism." Graduate students James Weinstein and Martin Sklar, in their journal *Studies on the Left*, argued that state intervention in economy served mainly to insure stable market conditions for capitalist growth, resulting in a welfare state better labeled "corporate liberalism."[24] Indeed, the main current of American historical writing in the 1960s would reconstrue twentieth-century reform as a "search for order" (in Robert Wiebe's phrase), and young scholars built a new, critical social history of public schools, mental asylums, and other institutions—all products of proud American reform movements. The new historians now skewered reformers for seeking "social control," a middle-class desire to establish or restore authority over unruly lower classes in social institutions that governed behavior strictly.[25]

The suspicion of systematic order in the 1960s could, nonetheless, take various forms. The radical theorists of corporate liberalism were most devoted to exposing the elite interests served by the much-vaunted stability achieved in American life, but here, as in any kind of systems theory, the temptation was to exaggerate the degree of order that actually prevailed. A different response appeared in the parodic fiction of Joseph Heller, Kurt Vonnegut, and John Barth, where Rabelaisian laughter derided order and called it madness. In works such as *Catch-22*, *Slaughterhouse 5*, and *Giles Goat Boy*, the sense of an overarching, coercive order looming beyond one's control joined with a portrait of events experienced as disorder, chaos, and dislocation—in other words, as the sheer nonsense of the world at large. In quite another vein, writers of the so-called Frankfurt school offered an extreme image of modern society organized in a virtually faultless system, but in rebelling against it, they insisted that systematic styles of thought be repudiated *tout court*. The best known of these exiled German philosophers, Herbert Marcuse, suggested in *One-Dimensional Man* (1964) that economic growth, consumer ethics, positivist philosophy, and engineering techniques had conspired to suppress any awareness of divisions or fractures in American life; the only worthy response was a "great refusal" to submit.

Other leaders of the school, such as Theodor Adorno, had returned to Germany after the war, and their work was not widely known in the United States, though an English translation of Adorno's *Prisms* (1967) started to revive interest in him. Of the Frankfurt writers, Adorno was most insistent on the need to reject the enticements of systematic thought. This attitude was not alien to American audiences. A commonplace of the "end of ideology" school held that nineteenth-century "grand systematizers" such as Comte and Marx, by denying a place for human volition in their deterministic schemes, had tilled the soil for totalitarianism. Adorno made the point somewhat differently, claiming that the actual imposition of systemic control on modern social life had vitiated the oppositional value of systematic presentation in theoretical, moral, and aesthetic expression. Consequently, in his 1951 book *Minima Moralia*, criticism appeared in the form of collected aphorisms rather than extended argument. As Martin Jay explains, "negation [or criticism of what exists] and the truth it precariously preserved could be expressed only in tentative, incomplete ways. Here [Adorno's] fundamental distrust of systematizing was carried to its extreme. The location of philosophical insight was no longer to be found in abstract, coherent, architectonic systems, as in Hegel's day, but rather in subjective, private reflection."[26]

Adorno's attitude, even if largely unknown at the time, found many parallels in American letters during the 1960s. Susan Sontag echoed Adorno when she introduced her essay "Notes on 'Camp' " by stating that "the form of jottings, rather than an essay (with its claim to a linear, consecutive argument) seemed more appropriate for getting down something of this . . . fugitive sensibility." She elaborated in a 1967 essay presenting what seemed like an agonized version of the "end of ideology." The scope of human disaster in the modern world, she wrote, had ushered in a "post-philosophical" age, in which the pursuit of abstract universal principles promising "order, harmony, clarity, intelligibility, and consistency" was no longer tenable, and ideologies of historical destiny as well as the positive "sciences of man" lacked conviction. One "response to the debacle," she wrote—Sontag was drawn to a rhetoric of "collapse," "ruins-in-the-making," and "apocalypse"—"was a new kind of philosophizing: personal (even autobiographical), aphoristic, lyrical, anti-systematic," of which Nietzsche's work was the best example. In this manner, one faced the acute crisis of order and meaning with no recourse to assurance in either science or faith, insisting instead on "the unending disclosure of difficulty." That was why, she wrote with reference to cubism, dada, and absurdism, "the important works of art of the twentieth century [did not aim at] creating harmonies but of overstraining the medium and introducing more and more violent, and unresolvable, subject matter. . . . Only 'fragments' are possible."[27]

This kind of deconstructive hostility to systematic order marked classicist Norman O. Brown's *Love's Body* (1966). Brown ended his earlier book, *Life against Death* (1959), with a call for "the resurrection of the body"; his wordplay with the Christian image of salvation was intended to advocate liberating the omni-erotic impulses at the core of human motivation ("the polymorphous perverse") from the forces of repression, which Brown claimed were simply obsolete. *Love's Body*, which sought to depict that resurrection, came in the aphoristic form of the antisystematic imagination. Chapters were collections of short paragraphs, annotated with diverse references to Christian scriptures, Freud and other psychoanalysts, classical literature, Western philosophy, and Eastern religion. Through the succession of chapters, each having a one-word theme—"Liberty," "Resurrection," "Fulfillment," "Judgment," "Freedom"—Brown would unmask the deceptive character of these terms and show how a sensitivity to symbolism could reveal the multiple and varied meanings of experience. Brown's ecstatic, Dionysian mood evoked that "sudden breakthrough" when "free associations, random thought [and] spontaneous movements" would leave "the natural order broken," Freud's reality principle and all repressive power dethroned, and the erotic principle triumphant in a free-flowing sense of communion with all things. Brown prophesied a Zen-like transcendence: as the superego of morality was abolished, so the ego and all kinds of distinction upheld by the discriminating intellect (the basis of "mind" in Bateson's cybernetic vision) collapsed. "Overcome the opposition of darkness and light, cleanliness and dirt, order and chaos," Brown advised, to achieve the fusion of all things, which was, for lack of distinctions, the same as Nothing, the topic of his final chapter. Here, "when the ego is broken," was satori, "not final victory but final defeat," and serenity.[28]

Brown claimed radical credentials. He demanded "no respect for persons, not to be fooled by masks; no clothes, no emperor. All power is an impostor; a paper tiger, or idol; it is Burnt up the Moment men cease to behold it."[29] In *Commentary* magazine, Herbert Marcuse argued against Brown that social power was real as well as symbolic, but Brown was unmoved, reasserting his notion of revelation as revolution: "What needs to be reiterated is ... that the kingdom of heaven on earth is possible; and that other world, the negation of this jungle, cannot possibly be anything except Communitas. A higher form of chaos."[30]

Brown's style of expressive radicalism, his Dionysian dance against order, had some purchase on the radical political imagination of his time. The idea that protest was most effective when it punctured the air of reality surrounding figures of power and authority, to be replaced by the imagination and will to enact a different kind of life *now*—these were principles embraced by the Diggers, a small band of activists in Haight-Ashbury led by a vigorous young tough named Emmett Grogan. Fusing the absurdist temper of avant-garde theater with utopian communism, a new-age consciousness, the anarchist "propaganda of the deed," and a hard-bitten ethic of the streets, the Diggers strove to make everything and everyone "free!" by declaring it so. (To reach the free food, some of it donated and some stolen, that the Diggers distributed in the Haight, the hungry had to pass through a 13-foot gate called the "frame of reference," symbolizing the change of consciousness they needed to help make the world free.) The Diggers defined their public events as theater, regarded theater as life, and advocated "life-acting" as the way to build a new society and exit the old. "Our authorized sanities are so many Nembutals [sedatives]," they wrote in one mimeographed broadside. " 'Normal' citizens with store-dummy smiles stand apart from each other like cotton-packed capsules in a bottle.... And we all know this." So they proposed an insurrectionary Happening "for the main business district of any U.S. city":

> Infiltrate the largest corporation office building with life-actors as nymphomaniacal secretaries, clumsy repairmen, berserk executives, sloppy security guards, clerks with animals in their clothes....
>
> At noon 1,000 freed beings singing and dancing appear outside to persuade employees to take off for the day. Banners roll down from office windows announcing liberation. Shills in business suits run out of the building, strip and dive in the fountain. Elevators are loaded with incense and a pie fight breaks out in the cafeteria.
>
> *Theater is fact/action*
> Give up jobs. Be with people. Defend against property.[31]

The Diggers aimed to dislocate perceptions of normality in favor of a future community, orchestrate chaotic scenes of gratification, provoke their friends as well as enemies, and flirt with the life of outlaws. They carried on the spirit of disruption, a rough rejoinder to the Apollonian search for order in the 1960s.

The Polar Sounds of System and Chance

The history of art music in the 1960s can also be viewed as a contest between systems and the suspicion of order. Although any sharp dichotomy somewhat oversimplifies the field of new composition in the 1960s, it is possible to recognize at least two poles of attraction that, in their principled extremes, represented diametrically opposed conceptions of modern music: one devoted to methodical, systematic composition and the other to the uncontrolled assemblage of sounds. The world of new music was divided between a highly self-conscious modernism, encamped in the major university music schools and identified with the Princeton-based composer Milton Babbitt, and an extra-academic avant-garde headed by the charismatic and puckish John Cage.

Both currents traced their origins to the innovations of the German Jewish atonal composer Arnold Schoenberg and the advent of new musical technologies after World War II. Early in the century, Schoenberg led the move away from compositions focused on key, in which a tonal octave determined the bounds of melody and harmony, toward the use of a full 12-tone row including all sharps and flats. During the 1940s, his influence grew in the United States, where he lived in exile. Meanwhile, Schoenberg's associate in Austria, Anton Webern, helped formalize the 12-tone method into what became known as serialism, a rigorous system of composition that would focus a composer's attention on all the technical elements of musical sound (pitch and intervals, duration, etc.) and the ways they might be controlled. While young European modernists such as Karlheinz Stockhausen and Pierre Boulez, meeting together annually, made the German city of Darmstadt a postwar center of musical innovation in Webern's mode, serialism sank roots in postwar American universities. Technology for the new music was soon forthcoming. The magnetic recording tape developed by Germany during the war entered the toolbox of avant-garde composers by the mid-1950s, and the first electronic music synthesizer, developed by RCA in 1955 to 1956 and improved by 1959, was installed that year at a new Columbia-Princeton Electronic Music Center. From 1959 to 1969, there was a boom in electronic art music as 50 more electronic studios were built across the country, mostly at universities.[32]

Both currents were acutely aware of inhabiting a "new" musical scene, where wide-ranging possibilities beckoned and old limits expired. Having encountered Schoenberg's work—a "revolution in musical thought"—as a music student in the late 1940s, Babbitt believed the "informed musician ... lives no longer in a unitary musical universe of 'common practice' " and had to recognize "alternatives to what were once regarded as musical absolutes." But as the materials of music, such as the choice of permissible pitches, had been vastly expanded, thus reducing the "redundancy" and predictability of musical language, both the maker and the listener required a far more precise understanding of musical events, variations, and structural patterns that make up a composition. In the scholarly journal Babbitt began with his students in 1963, *Perspectives of New Music*, the systems mentality was clear: the aim of his school was to "create structural coherence in the unique relativistic context of the compositional present" and "to construct musical syntaxes that can be controlled precisely." To achieve these ends and ensure "increased accuracy from the transmitter" of musical communication, the synthesizer (first installed at the experimental center Babbitt directed) was especially apposite.[33]

Electronic music was not entirely dominated by Babbitt's academic serialists. Across the country, avant-garde musicians Ramon Sender and Morton Subotnick founded the San Francisco Tape Music Center and electronic studio, and there, in 1966, Pauline Oliveros, one of the few well-known women working in new music, recorded her irreverent *Bye Bye Butterfly*, a spontaneous performance on synthesizer, emitting long, weird sounds like cricket choruses, against the background of a scratchy record of a Puccini aria. Nevertheless, the serialists dominated the field of electronic music. Unsurprisingly, the academics gained a very small audience for their music, and most music prizes in the 1960s, like the Pulitzer, typically went to moderate atonalists who worked with conventional instruments, such as Elliott Carter, or to composers such as Leonard Bernstein and Ned Rorem who still wrote tonal, lyrical music. In 1970, however, Charles Wuorinen, a young associate of Babbitt's electronic music center, won the Pulitzer for *Time's Encomium* (1970), a composition that paraded the features admired by the systematizers. In this piece, Wuorinen aimed to make the most of his medium by relying solely on techniques of "precise temporal control," since electronic music had no room for the "inflection" or "accent" that performers with instruments use to help realize the rhythm of a piece. Here, he wrote, "rhythm is always quantitative, never qualitative. Because I need time, I praise it; hence the title." The music had an austere, cerebral aura, though in the fleeting bleeps of the high register and rumbling electronic low tones one caught intimations of a church organ, Wuorinen's first instrument.[34]

John Cage's approach to the new realm of music differed profoundly. Born in southern California in 1912, Cage traveled to Paris in the late 1920s, imbibing the anti-art sensibility of the dadaist Marcel Duchamp before he returned and studied with the exiled Schoenberg. Schoenberg considered Cage "not a composer but an inventor of genius," and Cage applied his talents in the 1940 creation of a "prepared piano"—in which various objects attached to the strings (nails, rubber bands, feathers) helped the instrument produce sounds resembling at times a Balinese gamelan. Later, in such works as *Williams Mix* (1958), which drew competing catcalls and hurrahs at its performance in New York City, Cage demonstrated his conviction that the ability to manipulate sound on magnetic tape had revolutionized music. But the expanded scope of "sound-space," rather than demanding systematic precision, implied for him the radical openness of "free-ranging" creation. By the beginning of the 1960s, Cage concluded that the Darmstadt modernists were too wedded to the project of controlling sound, whereas he would "give up the desire to control sound, clear his mind of music, and get about discovering means to let sounds be themselves, rather than vehicles for man-made theories or expressions of human sentiments."[35] Hence his interest in the properties of "natural" or "found" sounds and in the aural experience of silence. Having developed an interest in Asia along with fellow California composers Henry Cowell and Lou Harrison, Cage studied Zen Buddhism with D. T. Suzuki and embraced the Chinese *Book of Changes (I Ching)* as a guide for incorporating the principle of chance into composition.

In some respects, the uses of chance in music were no less recondite than the serialists' experiments in control. In one composition of 1961 *(Variations II)*, Cage's score consisted of a number of transparent sheets marked by lines and points, which, when superimposed on each other, produced certain measurable lengths. These, which differed each time the exercise was repeated, were to define the values of sound dimensions (frequency, timbre, duration, and so forth) that would then be "realized" on one or more instruments chosen by one or more performers. Here, Cage wrote, was a "composition indeterminate of its performance."[36] During the 1960s, most of Cage's major musical compositions lay behind him, but he became a ubiquitous figure and mentor in avant-garde arts of all media, and several volumes of collected writings gave him a reputation as a major theorist of art and criticism. Cage's aesthetic—anarchic and "democratic" in its embrace of all sounds, its hostility to the imperatives of "control" and "hierarchy" in either the production or the evaluation of formal arts—came to echo the conclusions of his friend Norman O. Brown. Cage advocated meditative principles of "acceptance" and "attentiveness" that would point the listener (considered as much a maker of music as the composer or performer) toward the existence of things in their particular qualities, away from abstract generalization and causal explanation, and finally to "*dis*organization and a state of mind which in Zen is called *no-mindedness.*"[37]

The two wings of art music freely vented their hostility toward each other throughout the 1960s but actually shared more than they recognized. The serialists' emphasis on extreme precision and Cage's chance methods seemed to create like-sounding music. An antagonistic critic noted that Milton Babbitt's works paradoxically gave a "chaotic impression," for "whatever control there is cannot be heard [and] what is heard is atomized sound, without themes or continuity."[38] A friendlier view came from a European composer of the Webern school who conceded that music based on "the most abstract constructions" often seemed to be the result of "free play," a paradox that reflected the phenomenon of order within chaos apparent in natural events like "the unhurried dispersion of passing clouds, the twinkle of pebbles in the bed of a mountain stream, or the breaking of surf against a rocky coast."[39] Besides the unintended similarity of sound, both schools concurred in excluding expressivism from their music. Wuorinen's exclusion of "inflection" echoed Cage's "treatment of music simply as unemotional sound material."[40] Cage insisted that art depended on getting "one's mind and one's desires out of its way," for "love makes us blind to seeing and hearing." Mirroring Norman O. Brown's deconstruction of ego, Cage declared, "subjectivity itself [is] an authority structure," one to be refused.[41]

Both main currents had some influence in broader reaches of American music. Electronic music entered the pop idiom by the end of the 1960s, and Cage's principles of chance music and "found sounds" found their way, consciously or not, into Frank Zappa's experimentalism and Jimi Hendrix's expansion of the rock guitar's sonic field. The rigors of system versus chance started to break down before the decade was out; a few composers such as George Rochberg and George Crumb began working at least partly in a tonal vein as they sought to revive a sense of spirit, emotion, and mystery in music. It was in the expressive realm of jazz, however, that the divergent musical camps of the 1960s were both rebuked and synthesized most effectively. Steve Reich, a student of the serialist Luciano Berio and a leading young voice first in tape music and then in "minimalism," or "musique repetitive," was one of the composers who recognized contemporary jazz as an alternative to both the serialists' methodical straitjacket and the Cageans' anti-art rejection of musicianship. John Coltrane's modal jazz of the early 1960s anticipated the meditative dimension of Reich's minimalist compositions. From Coltrane's more unbounded improvisations of the mid-1960s, Reich gleaned other lessons. "What Coltrane was saying was that over a held harmony finally any note is possible, including noise. But this was very different from John Cage, and certainly from Boulez, Stockhausen, and Berio." The difference, Reich suggested, was both aesthetic and ethical. Students in music composition "were writing pieces which they didn't play, which one could doubt whether they *heard* in their heads, and ... you wondered if they'd ever be performed.... Coltrane picks up his saxophone and *plays* and the music comes *out*. ... It would've been almost immoral not to follow in Coltrane's direction because of the musical honesty and authenticity involved."[42]

Moreover, jazz in the 1960s pioneered a method that overcame the opposition of order and chaos. *Free Jazz* was the title of a 1960 recording by Ornette Coleman and his "double quartet" (two small ensembles). The piece consisted of 30-odd minutes of uninterrupted collective improvisation. In it each player worked, apparently unconstrained by any common melodic or rhythmic motif, creating a continuous movement that achieved, after the fact as it were, a coherent identity. The raucous music, marked by spontaneous harmonies and cadences, could reach points of elegant beauty, at least for listeners who, like readers of fragmented narrative in modernist fictions, could defer the demand for quick recognition of a predictable form and identify with the flow of sound.

Muhal Richard Abrams's Association for the Advancement of Creative Musicians (AACM) in Chicago became a key center for free jazz, a laboratory for exploring the individual and collective dimensions of musical expression. AACM membership demanded a strong sense of duty. All members joined in musical discussions and the organization of performances, voted on the group's corporate activities, vowed to build their musical ensembles mainly of fellow AACM members, and helped train teenage musicians on Chicago's South Side. Abrams aimed to foster "genuinely individual expression from each musician" while cultivating "a compositional procedure that made group awareness a fundamental part of successful music-making." In his study of Abrams's acolyte Anthony Braxton, Ronald Radano offers a compelling description of the AACM's kind of "collective improvisation," in which every member engages simultaneously in free exploration:

> The improvisations *work*, and they work because of the performers' uncanny ability to discern interesting improvisational pathways during the moment-by-moment act of creation. The musicians are constantly faced with decisions of where to begin and end phrases and sections, when to play and not to play. And they make these decisions to shape a composite texture, while also paying attention to signs of where the improvisation might lead. Such acute sensitivity developed from years of continuous ensemble playing and perhaps more generally from the collective orientation of African-American musical practice.... It also pays tribute to the organization's communal ideal ... : at moments of true union, the performers offer convincing evidence that they have achieved their ultimate aesthetic end, having melded together their respective musical personalities into an all-encompassing, spiritually unified whole.[43]

Although the AACM artists moved apart in various musical directions after the 1960s, the association's commitment to the communal dimension of free self-expression marked one of the decade's unique achievements. It demonstrated that the ideal of personal autonomy need not be corrosively individualistic and that collective action might give vent, and meaning, to the individual's voice rather than suppressing it. The AACM's free-jazz methods managed to combine order and disorder and indicated a way to surpass the antinomy of system and chance.

Clandestine Order and
the Writing of Thomas Pynchon

Among its many consequences, the fascination with, and suspicion of, systems helped foster the 1960s vogue of the spy novel. The most popular entries, the many titles of Ian Fleming's James Bond series, built their appeal largely on tales of technical wizardry, adventure, and sexual dalliance, but something more than these raised the genre to prominence. The spy novel plied the theme of the person reduced to a manipulated figure at the center of a game played by others. This was the telling motif in the decade's most acclaimed novel in the genre, John Le Carré's *The Spy Who Came In from the Cold* (1964). In this story, the hero, Leamas, comes to learn that even beyond the carefully plotted game plan he has executed, *all* the seeming contingencies and accidents that lead finally to his betrayal at the hands of his own superiors have been scripted, and that while something beyond his ken is happening to him, knowledge of the infernal whole is concentrated in the mind of the intelligence officer fittingly called Control. Furthermore, the spy novel thrived on a profound paradox: in an age when institutional concentration and wide-ranging communications made the production and distribution of knowledge increasingly a public resource, powerful apparatuses of secrecy engaged in Cold War adventures helped make it seem that the real order of things was less knowable than ever. The age of systems and their critique was also a time that aroused suspicion of a clandestine order to things, a secret history lurking beneath the surface of events.

Rampant distrust and suspicion hit a high pitch in popular responses to the assassination of John F. Kennedy. The official report on the assassination, fingering Lee Harvey Oswald as the sole killer, was greeted by a string of rebuttals, led by Edward J. Epstein's *Inquest: The Warren Commission and the Establishment of the Truth* (1966) and Mark Lane's *Rush to Judgment* (1966), not to mention Jim Garrison's failed prosecution of an alleged conspirator, businessman Clay Shaw, in 1969. Critics claimed that conspiracies involving the Central Intelligence Agency and related circles in government, organized crime, and the far-right fringe had plotted and carried out a political execution in Dallas—a claim that gained a good deal of credence among left-wing and liberal intellectuals and protest movements. Given Kennedy's ardent and reckless pursuit of the Cold War, these dissenters should have known better, for nothing in the record suggests Kennedy posed any threat to the national security apparatus or its Cold War aims. The CIA indeed manipulated the Warren Commission, but not by foisting on it the blanket cover-up the conspiracy mongers claimed. Rather, the CIA's reluctance to report its sordid campaign against Fidel Castro helped obscure a possible motive for Castro admirer Lee Harvey Oswald: revenge for United States assaults on revolutionary Cuba.[44]

The writing of the young novelist Thomas Pynchon became compelling in a time when conditions and events piqued the clandestine imagination. Combining the spy novel and the historical novel, adding a measure of the picaresque and sustaining the offbeat, outraged sensibility of the Beats, Pynchon repeatedly depicted an alienated or oppositional consciousness, beset by intimations of systems and driven by the desire both to plumb them and to get outside them. Having read Norbert Wiener as an engineering student in the 1950s, Pynchon brought to his writing an understanding of cybernetics and the problematic issues that surrounded it—the ambiguous relation of life and mechanism, the perception of order as both hope and danger, the contradiction of communication and clandestinity. He spoke like a systems enthusiast when he described the "discovery that everything is connected." Meanwhile, his books dwelled on his characters' suspicion of the forces that knit the world together *and* on the anxiety that their very perceptions of an order in things were unreliable. To believe *everything* is connected, Pynchon pointed out, is paranoia—though that diagnosis alone could not rule out the presence of real enemies at large in a threatening world.

All Pynchon's novels in this period magnify themes of the spy novel. They depict one or more characters in a long venture of gathering intelligence, which always leaves them short of definite conclusions but tantalized (or terrorized) by their growing suspicion that a conspiratorial order of some kind governs events. In *V.* (1963), Herbert Stencil follows a multitude of leads splayed across the stage of twentieth-century world history in hopes of determining the identity and fate of a woman named only as V. in the diary of Stencil's father, a British agent who died mysteriously in 1919 off the Malta coast. In *The Crying of Lot 49* (1966), Oedipa Maas tries to unravel the hints of an elaborate conspiracy that has something to do with a mysterious underground postal system and the estate of stamp collector Pierce Inverarity, a former lover who named her executor of his will. *Gravity's Rainbow* (1973) recounts a chase at the end of World War II to recover the German plan and prototype for Rocket 00000, a special V-2 rocket that will carry a human payload—and the part in that search played by Tyrone Slothrop, first recruited by Allied spymasters in England, who learned of his strange ability to predict, by the occurrence of his erections, the time and place of V-2 landings. In the bizarre concatenation of events that Pynchon relates, the German scientist whose behaviorist experiments on the infant Slothrop set the pattern for his conditioned erections, returned to Darmstadt (the postwar center, Pynchon remarks, of "dodecaphonic democracy" in music), where the scientist synthesized Imipolex G, a plastic to be used as the prophylactic sheath for Rocket 00000's human cargo; his employer is I.G. Farben, whose ties to American corporations reveal the formation of giant cartels with the power to pull the strings behind world affairs.

Throughout the long, fruitless quests in these books, the number of links, connections, suggestive parallels, and analogies multiplies to the point that leading characters are increasingly convinced that "something is happening," subjecting them to potent, integrated forces beyond their control; but they are also utterly bewildered by the spectacle of growing complexity. Pynchon's conspiratorial imagination mocks itself: his books tell enough, with sufficient historical verisimilitude, to suggest kinds of concentrated power lurking behind innocent appearances, but they also circle back to make the suspected order of things appear so monstrously extended as to be impossible or absurd. As Oedipa Maas encounters the signs and shadows of a vast network whose message (like hieroglyphics without a key) remains obscure, she asks, "Shall I project a world?" She wonders whether the order she perceives really lies behind the clues or whether it is only her own imposition of meaning that gives form to a mass of data. Although some readers infer that Pynchon advocates paranoia as a safe bet, uncertainty is the predominant note.

Yet if Pynchon is too self-conscious to propose the veracity of paranoia, he is too serious about the dangers posed by reality to conclude, as one critic put it, that "order is only a fabricated imposition placed on inherently random events by human desire."[45] Just because his characters are paranoid does not mean there is no order. In fact, in a kind of answer to Paul Potter, Pynchon comes close to recognizing the order that prevails as a system with a name, one not bizarrely conspiratorial but all too practical in its embrace of global terrain—capitalism. In *Gravity's Rainbow*, it is said that "the true war" is "a celebration of markets," a venture whose "real business . . . is buying and selling," a war that after 1945 was "adjourned and reconstituted as a peace."[46] In *V.*, despite the madness of Stencil's search for the mystery woman, there is in Pynchon's review of the twentieth century the unquestionable reality of imperialist depredation that stretches from the big-power diplomacy setting off World War I, to the appallingly brutal suppression of the Herrero insurrection in Southwest Africa, and on to an event—the Suez crisis of 1956—so often mentioned that it seems to be, like the eye of a storm, the source of the book's energy, the spark to Pynchon's imagination. Whatever wild fantasy may be involved in the far-flung conspiracies Pynchon's characters imagine, the uses of economic and political power growing throughout the twentieth century into more concentrated form with wider reach are compellingly real.[47]

Furthermore, for Pynchon and his characters, "projection" in Maas's sense is in some way necessary to establish meaning and, against the odds, to find one's place in the world. The references to concatenated events and persons suggest, as critic Leo Bersani writes, "a dazzling argument for shared or collective being . . . Singularity is inconceivable."[48] Here Pynchon upholds the import of Norbert Wiener's Apollonian search for pattern, for the counterentropic force of life.[49] Paranoia may be suspect, but Pynchon also distrusts "anti-paranoia"—"where nothing is connected to anything, a condition not many of us can bear for long."[50] Indeed, the obverse of paranoia, the good that lurks in the paranoid's manic perception of evil, is the promise of communion.

Throughout Pynchon's stories and novels, there is a disarmingly innocent search for human warmth, expression, and contact. Amid the swirling historical data of *V.* there is the saxophonist Sphere, who declares, "Be cool, but care." And in *Gravity's Rainbow,* Pynchon's phantasmagoric, sometimes pornographic passages often come to a close (like the free-jazz fury that ends in fortuitous but exquisite beauty) in elegiac expressions of love (if only in dreams or recollections), which might compensate for present pain. As one critic wrote, Pynchon can use "the most powerfully aching language" to make readers "feel ... keenly the moments of loss, separation, impingement, and simple sheltering human gestures."[51] The point was present in an early Pynchon story, "Entropy," aimed against the atomization of people that threatens the "heat-death of society." Contact constitutes meaning; connection is the gesture that chooses life.[52]

Postmodern critics often celebrate Pynchon's work for exposing how written texts create an illusion of making sense; his texts, they say, tease the reader to imagine that things "add up" but at best only reveal the tenuous and contingent ways writing has to define anything meaningful. In that view, writing neither gives voice to an expressive personality nor describes a reality "outside"; Pynchon, it is said, derides both these illusions. The interpretation offered here, on the contrary, finds in Pynchon's work a simple humanism and insistent realism. His novels evoke a persistent desire for human fulfillment that protests against the crushing order of things *and* hopes for a change that would create a home in the world for human subjects. The expressive voice of Sphere stands for the important role Pynchon ascribes to the feeling and thinking subject; meanwhile, the perception of some order in things suggests that the structure of social life might be known and hence changed. Because Pynchon's literary art is more like music than social theory, it need not be tested for its analytical acuity.[53] His hints about a global capitalism are about as far as he goes; otherwise, his "paranoid" vision suggests, in line with a common form of radical hyperbole in the 1960s, the image of a technocratic social machine that brooks no challenge and suffers no faults, an image of total domination that can be escaped only by dropping out. Yet Pynchon's mood of suspicion implies a kind of realism strong enough to offset any suggestion of quietism.

The same cannot be said of the most adamant antisystematic thinkers of the 1960s, Norman Brown and John Cage. In *Love's Body,* Brown argued that coercive power lay in the reality principle itself, in the very belief that a reality, stoutly resisting our wishes, lay outside ourselves. Power, Brown said, was Moloch, "a false god fed with real victims" upheld only by our willingness to submit, and its dread effects would unravel once Eros was liberated to overcome the separation of the ego from the world and realize the poetic spirit of symbolic communion. Brown's challenger, Herbert Marcuse, answered this view with a demand for social realism. Perhaps, he said, Brown's "extreme imagery" suggested a righteous impatience with the spectacle of human oppression throughout history, but

> imagery is not enough; it must become saturated with its reality.... The king must be shown not only as father but as king, that is to say, as master and lord; war and competition and communication must be shown not only as copulation but as war and business and speech. Unless the analysis takes the road of return from the symbolic to the literal, from the illusion to the reality of the illusion, it remains ideological, replacing one mystification by another.[54]

John Cage's antipathy to systems yielded a similar result. In a Whitmanesque vein, Cage often described his aesthetics and poetics as deeply "American," not "European," as democratic rather than hierarchical, devoted to undermining the working of power and control. He believed, however, that critical theories of social reality were bound to exaggerate the potency of will and hence exacerbate human ills. A Zen ethic of "attentiveness and acceptance" promised a new pacific world. Asked "how to improve the world," he answered, "you will only make matters worse."[55]

If antisystematic thought encouraged quietism, systems theory proposed an excessive holism, tending to exaggerate the perduring stability, the coherence of things in reality. American philosophers William James and John Dewey had historically challenged the notion of systematic order, the image of a "block universe" James thought was implied by Hegelian and other forms of idealism; they preferred to make way for change by stressing the open, unfinished, and incomplete character of reality. Still, without recognizing the degree of orderliness that does inhere in things, people remain powerless for lack of access to determinate levers of change. There is some systematic order in social affairs, and it must be examined to be challenged, even if it is not so systematic as modern systems theory suggested. The idea of an order that was not faultless but structured by recognizable lines of conflict—a mode of production, in Marx's sense—did not have much purchase on the social imagination in the 1960s, a time when great hopes for change were for the most part unmatched by a strategic sense of how to achieve it. Meanwhile, Pynchon's mode of paranoia—its odd intimations of order, its call for restoration of expressive human bonds—played a role in sustaining hope for renewal in social life.

seven

Peace and Violence

"Chickens come home to roost," said Malcolm X after John F. Kennedy was killed—a remark that drew a public rebuke from his mentor Elijah Muhammad and opened the breach that led to Malcolm X's departure from the Nation of Islam and the deadly rivalry between them. His point was simple: in a society maintained by the rule of violence, at some point, violence would make victims of its rulers. Before 1963 this perception of America as a peculiarly violent society was held largely by those who belonged to its subjugated classes, particularly blacks and other "racial" minorities who suffered the regular threat of police brutality, racist assault, and personal harassment. Malcolm X's meaning went right over the heads of most Euro-Americans, who tended to assume that racist violence, or militant resistance to it, was an aberration rather than the norm. Within a few years, however, in the half decade after Malcolm X's assassination, his perspective would gain a much wider hearing. In foreign wars, political assassinations, and street crime, in the violence of poverty, of rebellion, and of repression, the United States was surely a more violent country, or at least more *openly* so, at the end of the 1960s than at the beginning. Indeed, it became commonplace to recognize a propensity for violence as nearly a national character trait. Although it is "part of our buried history," the historian Richard Hofstadter wrote, "violence has been frequent, voluminous, almost commonplace in our past," and "the rediscovery of our violence will undoubtedly be one of the important intellectual legacies of the 1960s."[1]

The question of violence can hardly be separated from the issues of war and peace that polarized the American intelligentsia in the 1960s. Growth of the academic system in the era of the Cold War had created a corps of specialists, supported by government funds, who were devoted to studying problems in weapons development, military strategy, Great Power diplomacy, and counterinsurgency. On the other hand, college and university faculties also became the home for intellectuals whose ties (however attenuated) to old movements of dissent or commitments to humanist traditions inclined them to protest as the nuclear arms race quickened and Cold War confrontation hit a new high pitch around 1960. Academicians were part of an early peace movement that, along with the nonviolent resistance practiced by the civil rights movement, helped lay the basis for the next stage of large-scale protests, beginning soon after U.S. military escalation in Vietnam during 1965. Combined with the righteous indignation and impatience of African Americans in pursuit of freedom, the war and the antiwar movement of the mid-1960s helped radicalize the left-wing critique of American society. By 1966 to 1967, the war and the challenge of ending it even led some oppositionists, including activists first drawn to protest movements with commitments to pacifism or nonviolence, to tout tactics of militant confrontation and armed conflict, often with startling indifference to the utility or disutility of those tactics for advancing the movement's political aims. Alongside the continuing debate over war and peace in Vietnam, this shift in the sensibility of protest from nonviolence to violence surely signaled one of the era's most striking contradictions.

The War Intellectuals and the Peace Party

As part of the postwar academic revolution, a new field of "policy science" took shape around issues of military strategy raised by the ongoing development of nuclear weaponry. Policy science was a field developed by civilians working in special institutes such as the Princeton Center of International Studies and in extra-academic "think tanks" such as the RAND Corporation and the Hudson Institute, and though their efforts were designed to serve the interests of national security, they saw themselves as independent-minded critics of official policy. Leading scholars Bernard Brodie and William W. Kaufmann, at RAND and Princeton respectively, were convinced that the enormous intellectual resources devoted to technical matters of building nuclear bombs had not been matched by sustained thought about the role these weapons were to play in war and peace.[2] Both men criticized the Eisenhower administration's policy of threatening adversaries with "massive retaliation" because the policy relied on an evanescent U.S. monopoly or preponderance of nuclear force and disregarded the enormously destructive power of the thermonuclear weapons (hydrogen bombs) first tested in 1952. From then on, Brodie and his colleagues came to recognize "the absurdity of all-out war when each side had developed the means of utterly devastating the other," leading to Brodie's conclusion in *Strategy in the Missile Age* (1959) that policy had to emphasize "deterrence" of war rather than threatening to commence it.[3] Even deterrence, however, entailed a threat, and it was hard to determine for sure whether a particular strategic move would effectively check an adversary's inclination to aggression or goad it into war. RAND strategist Albert Wohlstetter, author of an influential paper called "The Delicate Balance of Terror" (1959), showed that a "logic of preemption" could entice either the United States or the Soviet Union to attempt a "first strike": believing that defense against thermonuclear destruction would be ensured only by knocking out the opponent's weapons, either side might be driven by a sense of fear and urgency to act before the other did.[4] And the desire to deter a first strike by answering each new weapon the opponent deployed with development of a more threatening one only led to an arms race ratcheting ever upward.

A number of RAND's scholarly strategists joined the Defense Department under the patronage of Robert McNamara in the early 1960s, marking the political arrival of policy science. With the advice of young intellectuals such as Adam Yarmolinsky, Alain Enthoven, Henry Rowen, and Daniel Ellsberg, McNamara first embraced a RAND-fashioned "counterforce" strategy ensuring that enough American missiles would survive a Soviet attack to retaliate and destroy Soviet nuclear forces. By 1964, however, McNamara and others concluded that this strategy rendered nuclear affairs dangerously unstable; targeting the enemy's nuclear forces and openly striving to make one's own invulnerable excited the adversary's fear of a first strike and kept the ante up too high.[5] The search for a "stable nuclear balance" led toward a posture of threatening the enemy's cities, based on the assumption that "maintaining at all times a clear and unmistakable ability to inflict an unacceptable degree of damage upon any aggressor" was the best deterrent.[6] Under this strategy of "mutual assured destruction" (MAD), McNamara's aides calculated just how much nuclear force was needed to inflict catastrophic damage on the Soviet Union, hoping to determine a level of sufficiency *below* the constantly escalating demands of military men for more armaments. Notwithstanding his espousal of MAD, however, McNamara also ordered that research begin on multiheaded missiles (MIRVs), and a rapid buildup of nuclear arms on both sides of the Cold War persisted through the 1960s.

Nuclear strategy was not the only precinct in which academic intelligence came to play a prominent role in official policy making. McGeorge Bundy, former Harvard College dean, and Walt W. Rostow, an economic historian, served in succession as national security adviser to the president, setting a precedent of academic intellectuals holding that post, to be followed in later years by Henry Kissinger and Zbigniew Brzezinski. As the younger colleagues and students of these men, such as Kissinger's assistants Morton Halperin and Anthony Lake, were brought into the National Security Council, another link between academic intellectuals and policy making was fastened. Schools such as Harvard and Yale became "national security managerial training and recruitment centers," while major state universities occupied another niche, providing teams of researchers to carry out "field operations" in various Third World countries on contract with the Defense and State Departments.[7] A Michigan State University project led by political scientist Wesley Fishel, intended to upgrade the administrative efficiency and political legitimacy of the U.S. client government in Saigon, was only the best known of these efforts. Among the project's tasks was helping to draft a constitution for Ngo Dinh Diem's government of South Vietnam.[8] In time, a few participants in such projects questioned the validity of scholarship determined by the political goals of government, but in most cases, the largely unquestioned dominance of Cold War anticommunism inside the academy and out made this work seem unexceptional or virtuous to the scholars involved.

As the apparatus of war intellectuals developed, protests devoted to the cause of "peace" also revived. The first signs of public concern about fallout from nuclear bomb tests encouraged the new move to organize. Pushed primarily by *Saturday Review* editor Norman Cousins, a group of liberal pacifists founded the Committee for a Sane Nuclear Policy (SANE) in 1957 to lobby for a ban on bomb testing. A more militant group, the Committee for Non-violent Action (CNVA), was founded that year by A. J. Muste, veteran labor agitator and Christian pacifist, and David Dellinger, who had been jailed for refusing military service in World War II. The CNVA organized small groups of trespassers at the government's Nevada nuclear test site and sponsored the 1958 protest voyage of the sailboat *Golden Rule* into a Pacific Ocean testing zone. SANE, which drew endorsements by prominent figures such as actors Steve Allen and Robert Ryan, singer Harry Belafonte, and the missionary doctor Albert Schweitzer, grew rapidly to a national membership of 25,000 but was weakened in 1960 by an internal controversy over whether to permit Communists to belong. A group formed in 1961, Women Strike for Peace (WSP), thrived, however, rallying women to "make the whole world a home" (as one organizer, Elise Boulding, put it) in demonstrations and picket lines promoting a test ban and nuclear disarmament.[9] Also in the early 1960s, the Student Peace Union (SPU), inspired by SNCC's direct-action campaigns, emerged as a new milieu for radical sentiment as the energies of SANE flagged.[10]

A contingent of American intellectuals played a part in these moves. In 1956 Barry Commoner of Washington University organized the St. Louis Committee for Nuclear Information to publicize effects of radioactive fallout (particularly evidence of Strontium-90 in milk supplies). A year later, Nobelist Linus Pauling sponsored a petition calling for a nuclear test ban, soon signed by 2,000 American scientists. Shortly afterward, in July 1957, a meeting at Pugwash, Nova Scotia, of 22 scientists from around the world, including Eugene Rabinowitch, Leo Szilard, and Victor Weisskopf from the United States, issued a statement urging a test ban and declaring that "the paramount responsibility of scientists outside their professional work is to do all in their power to prevent war and to help establish a permanent and universal peace."[11] A kind of peace party was taking shape in the late 1950s and early 1960s, and though it lacked any firm or definite platform beyond the minimal demand for a test ban, it was distinguished by its advocacy, however vague, of disarmament. The war intellectuals dismissed that possibility, claiming nuclear arms were needed for deterrence and that a stable balance, perhaps supported by "arms control" agreements, was the most to be expected. Only a few weapons experts such as Seymour Melman and Richard J. Barnet wrote favorably of disarmament.[12]

Among the peace party, the left wing was marked by the radical pacifists associated with the magazine Muste and Dellinger founded in 1956, *Liberation*, which called for the abolition of nuclear weapons and advocated unilateral disarmament by the United States.[13] Harvard historian H. Stuart Hughes, who undertook a quixotic peace campaign for U.S. senator from Massachusetts in 1962, tentatively endorsed unilateral disarmament, on the grounds that the risks of giving up the arms race with the Soviets were less serious than the risks of thermonuclear war perpetuated by the "delicate" policy of deterrence.[14] As it turned out, the minimal program of the peace lobby, a test ban, was met partially with the 1963 treaty banning atmospheric tests—a modest step back after John Kennedy's frightening brinkmanship over Cuban missiles the year before—but the administration had already lost whatever degree of confidence the peace party had vested in it. Having joined the Kennedy administration with hopes for a liberal turn in military policy, Richard Barnet and Marcus Raskin quit; from 1963 on, their Institute for Policy Studies (IPS) set out to challenge the established policy scientists who mulled over the intricate logic of deterrence.[15]

In these years of its debut, the peace movement was closely associated with the black freedom struggle. The link between the two went back to the early 1940s, when the pacifist organization Fellowship of Reconciliation (FOR) gave birth to the Congress for Racial Equality (CORE), and the connection survived into the 1950s as FOR organizers Bayard Rustin, Rev. Glenn Smiley, and Rev. James Lawson served as prominent SCLC and SNCC advisers. *Liberation* magazine became a clearinghouse for activists in the freedom struggle and the peace movement and provided some of the earliest ideas about what made the revival of protest a "New Left." *Liberation* writers, who sought to revolutionize society by nonviolent means, argued that the new conditions of the nuclear age gave the philosophy of nonviolence special relevance, for the danger of annihilation made war itself obsolete. They insisted also that radicals needed to maintain the consistency of means and ends—peaceful methods in pursuit of a pacified society—if they would avoid the fate of the "Old Left" (mainly the Communist Party), whose acceptance of violence, it was said, led old radicals to make apologies for Soviet dictatorship.

This interpretation of the Old Left was simplistic, neglecting a careful analysis of the causes of Stalinism and verging on a kind of ethical absolutism, or moralism. To be sure, activists in the black freedom struggle and the direct-action wing of the peace campaigns possessed a high degree of moral purpose and dedication, granting the new movements a special appeal to the young and a formidable strength and authority; but morality, if raised to an absolute criterion in public action, could turn into moralism, a politically disabling sort of purity and self-righteousness. The New Left sensibility of the *Liberation* circle was correct to insist that revolutionary movements for peace and social justice never surrender their moral vision of a new society and, at the very least, treat the dreaded tools of violence with the most disciplined reserve. But the doctrine of strict consistency between means and ends evaded the troubling ambiguities of political action, particularly for social movements of the oppressed, which have rarely been able to forswear violence of a defensive or tactical sort when beset by an armed and determined enemy. Moreover, a moralistic approach to politics, when faced with stiff obstacles or reversals, may turn into a hardened sense of separation from all who are not part of the cause. Once the committed are steeled against outsiders, the absolute tenor of the struggle can justify a great deal, perhaps even violence itself. In this sense, the contradiction between violence and nonviolence was fraught with bedeviling ambiguities.

Martin Luther King Jr. occasionally wrote in the pages of *Liberation*, propounding nonviolence in Christian terms. He argued that agape, the disinterested love or goodwill for all humans as creatures of God, sustained the strength and resilience of the freedom struggle and marked the path toward the realization of community, first within the movement itself and later among all participants in a reformed society. Defending the technique of nonviolence as an active program for making change, not one of passive submission, King insisted on "refusal to cooperate with evil" as the watchword of a moral politics.[16] More than a moralist, however, King was, at his best, an inspired organizer of mass action, and his commitment to nonviolence was complemented by political vision. For King, writes philosopher Greg Moses, the "love" one had for one's enemies was essential to keeping attention politically focused on changing the "structure" or "system" of oppression, rather than dissipating energy in anger directed at persons; this kind of discipline not only ensured personal dignity and perseverance to the dissenter but also kept the mind clear to calculate the maximum effectiveness of organized protest. King's political perspective, furthermore, was "pragmatic" or experimental in responding to the changing circumstances of time: in response to the setback he suffered in the 1966 open-housing campaign in Chicago, King proposed refocusing the movement on the grand task of eliminating poverty, hoping thereby to liberate African Americans *and* defuse the economic fear and insecurity that led many working-class whites to resist black progress. King was quite correct in his political calculation that armed struggle by racial minorities "will not work" to effect great change in the United States of his time.[17] Yet in stressing the discipline of nonviolence and the diffuse rage of violence, he did not see that violence, although always ethically and politically dangerous, might also be disciplined and then made effective, at certain times and places, in checking an oppressor's force or making way for free political action by the oppressed. Nor did he see that the moral politics he professed could become, in less supple minds than his own, the kind of moral absolutism that itself bore undisciplined, unpredictable effects.

Antiwar American Thought and Culture

Before the U.S. war effort escalated during early 1965, public criticism of the government's Vietnam policy was muted and dispersed. Journalist Bernard Fall and scholar Paul Mus (both Frenchmen working partly in the United States) had pointed out that the struggle in Vietnam was part of a long anti-colonial revolution possessing the will and ability to resist American designs, and American journalists I. F. Stone and Murray Kempton questioned the official rationale for the August 1964 Gulf of Tonkin Resolution, which granted the president unlimited war-making powers.[18] Generally, however, the American press, when it paid attention to Indochina, backed the government's view that South Vietnam was an ally under siege.[19] Even the radicals of SDS only began at the end of 1964 to address the war in Vietnam, suggesting the low priority it held in most Americans' consciousness. It was remarkable, then, that within only a few months following the 1965 escalation of bombing and U.S. troop strength, protest attained such large proportions as it did, drawing thousands or tens of thousands to a new antiwar movement condemning official American policy. The mobilization surprised even some activists, who had seen the energies of the "peace" movement flag by 1964 and civil rights workers grow more frustrated and bitter. Nonetheless, the recent heritage of the intertwined peace movement and black freedom struggle played the prime role in generating the critical sentiment, providing organizers, and shaping the tactical imagination of the new antiwar protest.

There were various ways of posing criticism of, or opposition to, U.S. policy in Vietnam. Some observers, such as the young reporter David Halberstam in his 1965 book *The Making of a Quagmire*, found that the U.S. war effort was failing, concluded it was unlikely ever to succeed, and argued for correcting the mistake of investing so heavily in a lost cause. One of the policy's main architects, Defense Secretary Robert McNamara, who came to doubt prospects for success as early as January 1966 and was convinced of failure by 1967, adopted this view, though he refrained from any public dissent.[20] Another view recognized a deeper flaw in U.S. policy. According to "realist" critics of Vietnam policy such as veteran diplomat George F. Kennan, respected political scientist Hans Morgenthau, Ronald Steel in his book *Pax Americana* (1967), and the most vocal early critic within the governing party, Senator J. William Fulbright, the problem lay not merely in a miscalculation of enemy strength but in a dogmatic foreign policy that exaggerated both the threats posed to essential American interests around the world and the need always to wield American power with force. Beyond the realists' objections, a broad criticism of the Cold War, finding that American motives after World War II had been aggressive and provocative—rather than benign, defensive, or misguided—emerged alongside the peace sentiment of the early 1960s and provided some war opponents after 1965 with an explanation of the root causes for U.S. involvement in Vietnam.[21]

By and large, the antiwar movement rested on the plain argument that the extreme violence used by the United States to defeat the indigenous enemies of the Saigon government, and the massive death and destruction it wrought, was morally repellent and ought to be stopped as soon as possible. Although demonstrators differed on how that could be accomplished (and for some time, only the most militant, politically self-conscious among them clearly understood their aim as immediate and unilateral United States withdrawal), the simplicity of the demand to "end the war" and the commitment to manifest opposition in public protest effectively distinguished the antiwar movement from "establishment liberals" who pressured the administration to modify its policies. Excepting figures such as J. William Fulbright and Wayne Morse, liberal objections to Vietnam policy were slow in coming. Eugene McCarthy and Robert Kennedy made their first major critical statements— quite mild ones—in early 1967. That April, Victor Reuther, Clark Kerr, Joseph Rauh, J. K. Galbraith, Arthur Schlesinger, and Marriner Eccles announced the formation of a group called Negotiations Now to nudge policy makers away from the pursuit of military victory. In contrast, the demands of the antiwar movement were bolder, its dissatisfaction with the unresponsive character of the government more acute, and its conviction far deeper that the war exposed basic flaws in American society and politics. In these ways, the antiwar movement became the center of the American Left in the 1960s. The war, its impact on American society, and the movement against it seemed to fuse most issues agitating radicals: U.S. responsibility for endangering world peace and survival, the destructive power of modern technology, the rigid controls that social institutions (here, the draft and military) imposed on personal life and destiny, government deceit, inequality and racism in American life. Furthermore, the radicalization of sentiment occasioned by the war brought young radicals into contact with individuals from the so-called Old Left—from the Communist milieu as well as older anti-Stalinist revolutionaries—whose analysis of Western imperialism as a force exploiting peoples of the Third World became a keynote for far-left activists.

Antiwar leaders tended to be veterans of the peace and civil rights campaigns of the early 1960s or part of the radical student movement inspired by those campaigns. The linked arms of pacifist David Dellinger, SNCC's Robert Moses Parris, and radical historian Staughton Lynd, marching in August 1965 to declare their own peace with the people of Vietnam, symbolized the new movement's constituent elements. The salience of religious motives in the earlier peace and freedom campaigns foreshadowed the prominent role religion would play in Vietnam protest. The encouragement the Second Vatican Council gave to a church that was integrated with the society around it, bringing its message into the world, as well as recent Protestant ideas of a "servant church" that renewed itself as a moral guide in practical affairs, laid the groundwork for religious engagement in political affairs. The war had its supporters in churchmen such as New York's strident anticommunist John Cardinal Spellman, but he was answered by the antiwar activism of longtime Catholic pacifist Dorothy Day and the Catholic Peace Fellowship formed in 1964 by priests Daniel and Philip Berrigan. Protestants and liberal Jews gathered in Clergy and Laymen Concerned about Vietnam, founded in 1966 by Rev. William Sloane Coffin, Rabbi Abraham J. Heschel, and seminarian John Bennett. Boxer Muhammad Ali's refusal of induction manifested the religious resistance encouraged by the Nation of Islam, and the ecumenical Catholic monk Thomas Merton helped popularize Buddhist principles of resisting war.[22]

Opposition to the war arose quickly among the humanist intelligentsia. When poet Robert Lowell, recently converted to Catholicism, protested Johnson's war policy by publicly declining an invitation to the White House Festival of the Arts on June 14, 1965, Lowell was backed by a long list of distinguished writers and artists including Hannah Arendt, John Berryman, Philip Guston, Alfred Kazin, Dwight Macdonald, Mary McCarthy, Mark Rothko, William Styron, Robert Penn Warren, and Edgard Varèse. In the years to come, a number of writers were deeply involved in antiwar protests, notably the poets Denise Levertov, Muriel Rukeyser, and Robert Bly, and the short-story writer Grace Paley. Novelist Mary McCarthy, who was one of the best-known writers to dedicate a good part of their work to polemicizing against the war, traveled as a sympathetic observer to Hanoi and published two angry and anguished books about Vietnam.

An outpouring of creative writing on the war and its meaning came from figures both well known and obscure. Begun in 1965, Read-Ins for Peace brought poets together in scores of cities around the country, and their work was published in the anthology *Where Is Vietnam? American Poets Respond* and other collections. Much of the poetry dwelt on grotesque images of war, as in Olga Cabral's lines: "I saw the enemy, a seven-year-old boy. / I heard him screaming for his cooked / eyeballs. / I saw the granny blazing like a bundle / of reeds, / heard the infant wailing in a winding-sheet / of flame / in a village of thatched huts / hit by napalm." Other poets mocked the rhetoric of the war, "that mushroom mania where / offense is defense," or, as in Allen Ginsberg's most famous antiwar poem, linked American traditions of sexual repression to the "vortex of hatred that defoliated the Mekong Delta."[23] Above all, antiwar poets expressed a sense of awakening to horror—hearing, Galway Kinnell wrote, "above me / a wild crow crying '*yaw yaw yaw*' / from a branch nothing cried from ever in my life"—and the need to reject anything insulating the poet from a wider world of pain. Marge Piercy wrote, "We can no longer shut out the screaming / that leaks through the ventilation system, / the small bits of bone in the processed bread."[24] Such longing for a more direct connection to the world and to audiences led Walter Lowenfels to suggest that "we are going through our own birth of public poetry" and a "historic shift" away from the view that "social commitment [is] suspect in literary circles."[25]

The suspicion of commitment had been even stronger in the world of painting and sculpture, but antiwar sentiment grew there, too. Collective action akin to the read-ins emerged in 1966 and 1967, in a Los Angeles *Peace Tower* and New York's *Collage of Indignation*, each composed of contributions by a hundred or more antiwar artists. The most noted and effective collective action came in 1969 with the publication by the Art Workers' Coalition of an antiwar poster based on the March 1968 massacre of hundreds of noncombatants, including children, by American soldiers at My Lai hamlet in Vietnam: a large photograph of bodies lying tangled on a dirt path, stamped on top with the line "Q: And Babies?" and on bottom, "A: And Babies." Paintings by R. B. Kitaj, Leon Golub, Rudolf Baranik, Nancy Spero, and May Stevens depicted stark or brutal scenes of American military men and Vietnamese victims.[26] Some striking antiwar work came from Edward Kienholz, the California maker of assemblages, something like weird stage sets composed of everyday objects or icons. His *Portable War Monument* (1968), like Marge Piercy's poem, bitterly scorned the insulation of American consumer life, depicting a replica of the Iwo Jima marines raising a flag in the center of an outdoor café's picnic table while a nearby couple, turned away, drink Cokes. An uncluttered piece, *The Eleventh Hour Final*, featured a television set with a week's body counts frozen on the screen. As Arthur Danto has pointed out, Kienholz's art rejected attempts at beauty and assumed "a mode of presentation appropriate to the moral ugliness . . . his art [was] to reveal."[27]

Substantial academic opposition to government policy was also evident immediately after escalation. A May 1965 *New York Times* ad featured 750 signatures from the Greater Boston Faculty Committee on Vietnam, attacking the administration's war rationale and calling for an immediate bombing halt and cease-fire. Surveys of faculty members in the humanities and social sciences found large majorities professing liberal or radical criticisms of the war. Hawkish sentiment was high in fields such as business and engineering, and natural science faculties were relatively quiet, though distinguished scientists such as Harvard biologists George Wald and Ruth (Hubbard) Wald became prominent antiwar speakers.[28] A few academics became key protest organizers. Math professor Stephen Smale headed Berkeley's Vietnam Day Committee (VDC) with community activist Jerry Rubin. The clearinghouse for major street demonstrations from 1966 to 1968, the National Mobilization Committee to End the War in Vietnam (or Mobe) was led by activist professors Douglas Dowd of Cornell and Sidney Peck of Western Reserve.[29]

Pro-war sentiment was also prevalent on campuses. Leading academics who defended government policy included political scientists Ithiel de Sola

Pool (MIT), Robert Scalapino (Berkeley), and Wesley Fishel (MSU). Although the Johnson administration considered vocal antiwar opponents a fringe element of the populace, and a majority of students and faculties (at least before May 1970) disliked radical protesters, war policy appeared to be on the defensive. In 1965 McGeorge Bundy and Walt Rostow tried to give it intellectual legitimacy by debating academic critics Hans Morgenthau and Stanley Hoffman, but before long, picketers and hecklers kept officials from making many public appearances.[30] Later, Johnson's hawkish adviser John P. Roche formed a pro-administration Citizens Committee for Peace with Freedom in Vietnam but found it hard to round up prominent intellectuals; former Harvard president James Bryant Conant, novelists Ralph Ellison and James Farrell, historians Oscar Handlin and Allan Nevins, and scientists Ralph Lapp and Harold Urey signed up, convinced that the Vietnamese Communists promised only a brutal future for South Vietnam and could be fought back.[31] In contrast, right-wing intellectuals Russell Kirk, Peter Viereck, James Burnham, and William Buckley attacked the administration for weak resolve in the pursuit of victory in Vietnam. Their hard vision of a global anticommunist struggle and the danger of liberal government policy "retreating" before the enemy found an academic voice in conservative foreign policy institutes at Pennsylvania, Stanford, and Georgetown University. Although intellectuals associated with these outfits gained some prestige in the 1960s (and more later), the Vietnam debate remained largely a debate between administration backers and their liberal and left-wing opponents.[32]

The antiwar movement soon moved from debate and protest to tactics of noncooperation, inspired by King's principle of "refusal to cooperate with evil." By summer 1965, VDC protesters in California tried to block trains carrying troops to an embarkation point for Vietnam.[33] By 1967 noncooperation with the draft became a focus of antiwar agitation, and dozens of prominent intellectuals, including Hilary Putnam, Marshall Sahlins, and Linus Pauling, endorsed this tactic by signing the "Call to Resist Illegitimate Authority" issued by Noam Chomsky and Dwight Macdonald's organization Resist.[34] In this spirit, antiwar rhetoric typically attacked complacency. Perpetuation of the war, opponents argued, signaled a common willingness to neglect horror and one's duty to stop it. Beyond mere complacency lay the more deep-set moral malaise of "dissociation," the capacity or inclination to separate oneself from one's surroundings and the consequences of one's acts. Robert Jay Lifton recognized this in a GI's recollection of the scene at the My Lai massacre: the soldier remembered "the kind of unreality of the thing.... There was something missing in the whole business that made it seem like it really wasn't happening."[35] Here was the "psychic numbing" Lifton first described in his study of Japanese bomb survivors, *Death in Life:* a profound insensitivity to death and suffering that characterized both the perpetrators and victims of massive violence—and a key element conducive to what Lifton called "atrocity-producing situations."[36]

At My Lai, dissociation occurred in violence close at hand, but antiwar activists argued that dissociation marked the whole war, especially as the high technology of air war enforced moral indifference. "A man has to be indeed evil ... to kill a human being with a knife," said systems theorist Anatol Rapoport, but "*anyone* can sit in a comfortable control room and move levers in response to flashing lights."[37] Beyond complacency and dissociation lay the problem of complicity, and much of the intellectual antiwar movement was devoted to exposing manifestations of complicity in academic life. The icono-clastic magazine *Ramparts* ran a series of articles by Sol Stern outlining the Michigan State University advisory role in Saigon, manipulation of the National Student Association by the CIA, and manifold links between mili-tary institutions and the University of Pennsylvania. In August 1966, Stern described the discovery by student activist Robin Maisel that the University of Pennsylvania–affiliated Institute for Cooperative Research was studying techniques of chemical-biological warfare, including new strains of rice-crop disease that could be used against NLF strongholds. One faculty member protested, with reference to Nazi barbarism, "I am ashamed to be associated with a university that has a bunch of Dachau Doctors."[38]

Moral outrage, of course, played a prominent part in the antiwar move-ment. Indeed, insistence on a morally motivated politics inherited from the earlier civil rights and peace movements gave the campaign against the Viet-nam War much of its vigor. Still, the moral emphasis built in to criticisms of insulation, complacency, dissociation, and complicity always threatened to veer into a distinctly moralistic point of view. Michael Walzer and other writ-ers associated with *Dissent* magazine noted this trait, but since these critics usually urged protesters to have greater faith in the legitimacy of the estab-lished political system, their remarks were brushed off by radical war oppo-nents.[39] Still, there was something instructive in their argument that ardent demands for noncooperation and "resistance" betrayed a self-indulgent and apolitical attitude. The attempt to achieve moral purity by doing one's utmost to break the machine of death, while disdaining the moral sensibility of others who found themselves, willy-nilly, more implicated in it, erected too high a barrier between the movement and a potentially sympathetic public. Such moralism limited the movement's capacity to build solidarity with a larger portion of the people. Indeed, the temptation, once the moral stance was assumed, to denounce the American people as a whole for their government's crimes affected even a steady light of the antiwar movement, Noam Chomsky, who said citizens who refuse the "duty ... to resist ... can justly be accused of complicity in war crimes."[40]

An instructive contrast to such rhetoric could be found in the International War Crimes Tribunal, convened in Europe from fall 1966 to spring 1967 by the venerable British philosopher Bertrand Russell. Established as an attempt to make the principles of the 1946 Nuremberg war crimes trials universally applicable and create a precedent "enabl[ing] private citizens to make compelling judgments on the injustices committed by any great power," the tribunal issued its report on U.S. actions in Vietnam in 1968. Based on information generated either by several teams of Western investigators who traveled to Indochina or by North Vietnamese and NLF reports (U.S. officials who were invited to testify declined to appear), the tribunal's report established, Russell said, "the facts about aggression and torture, anti-personnel weapons and aerial bombardment, the systematic destruction of civilians and their agriculture, hospitals, schools and homes." Statements by Russell and his young American assistant Ralph Schoenman were frankly anti-imperialist, denouncing "the American empire [as] a world system of exploitation backed by the greatest military power in history," and although the tribunal was admittedly "biased" in its opposition to the war, Schoenman denied that men of such scholarly repute as those who led the tribunal would "fake or exaggerate evidence." Assisting Russell was Jean-Paul Sartre, whose inaugural address to the hearings set the tone. Nuremberg principles should be more than a matter of "victors' justice": in fact, Sartre stated, the tribunal's independence of any state power, hence its very "powerlessness," ensured its integrity. The commission, he said, was not so much a trial as a grand jury, considering an indictment of the United States for war crimes. "We, the jury, at the end of the session, will have to pronounce on these charges: are they well-founded or not? But the judges are everywhere: they are the peoples of the world, and in particular the American people. It is for them that we are working." Thus the tribunal addressed the American people, not as morally debased, but as a public capable, if awakened and informed, of judging its own government.[41] Intellectual opponents of war could do no more, and no better, than that.

Dynamics of Violence in the Movements

The year 1967 marked a turning point. In that year and afterward, overt manifestations of violence in American life—uprisings by African Americans in urban ghettos; the adoption of more provocative tactics and, later, frankly violent means of protest by some elements of the antiwar movement and the young Left; and increasing rates of violent crime, assassinations, and advocacy of armed ventures by some black and white leftist militants—fed impressions of a breakdown in civil order or a national proclivity to violence. A series of presidential commissions issued public reports on the reasons for civil strife, violent crime, and disruptive protest. Popular movies such as *Bonnie and Clyde* (1967) and *The Wild Bunch* (1969) dwelled on the bloody side of American experience in what were deemed unprecedentedly graphic images of murder and mayhem. Meanwhile a mounting cry for law and order (finding voice in the 1968 presidential campaigns of George Wallace and Richard Nixon) lumped together the varied forms of disruptive violence and failed to acknowledge its diverse causes. No doubt, the persistence of white racial violence and the use of repressive force (especially in the measures taken to suppress the urban uprisings) had excited the growth of an ultramilitant protest rhetoric among black liberation activists. In only a few of the less well known incidents, for instance, police shootings left four African Americans dead in Chicago in April 1968; six in Augusta, Georgia, in May; and three in Miami that June. Furthermore, politicians who intentionally stirred public fear of disorder in the coming years, such as the Ohio governor who irresponsibly ordered heavily armed National Guard troops to the campus of Kent State University in May 1970, were chief among those who fostered growing violence in the United States.[42] The bitter political ethos of the Nixon administration, which regarded protest virtually as treason, and the use of the FBI to harass left-wing organizations also played substantial parts in stoking American violence.

Many antiwar activists, responding to criticism of violent protest, argued cogently that moral censure had to be focused on the far greater violence committed by the American military in Vietnam. Nonetheless, the surfacing of violence—in rhetoric and practice—as a tool of the protest movements themselves rightly demands attention, particularly from partisans of those causes. Under certain conditions, violence can be a viable means of political struggle, but by the late 1960s, violence often appeared in frenzied form, bound to alienate large parts of the populace and characterized by a dangerous mystique that made it, for some protesters, more than a means to an end. Most participants in antiwar protest and other social movements eschewed violence and bemoaned its appearance in their ranks. That a radical romance of violence, however, could achieve some prominence within movements begun in commitments to nonviolence remains a puzzling contradiction.

The place of violence in the imagination of protest movements cannot be understood apart from the main acts of civil unrest during the 1960s: uprisings in mainly black ghettos that began with troubles in seven cities during the summer of 1964, all of them sparked by outrage over cases of police brutality. That summer's toll in the numbers killed, injured, and arrested paled in scope compared to the great Watts revolt of August 1965, which ran for six days and left 34 people dead. (All but 3 of that total were black residents of the district; 23 of the deaths were officially declared caused by Los Angeles police or the National Guard.)[43] A crowd gathered after police stopped a car near Watts and arrested the driver, a 21-year-old black man named Marquette Frye, for failing a sobriety test, along with his brother and mother when they arrived to challenge the police officers. Angered by the rough handling the cops gave the Frye family, small groups of onlookers stoned passing cars and reportedly beat some white drivers. In the coming days, as the police rejected a proposal to calm the scene by replacing all white patrolmen in Watts with black officers, street crowds commenced looting and burning white-owned stores—in some cases, after first destroying the merchants' hated credit records. Finally, with a 46.5-square-mile area under curfew and 14,000 National Guardsmen called in, the violence ran its course.[44]

The Watts uprising brought the first major commission report, from a panel led by former CIA director and wealthy shipping executive John A. McCone. The report recommended better schooling, job training, and equal opportunity to repair the disadvantages that laid the "seedbed of violence" but resolutely defended Los Angeles police against charges of racism and "police brutality" (always in quotation marks) while condemning people in the streets. Negro rioters, the report stated, were "caught up in an insensate rage of destruction"; excessive hopes aroused by the new federal poverty program and a national epidemic of "unpunished violence and disobedience to law" had encouraged the rioters "to take the most extreme and illegal remedies to right a wide variety of wrongs, real and supposed." According to dissenting writer Paul Jacobs, McCone's personal insistence on a report emphasizing "respect for law" and for the police ("the thin thread that enforces observance of law") required the commission to ignore the information it gathered from Watts residents. In his 1967 book *Prelude to Riot*, Jacobs aimed instead to expose the Los Angeles police as a racist and abusive paramilitary force in the ghetto and to show how all dealings the poor had with government agencies (in welfare, housing, health, and schooling) were routinely punitive and demeaning. Condemning officials whose indifference to urban poverty "reinforced America's sickness, its disease of racial superiority," Jacobs predicted death-dealing violence between blacks and whites would only increase.[45] In another case across the country, the murder of a white shopkeeper stirred up a "lynch mob" hysteria in "white New York" and led to the frame-up of six Harlem teenagers. The radical novelist Truman Nelson said ghetto dwellers were "living in a police state"; soon, he wrote, Harlemites would "no longer [act] like perpetual victims but more like what they actually are—oppressed people in an occupied country."[46]

Recent studies of uprisings in the 1960s suggest that crowds behaved more rationally in protesting social and economic subjugation than politicians and media at the time let on, that a sizable proportion of ghetto residents supported or acquiesced in the disruptive actions usually led by young men in the streets, and that the greatest horror was the repressive violence used to crush them.[47] Besides ghetto residents themselves, only radical observers at the time recognized these points. One outsider, Thomas Pynchon, did not regard the Watts uprising as "formless … senseless … hopeless." Visiting Watts a year after the riot, he found little had changed in the "basic realities" of poverty. Well-meaning social workers offered job training but no jobs; they thought "violence is an evil and an illness."

> They remember last August's riot as an outburst, a seizure. Yet what, from the realistic viewpoint of Watts, was so abnormal? "Man's got his foot on your neck," said one guy who was there, "sooner or later you

going to stop *asking* him to take it off." The violence it took to get that foot to ease up even the little it did was no surprise.... Once it got going, its basic objective—to beat the Black and White [city] police— seemed a reasonable one, and was gained the minute The Man had to send troops in.[48]

Seeing the uprising as a reasonable reaction to insufferable oppression, Pynchon went beyond Jacobs's tragic sense of understanding, and even the indictment penned by Nelson, to acknowledge the utility of violence. By this time, a number of black writers had also tried to make vivid the anger that rose among African Americans and finally peaked in a resolution to fight violence. In John A. Williams's acclaimed novel *The Man Who Cried I Am*, a black writer who discovers government plans to intern African Americans en masse calls for taking arms and "putting an end to the peace in which Negroes died one at a time in Southern swamps or by taking cops' bullets, the dying from overwork and underpay, praying all the while, looking to the heavens."[49]

The idea of armed self-defense by blacks facing white terror had been raised in 1960 by Robert F. Williams, the head of an NAACP chapter in the white-supremacist town of Monroe, North Carolina, and was promoted by Malcolm X as well. In fact, a quiet practice of self-defense was not uncommon in the rural South, where a black man or woman might sit with a shotgun on the porch while civil rights workers slept inside. Still, vocal advocacy of self-defense by Williams and Malcolm X made them notorious in the white press, which reacted hysterically to any rumor of "antiwhite" resistance. In 1966, following the shooting of civil rights activist James Meredith, SNCC helped bring the issue out of the margins into the main currents of black activism when it "reaffirm[ed] the right of black men everywhere to defend themselves if threatened or attacked."[50] Soon, however, rhetoric moved beyond a justification for self-defense to more provocative talk of retaliatory violence and armed struggle for social change. In October 1966, SNCC's Ivanhoe Donaldson remarked, "We live in a violent country. If the establishment doesn't leave people any outs besides violence, we don't have any qualms about violence." In the next summer, there was nothing conditional about it: H. Rap Brown, the new head of SNCC, said, "Violence is necessary. It is as American as cherry pie."[51] And in an account of the 1967 Newark rebellion that was otherwise brilliantly perceptive, former SDS leader Tom Hayden went so far as to claim that "the conditions slowly are being created for an American form of guerrilla warfare based in the slums.... The role of organized violence is now being carefully considered ... [to] create possibilities of meaningful change."[52]

Gerald Horne, a historian of the Watts riot, is probably more accurate when he describes such events as a kind of urban Jacquerie, a "conscious, though inchoate, insurrection." The prospects for real guerrilla warfare were hardly present, and promoting it in the United States of the 1960s was irre-

sponsible at best, dangerous at worst. Some activists such as Hayden, radicalized by the prolonged struggle against the war, had adopted a muddled idea of
revolution, inspired by guerrilla movements in quite different settings—Vietnam, Cuba, China—and spoke romantically of "picking up the gun." More
disciplined activists, familiar with socialist traditions, knew that advocating
social revolution did not necessarily mean a literal call to arms: Marxists typically placed politics above violence, emphasizing the collective organization
and mass action of the working class, rather than mere military tactics, as the
key force for change. But in the period roughly from late 1966 to early 1968, a
process that can only be called the militarization of protest rhetoric clouded
the judgment of some elements on the far left of American dissent.

The fate of the Black Panther Party for Self-Defense (BPP) showed the
confusion of the times. Led by two former college students, Bobby Seale and
Huey Newton, and the flamboyant convict-writer Eldridge Cleaver, the BPP
was founded in the fall of 1966 in Oakland, California, with a bold program
calling for full employment, new housing and black-oriented schools, the
release of black prisoners, and military exemptions for blacks. Leading armed
street patrols intended to check the unbridled and brutal power of the Oakland police, the Panthers quickly gained notoriety. They promoted black
pride but rejected racial separatism in principle, propounding radical egalitarian social policies potentially beneficial to the nonblack poor as well; thus the
Panthers fashioned a heady mixture of black nationalism, socialism, and self-
defense that appealed to street kids as well as black intellectuals and much of
the white Left. Yet the Panthers also encouraged the final shift of the 1960s in
the rhetoric of violence, as stout assertions of the right to self-defense meta-
morphosed into a veritable cult of the gun. Their militance called forth from
local authorities and the FBI a vicious campaign of harassment and repression—marked most dramatically by the cold-blooded police murder of dedicated Chicago organizer Fred Hampton—and soon the Panthers were locked
in a running battle with police everywhere. Having recruited street corner
toughs as members, and having advertised their conviction that this "lumpen-
proletariat" formed a revolutionary force, the Panthers found themselves in a
deadly match with the curdled hatred of white cops. Leftists rallied to the
Panthers' defense but, in their sympathy for the besieged militants, failed to
look closely at the character and conduct of the BPP. The BPP comprised sincere revolutionaries—women as well as men—serving their communities
with free breakfast programs and other services, alongside a thuggish element
driven to flaunt their daring in an idiom of violent threat. Panther leaders
were known to discipline internal dissenters with beatings, threaten allies who
questioned them with violence, and boast of provoking firefights with police.
The internecine struggles that later broke out between Panther factions or
between Panthers and rival black nationalists, although often stirred by police
agents, were one consequence of indulging in a cult of violence.[53]

Meanwhile, the romance of violence flourished in small but forceful circles within the young white Left. Casual violence in antiwar demonstrations, such as "trashing" windows, cars, and occasionally offices, escalated to the point, in early 1969, when there were 84 bombings, attempted bombings, or arsons on college campuses in six months.[54] Destruction of property on campus—whether related to military research, the Reserve Officers' Training Corps (ROTC), or otherwise—and even cases of harassment and intimidation aimed at unsympathetic faculty members were incited by undisciplined leftists (though some cases stemmed from provocateurs aiming to discredit the antiwar movement). The worst glorying in violence, however, came from the so-called Weatherman group (or Weather Underground), one of the factions left by the breakup of SDS in summer 1969. Perhaps only 100 people remained with the group when it went underground to start a bombing campaign that hurt its own members more than it did the war makers. At the group's last open convention, in Flint, Michigan, leader Bernadine Dohrn lauded Charles Manson, murderer of Hollywood socialites, in effect, for "offing the pigs." Later observers can only wonder at the conversion of radical sentiment, sparked by revulsion from military violence, into what one movement veteran called a dark "death trip."

To understand why part of the protest movements came to embrace, or acquiesce in, the rhetoric and practice of violence, it is necessary to examine the meanings that became associated with violence by the late 1960s. It is one thing to accept the political utility of violence, but to do so also entails careful judgment of whether violent means, in particular circumstances, are likely to lead to desired ends. The most troubling problem lies not in this instrumental attitude but in a tendency to invest violence with meaning *beyond* strict utility, with value in its own right. In the 1960s, violence became associated with ideas of authenticity, thrived on an apocalyptic sensibility that contended with the reformist mood of the times, and grew in part from the very moralism that first sealed protesters in a commitment to nonviolence.

Thomas Pynchon's perceptive, but still romantic, essay on Watts was a telling example. In Watts, he wrote, "everything seems so out in the open, all of it real, no plastic faces, no transistors, no hidden Muzak, or Disneyfied landscaping." Amid the glitzy consumerism of the "L.A. Scene," where "illusion is everywhere," Watts "is, by contrast, a pocket of bitter reality." Pynchon's rhetoric then turned from recognizing the harshness in the life of the poor to a preference for a world that is "real":

[I]n the white culture outside, in that creepy world full of pre-cardiac Mustang drivers who scream insults at one another only when the windows are up; ... of an enormous priest caste of shrinks who counsel moderation and compromise as the answer to all forms of hassle; among so much well-behaved unreality, it is next to impossible to understand how

Watts may truly feel about violence.... Far from a sickness, violence may be an attempt to communicate, or to be who you really are.[55]

With the additional note that violence in Watts may be present at any moment, "because you are a man, because you have been put down, because for every action there is an equal and opposite reaction," Pynchon regarded violence as a sign of authenticity, and in particular, masculinity.

Novelist Saul Bellow illuminated another side of the problem. In his 1964 novel *Herzog,* Bellow already attributed a fascination with violence to a temperament too inclined to dwell on the end of things. "We love apocalypses too much," Herzog reproaches an existentialist author, "and crisis ethics and florid extremism with its thrilling language." Thus he reflects on the hardening of hearts:

> [W]hat is the philosophy of this generation? Not God is dead.... Perhaps it should be stated Death is God. This generation thinks—and this is its thought of thoughts—that nothing faithful, vulnerable, fragile can be durable or have any true power. Death waits for these things as a cement floor waits for a dropping light bulb.... this is how we teach metaphysics on each other.... "You think history is the history of loving hearts? You fool! Look at these millions of dead.... History is the history of cruelty, not love.... We have experimented with every human capacity to see which is strong and admirable and have shown that none is. There is only practicality.... This is how it is—without cowardly illusions."[56]

Bellow had a point. In John Williams's *The Man Who Cried I Am,* the protagonist's affirmation of violence comes with the expectation of a final showdown as well as a bitter, cynical conviction, stirred by a deep sense of unending disappointment, in "the bankruptcy of the human soul."[57]

In addition, however, the moralist streak running through the American Left ironically linked the extremes of peace and violence. For some partisans, the movement's moralism helped transform the extreme rigor of nonviolence and its ideal of noncooperation into a fascination with foreign guerrilla heroes deemed incorruptible. It also fostered an image of violence, cultivated by Frantz Fanon's doctrine of colonial rebellion and renewal, "as a cleansing force." Susceptibility to this shift in allegiance has something to do with the peculiar conditions of the American Left in the 1960s. Cut off by the postwar reaction from old radical traditions of popular struggle, young radicals of the 1960s had little confidence in the prospects of mass action for social change, compared to the virtue of dissent by small minorities. Still mesmerized by the postwar ideology of social stability and welfare state consensus, they tended to exaggerate the systematic coherence of American society, the successful incorporation of the working class within it, and hence the hopelessness of building a radical opposition within American life. Violence appealed to some disaffected young just as nonviolence might have, satisfying a desire to repudiate the existing order and make political action expressive, demonstrative, and exemplary—intent more on revealing the quality of one's commitment than recruiting other dissenters to join the cause (though, to be sure, many early leaders of nonviolent protest were very effective organizers of mass action). As Susan Sontag astutely remarked at the time, "revolutionary" commitment in American parlance was, as often as not, less a matter of struggling to transform society than "a form of action designed for the assertion of individuality against the body politic."[58]

The point becomes clearer with the help of Hannah Arendt's *On Violence* (1969). Arendt insisted that "power and violence are opposites; where the one rules absolutely, the other is absent."[59] Power was a distinctly political and collective phenomenon, the effectiveness of action derived from solidarity and the numbers of people giving assent; violence was a matter of sheer physical strength deployed by individuals or groups as a means to win an end. Violence might be impotent against real power, as shown by the U.S. failure in Vietnam; violence, on the other hand, came into play when power failed. When violations of authority are no longer deterred by public opinion, that is, authorities have recourse to the billy club. Arendt's argument applied also to the young Left, whose resorting to the romance of violence expressed, more than anything, the Left's weakness. The antiwar movement revived left-wing protest in the United States but was frustrated by its inability to reverse government policy quickly. The Left's quandary was but one more expression of the age of contradiction: lively hopes for dramatic social change persisted alongside the absence of well organized social forces capable of bringing change to fruition. Neither the aim of a new society nor the protest of existing conditions was wrongheaded or unrealistic; but lacking a strategic vision of how to tap the underlying conflicts in American life to build a mass revolutionary movement for change, or the wisdom of an ideological heritage that would justify digging in for a long struggle, they were stuck in moods of desperation. No matter how loudly radicals trumpeted the coming revolution, official intransigence on the war was taken, not incorrectly, as a sign of the Left's limited power; and given their lack of power, a romantic embrace of violence (more often in rhetoric than in practice) provided a kind of quick fix.

A unique response to violence, however, came from a new force in American life, the rise of women's liberation in 1967 and 1968. The term "women's liberation" came into use among groups of radical young women in Chicago, New York, and Washington, D.C. Spearheaded by figures such as psychologist Naomi Weisstein, art student Shulamith Firestone, writer Ellen Willis, and activists Jo Freeman, Heather Booth, and Kathie Sarachild, these groups drew together women experienced in the civil rights and antiwar movements who recognized the subordination of women in society (but also, and most gallingly, within the protest movements themselves) as analogous to racial oppression and imperial domination of Third World peoples. With the emergence in 1968 and 1969 of consciousness-raising circles encouraging women to discuss matters of their private lives as part of their common condition, and the advent of a cultural politics that challenged women's magazines, beauty pageants, and sexual mores, it was said that "women's liberation" differed sharply from "women's rights" campaigns early in the 1960s by widening the scope of criticism beyond the denial of opportunity in jobs and politics; criticism now targeted the structure of gender relations in private life, too, under the slogan "the personal is political." Before women's liberation, to be sure, older critics of gender inequality such as Alice Rossi and Jessie Bernard had addressed the disadvantage of women in the private as well as public domain. In this respect, the growing critique of social inequity wherever it was found, and the gradual emergence of a movement for women's emancipation, can be seen as almost a continuous process.

Yet women's liberation made explicit what was largely missing from earlier broadsides such as Friedan's *Feminine Mystique:* that women's disadvantage stemmed not from unenlightened public opinion about feminine limitations but from the concrete benefits that men as a group enjoyed as authorities over women. Fighting women's oppression thus depended on the solidarity of women organized in a struggle pitting power against power, their own against that of men.[60] Conjoined to this was a resolutely revolutionary point of view. Robin Morgan's compilation of early women's liberation documents, *Sisterhood Is Powerful* (1970), and especially Morgan's introductory essay to the volume, seethed with radical opposition to all of normal social life, convinced that it was corrupted throughout by oppressive gender hierarchy and that a break toward a wholly new order of social relations was conceivable, nay imperative.

Although the movement thrived on the revolutionary spirit of the Left, and some of its members admired the public role played by Vietnamese women in the NLF, women's liberation (or radical feminism, as many adherents soon called it) generally recoiled from the militarization of protest rhetoric that began after 1966. Even as male leftists and some antiwar women charged that it was self-indulgent for women to create their own liberation movement while a brutal imperialist war continued, the cresting rhetoric of violence helped make the older protest movements appear inhospitable to many women. Tied to an assertive masculinity in both black nationalist and white left-wing circles, the romance of rebel violence repelled them.[61]

Moreover, radical feminism set out to challenge sexual as well as military violence. Susan Griffin's *Ramparts* essay "Rape: The All-American Crime" was one of the first literary salvos in the antirape campaign that would grow in the 1970s. It was also part of the drive to expose an American national proclivity to violence. "Whatever the motivation, male sexuality and violence in our culture seem to be inseparable.... and though there is no known connection between the skills of gun-fighting and love-making, pacifism seems suspi-

ciously effeminate." Patiently refuting the myths that justified rape as the out-
come of impetuous male desire or secret female longing, scoring the law that
demeaned rape victims and reinforced men's authority over women, Griffin
concluded that rape was a "form of mass terrorism" denying women "the status of a human being." In response, Griffin recognized the place of self-
defense but wanted something more: "It is part of human dignity to be able to
defend oneself, and women are learning. Some women have learned karate;
some to shoot guns. And yet we will not be free until the threat of rape and
the atmosphere of violence is ended."[62]

Radical feminists did not claim that women were innately nonviolent; nor
was their movement immune to the ideological fanaticism and bitter factional-
ism that beset the male-dominated Left. But macho heroics on the violent
fringe of the antiwar movement helped make the feminist departure a protest
against the militarized rhetoric of the time. Schooled in the militant politics of
the late 1960s, women's liberation upheld the goals of bringing peace and
equality to social life. Force has utility and sometimes necessity in popular
struggles, but the telling feminist slogan "sisterhood is powerful" put the
political virtue of solidarity—achievement of collective effectiveness, or
power as Arendt defined it—back where it belonged, in the vanguard before
violence.

eight

The Push and the Shove

The impression that America in the 1960s experienced a cultural crack-up—even a kind of social disintegration—has become commonplace in retrospective images of the country "coming apart" or "unraveling."[1] The tone was set in 1970 by well-placed observers such as the President's Commission on Campus Unrest:

> The crisis on American campuses ... has roots in divisions of American society as deep as any since the Civil War. ... reflected in violent acts and harsh rhetoric, and in the enmity of those Americans who see themselves as occupying opposing camps. Campus unrest reflects and increases a more profound crisis in the nation as a whole. ... If this trend continues, if this crisis of understanding endures, the very survival of the nation will be threatened.[2]

This view of acute social crisis, remarkable in how quickly it skipped over careful comparison with other modern moments of sharp conflict (such as the depression era or the 1877 strike wave) to identify the 1960s with civil war, has persisted despite some obvious indications to the contrary. The quick falloff of large-scale disruptive protest after hitting its height in spring 1970, the aplomb with which the corporate-political elite maintained its position and its clout despite the sometimes panicky mood of the Nixon White House, the more or less undisturbed structure of wealth and poverty, and the ongoing rounds of middle-class degree getting and career making (even considering belated starts by some alienated youth) all suggest that the established order of American society proved more resilient than the crisis mongers suggest. This judgment does not deny the wide scope of the challenges facing the status quo, from student upheaval to an epidemic of disobedience in the military to awakened militancy among American workers; it only distinguishes the radicalization of sentiment that occurred in American life from the illusion of a revolutionary crisis or social breakdown, which excited alarm in some quarters and the fantasy of guerrilla struggle in others.[3] Yet although the basic structures of society were uncracked, cultural and intellectual life indeed suffered a deep crisis. Strikes on college campuses, the rise of dissenting caucuses breaking the consensus of scholarly disciplines, artists organizing to question the system of museum and gallery patronage, the flourishing of frankly revolutionary theories in and outside the academy, and the polarization of the American intelligentsia suggest that established norms of thought and culture passed through fire.

Terms of Engagement and the Polarization of the Intellectuals

Protest by students and youth occurred worldwide by 1968, but the American student movement was so widespread across the country in different types of academic institutions, and so prolonged over several years' duration, that it was virtually unique. It battered down the imaginary walls that gave university life a sense of insulation from social and political conflict. The first surge of campus activism in 1964 and 1965 posed the same challenge, but protests from 1968 to 1970 were no longer limited to matters of internal campus rules (as at Berkeley) or so governed by academic propriety as the Vietnam teach-ins. Campus radicals late in the decade raised pointed questions about the practical relations between universities, the surrounding community, and the national polity; they stirred polemics about the rightful place of political commitment in scholarship and challenged the very integrity of academic knowledge accumulated over past generations. Their recourse to disruptive tactics such as student strikes and building occupations indicated how difficult it would be to maintain university business as usual amid the controversy and conflict that coursed through society at large. But despite those who charged radicals with "politicizing" academic life, administrators who called on police or militia to constrain protesters also showed a willingness to level barriers between university life and the "real world." Each side had conflicting impulses to integrate the university in society at large *and* uphold its distinction from the outer world.

At Columbia in April 1968, students helped spotlight the university's role as an exploitative owner of real estate in surrounding black and Latino neighborhoods and as an adjunct to the military machine. Led by the Student Afro-American Society (SAS) and the aggressive "action faction" of Columbia SDS, activists occupied two university buildings, demanding that construction of a new gymnasium, planned for a nearby public park and long viewed as an affront to black neighbors, be halted and that Columbia sever all ties to a war-related institute. Others backing these demands took over several class-room buildings, staying for a week in self-styled communes as they awaited a long-rumored police assault. It came on April 30, despite faculty attempts to dissuade the administration from using force. The scene of young people with faces bloodied by blows from rampaging cops inflamed student opinion, and an ensuing strike ended classes for the year.[4] When SDS-led Harvard students occupied college offices there in 1969, university officials moved quickly to have club-wielding police clear the scene, sparking a six-day student strike and a sharp debate among the faculty, who were split between those offended by student tactics and those outraged by the heavy-handed administration. Finally, faculty voted to condemn the use of police force on campus and urge concessions to student demands that Reserve Officers' Training be eliminated, plans to raze university-owned low-income housing be cut back, and black students help govern a new black studies program.[5]

These episodes were overshadowed, in duration, militancy, and extent of community involvement, by the San Francisco State College strike begun in November 1968. More than a year of demonstrations, negotiations, and unfulfilled promises by the college administration preceded the strike call, by the Black Student Union (BSU) and other "Third World" students (Native American, Mexican, and Asian American), for independent black studies and ethnic studies departments and an open admissions policy for students of color. Denounced as a coercive minority promoting a new kind of segregation, the strikers actually won the sympathy of many students and faculty while demonstrating a keen sense of social need: only open admissions and programs controlled by students and faculty of color, they claimed, would effectively train more young people ready to lend their skills to improving the conditions of poor ghetto communities. Assaults on strike activists and by-standers by police, acting with the support of "hard line" college president S. I. Hayakawa, goaded teacher unionists to strike as well. Moderate black community leaders spoke out in defense of striking students, and the students even made tentative alliances with hospital and oil workers on strike elsewhere in San Francisco. Paralyzing the campus for more than four months, the strike continued until the mass arrest of almost 500 student protesters at one rally, along with flagging energy and cracks in the student-faculty-unionist alliance, took steam out of the movement.[6] Despite the inconclusive results, other militant campaigns by black students at Cornell University and the University of Michigan in 1969 and 1970 followed, as did a vital Chicano student movement and the beginnings of a young Asian American call for "Yellow Power." Then, in May 1970, when the invasion of Cambodia as well as National Guard and police shootings at Kent State and Jackson State universities sparked strikes at a third of the nation's campuses, protesters transformed colleges and universities into centers of agitation. Study time was devoted to writing antiwar leaflets, designing protest posters, and planning "street theater"; statements appeared on the social responsibility of young professionals, and manifestos called for campus self-rule by students, faculty, and staff together. Some observers saw the emergence of a new model university, making the campus a base for taking protest into public life beyond.[7]

All these events sparked polemics over the "politicization" of academic life. Philosopher Sidney Hook, an ardent opponent of the New Left, spoke for many liberals who identified academic freedom with disinterestedness and feared a right-wing backlash against universities: "If the university is conceived as an agency of action to transform society in behalf of a cause, no matter how exalted, it loses its *relative* autonomy, imperils both its independence and objectivity, and subjects itself to retaliatory curbs and controls on the part of society on whose support and largesse it ultimately depends."[8] At Columbia's commencement soon after the student strike, historian Richard Hofstadter made a similar point. "Here at Columbia," he said, "we have suffered a disaster whose precise dimensions it is impossible to state." As "an organization in which anything can be studied or questioned, ... whose business it is to examine, critically and without stint, the assumptions that prevail in ... society," the university "does not have corporate views of public questions." The university was "suspended" between the social world at large and the world of thought:

> That universities do share in, and may even at some times and in some respects propagate, certain ills of our society seems to me undeniable. But to imagine that the best way to change a social order is to start by assaulting its most accessible centers of thought and study and criticism is not only to show a complete disregard for the intrinsic character of the university but also to develop a curiously self-destructive strategy for social change.[9]

It is interesting that Dwight Macdonald, speaking at a "countercommencement" organized by student supporters of the Columbia strike, similarly warned that disruptive tactics endangered the protection that even a corrupted university gave to dissent.[10] Nonetheless, young radical intellectuals such as historian Jesse Lemisch were not convinced by defenses of the disinterested academy. Having been dismissed from a University of Chicago faculty post for his political activities, Lemisch issued a 1969 broadside called "On Active Service in War and Peace" that revealed Cold War political biases in mainstream historical scholarship and denied that the liberal doctrine of academic freedom protected dissent. Rather, it meant merely "that final power to make academic decisions should rest with those who rule the profession" rather than with outsiders, and that universities be free to administer their own repressive discipline. Thus, Lemisch stated, universities conducted a "housecleaning" of left-wing scholars during the anticommunist hysteria after World War II and seemed prepared to do so again.[11] (Although Harvard faculty condemned their administration's use of police on campus and asked civil authorities to drop criminal charges against protesters, for instance, the faculty backed the university in expelling 16 student strike leaders.) Lemisch's critique, however, alienated some other leftists. The Marxist historian Eugene Genovese, whose 1965 remarks welcoming an NLF victory in Vietnam had made him a cause célèbre for academic freedom, agreed that political motives always played a role in historical work, but he challenged those "opponents of Academia" who treated the university "as if it were just another corporation, just another part of the military-industrial complex, just another whore-house." Against "radical historians" such as Lemisch who called for a new scholarship in league with political struggle, Genovese insisted that the proper work of a dedicated socialist historian was consistent with "the responsibility of all intellectuals to defend and extend the critical spirit" and "to defend the universities and professional associations as places of contention."[12] But if the academy was to maintain its integrity by strictly avoiding political engagement, how could one deny the legitimacy of campaigns to expel ROTC and military research from campus (indeed, Genovese lauded those aims), and given such inevitably political issues in academic life, how would limits be set on acceptable tactics? At Harvard, liberal faculty said that the SDS building occupation set back their attempts to eliminate ROTC by legitimate means, but radicals responded that only the strike, in fact, finally accomplished that aim.[13] Academics had a hard time anyway maintaining the principle of political neutrality as departments, faculties, and professional associations began passing antiwar resolutions. In the wake of the Cambodia invasion, almost 200 college presidents declared their opposition to the war in what one historian called a "progressive swing" of the "academic elite."[14]

Debate over the problematic terms of engagement between scholarship and politics, the academic world and civic life, was echoed in the art world. During the 1960s, the most salient trait of the visual arts was the rapid-fire emergence of new styles, each offering a breakthrough in the scope and methods of art; meanwhile, the art world establishment of museums and galleries, welcoming every new style in turn, seemed to embrace the routine subversion of its own conventions.[15] Even more ironic, perhaps, was the way disparate artistic currents converged on the aspiration, historically associated with revolutionary avant-gardes, to overcome the breach between art and life. Artists committed to rigorous aestheticism—insistence on the special province of art and its formal concerns—aimed to resist the vulgarization of art by commercial or decorative imperatives: their distrust of the museum-gallery system on these grounds brought them near those artists of the 1960s who embraced the "anti-art" animus (or mockery of aesthetic privilege) promoted by dadaists and their descendants. The impulse in both these camps to escape the confines of traditional art venues gained ground even before the confrontational mood of the late 1960s suggested to some that political action was the way to meld art and life. In any case, the urge to dissolve the boundaries around art—

the "de-definition of art," in Harold Rosenberg's phrase—remained an elusive, problematic goal.

Eager to mark their own independence, leading artists of the 1960s responded ambivalently to the modernist traditions of art canonized in the years after World War II. Although they turned away from the styles of emotional expression identified with postwar painters such as Jackson Pollock and Willem de Kooning, younger artists of the 1960s upheld the belief that their job was to work out the formal problems of particular arts in a pure, disciplined manner (a hallmark of modernism, according to critic Clement Greenberg). If the spatter and arm strokes of paint on Pollock's canvases focused attention on the process and material of painting, then Frank Stella, who painted neatly ordered pinstripes and chevronlike bands of color, would purify the art even of personality, leaving nothing to be observed "besides the paint on the canvas." Of the older New York school, austere color-field painters such as Mark Rothko garnered special attention in the 1960s, and Ad Reinhardt kept trying to strip art of all excrescences, until only paintings of one color—his all-black canvases—were left. Reinhardt's "painstakingly worked surfaces" disclosed faint hints of form and color variation to very close viewing, suggesting that art must be made and observed in the egoless spirit of disciplined meditation.[16] Something of the same sentiment figured in sculptural work of the mid-1960s, dubbed "minimalism," by Donald Judd, Sol LeWitt, and Robert Morris: displays of the simplest three-dimensional forms, arranged in rows or grids, that drew attention to the elemental attributes of sculpture—shape, surface, structure, and setting. Such principles seemed turned on their head when Robert Morris, trumpeting an aesthetic of "antiform," organized a show devoted to eccentric works in soft, structureless materials, such as clumps of earth and fabric covering a gallery floor—but there still was an insistent focus on the brute stuff and conceptual foundations of an art form. Linking all these ventures in aestheticism was a desire to create, as one artist put it, "an antidecorative difficult art" that resisted facile assimilation by a sensation-seeking art audience and made artworks difficult to peddle as discrete, priced objects.[17] Driven to deny conventional marks of artistry and resist assimilation by art institutions, the wish to uphold the autonomy of art for its own sake ironically verged on an anti-art ethos.

On another side of the art world, sentiments common to dada and surrealist movements from 1910 through the 1930s returned in the desire to trample on conventions that isolated pure art forms or held art apart from life. The use of common objects, from Coke bottles to bowling pins, wrecked auto fenders, chicken wire, and long sheets of cheesecloth by artists Robert Rauschenberg, Louise Nevelson, Eva Hesse, and Edward Kienholz; the mixed-media action environments of Happenings; the purposeful exploration of the "unbeautiful side of art" in the gross, unwieldy objects fashioned by California's "funk" artists; and the insistent quotation of popular culture and commerce in pop: all evoked older practices of Max Ernst, Kurt Schwitters, and the organizers of dada "manifestations."[18] The desire to mock the mystique of art flourished particularly in Andy Warhol's deadpan comparisons of upholstery and painting or a child's Colorform stickers with Roy Lichtenstein's bendayed pictures.[19] Some veteran surrealists gained a new lease on life in the 1960s, such as the Spanish filmmaker Luis Buñuel, whose depiction of dream imagery and sadomasochistic fantasies in *Belle du Jour* still aimed to puncture middle-class complacency. That such gestures of offense and rebellion generally no longer appeared scandalous but became warrants of celebrity was a dilemma not lost on contemporary dissenters. A major show, "Dada, Surrealism, and Their Heritage," organized by William Rubin and opening at the Museum of Modern Art (MOMA) in March 1968, recognized the long shadow cast by these historic movements on the decade's artistic imagination, but the show was greeted by 300 demonstrators who denounced the "Mausoleum of Modern Art" for ignoring the genuinely disruptive intent of the movements and reducing them to a legacy of formal styles now soundly wrapped in the "tradition" of modern art.[20]

Artist involvement in antiwar protest had emerged in 1965, but protest against the institutions of art was new. In early 1969, an Art Workers' Coalition (AWC) appeared in New York, its name obviously claiming alienation from art world bosses. For the Vietnam Moratorium protests of October 15, 1969, the AWC convinced major showplaces of contemporary art—MOMA, the Whitney, the Jewish Museum, and most galleries—to close for the day and picketed the Guggenheim and Metropolitan museums for staying open. The next year, AWC issued a program calling for free, decentralized museums—run by artists, staff members, and the public, rather than by trustees and curators—that would recognize works by black, Puerto Rican, and women artists.

The AWC and like-minded artists began addressing links between art institutions and forms of abusive power in American life. One vehicle for political assertion was conceptual art, which expressed its contempt for the salable art object by offering as a "work" some kind of statement or event (or mere documentation of activities that were, or might be, carried on elsewhere) that would spur questions about the nature of art and its place in the wider social world.[21] Conceptual art was one current that aimed to "de-aestheticize" art, or sharpen its polemical thrust by excluding from artwork any sense of beauty or sensual appeal. At a 1970 MOMA show on uses of information in contemporary art, Hans Haacke, a German-born New York artist, set up a polling station to ask visitors their opinion of Governor Nelson Rockefeller, a prominent MOMA trustee, and his failure to denounce Nixon's Indochina policy. The next year, Haacke proposed an exhibit exposing respectable slumlords in New York, but it was deemed too sensitive to show at the Guggenheim; a few years later, he extended his critique of private property in housing to the art market with displays documenting the changing, speculative ownership of great paintings.[22] Lucy Lippard, a critic who joined the political camp after 1968, said such ventures aimed to "weaken the hold a single moneyed and educated class has on the art world" and undermine the image of "the art world [as] a safe and superior little island."[23] *New York Times* critic Hilton Kramer, in response, tried rallying all "who believe in the very idea of art museums ... to say loud and clear that we will not stand for the politicization of art."[24]

A bold contrast to the de-aestheticized vision of conceptual art appeared in the urban mural movement, begun in 1967 with the *Wall of Respect* on Chicago's South Side by painter William Walker and the Organization for Black American Culture, and adopted by 1970 as a mode of collective expression by Chicano activists. By bringing art onto street corners and drawing on styles associated with folk art, muralists challenged museum culture, but rather than desert the aesthetic dimension, they frankly relied on the appeal of beauty (albeit not the art world's rarefied notions of it) for purposes of political education and communal solidarity. Muralism grew until the mid-1970s, when poor funding, the ebbing of activism, and worsening conditions of inner-city neighborhoods began draining the movement's energy. Still, it was relatively successful in its attempt to fashion a political art; in comparison, movements that aimed to bridge art and life by denying the specificity of the aesthetic proved self-defeating. Conceptual and de-aestheticizing moves failed to escape the special preserve of the art world, for conceptual works (or their documentation) could be treated still as precious artifacts available to collectors.[25] At the same time, neo-dadaist anti-art gestures paradoxically tended, by leveling the boundaries around art, to aestheticize everything. Andy Warhol's persistent attempts to mock art's claim to exalted status, for instance, were accompanied by a tendency to subject *all* experience to casual, arbitrary judgments of taste. The muralists, however, sensed that any attempt to draw art and life together would be purposeless if aesthetic value had no distinctive meaning. William Walker's art group declared, "Our murals ... speak of an end to war, racism, and repression; of love, of *beauty,* of life. We want to restore an image of full humanity to the people, to place art into its true context—into life."[26]

In their own way, though, avant-garde trends of the 1960s—purist and anti-art alike—made a significant point, for they recognized, if only vaguely, that the character of contemporary art had changed profoundly: it had become deeply *socialized.* The writer Harold Rosenberg, who was often dismissive of new art in the 1960s, captured this trend well when he wrote,

> The basic substance of art has become the protracted discourse in words and materials echoed back and forth from artist to artist, work to work, art movement to art movement, on all aspects of contemporary civilization and of the place of creation ... in it. ... Begin by explaining a single contemporary painting ... and you will find yourself touching on more subjects to investigate—philosophical, social, political, historical, scientific, psychological—than are needed for an academic degree.[27]

Disputes over knowledge and art and the integrity of the institutions governing them helped polarize intellectual life between an academic and aesthetic Left and the conservative reaction against it. A number of intellectual figures who had begun promising careers a decade before, either holding liberal views or professing no particular politics, found themselves driven to postures of opposition. Poet Adrienne Rich, deeply engaged in antiwar activism, moved from the formalist verse of the 1950s to a politically charged feminist poetry by 1970. Government adviser Daniel Ellsberg, who released the Pentagon Papers, turned to the Left. Former *National Review* writers Garry Wills and Joan Didion shifted from one side of the political spectrum to the other.

At the same time, many figures who began the 1960s as moderate social democrats were outraged by the escalation of student protest and became dedicated opponents of the New Left. Even the relatively well-mannered Berkeley protests of 1964 appeared to professors Nathan Glazer and Seymour Martin Lipset as the work of coercive extremists. Later, others would compete to offer the most vitriolic denunciations of campus radicals: child psychologist Bruno Bettelheim viewed protesters as "very, very sick" people who were motivated by Oedipal resentments of father figures; Lewis Feuer, another Berkeley faculty member, regarded demonstrators as "morally corrupt"; and historian Daniel Boorstin, who termed student radicals "dyspeptics and psychotics," claimed universities need not tolerate dissenters who were guilty of "treason" against the culture and mission of academic life. Inclined to view the new student radicals as "fascists," Sidney Hook organized a group called University Centers for Rational Alternatives, which justified the use of police force against campus protesters and rallied people such as Oscar Handlin, S. I. Hayakawa, Leo Strauss, and John Roche to build a hard opposition to the New Left.[28] Also by 1966, *Commentary* editor Norman Podhoretz, who had supported the new radicalism in 1960, grew appalled by the apparent anti-Americanism of a movement he once thought would build a loyal opposition of "social criticism." In June 1970, he committed *Commentary* to making "an all-out offensive against the movement," assailing the assorted psychological, political, and literary dispositions he and others called "the New Sensibility."[29] With Podhoretz's battle cry appeared one of the first signs that a camp of liberals and former radicals were drifting, first in cultural matters and a few years later in political and economic affairs, toward a "neoconservatism" destined to flourish in the 1970s.

In this context, several cultural critics reconsidered the heritage of modernism, the experimental arts of the early and mid–twentieth century, and decried the enduring legacy of that movement. What had begun as the effort of a creative, embattled minority to break the bonds of artistic orthodoxy had grown into a widespread attitude—an "adversary culture," Lionel Trilling called it—suspicious of any restraint or obligation in social living. The critics, most of them New York intellectuals who had grown up with the triumph of the modern arts, could not avoid a good deal of ambivalence, uncertain whether the problem lay in modernism itself or only its vulgarization. Yet Irving Howe, who had mourned the lapse of modernist experiment in 1959, now pointed out the subjectivism, apocalyptic despair, disdain for social institutions, and flirtation with nihilism that characterized that tradition; whereas the great artists of the modern past, he thought, had at least recognized these as demonic forces, the current popularizers indulged them all. Around this time, Daniel Bell also drafted a critique of modernism, to appear a half decade later as *The Cultural Contradictions of Capitalism.* According to Bell, the hedonism and irrationalism of modernism and particularly its cult of immediacy—what Bell called an "eclipse of distance" fostered by all avant-garde currents seeking a fusion of art and life—had effectively deprived people of the capacities for self-restraint and realism that were desperately needed to cope with the practical demands of modern life.[30] And in the drive to unleash all passions and interests, culture had devolved into a perverse celebration of desire, a "pornotopia" as the scholar Steven Marcus put it.[31]

For many of these writers, it was clearly the prospect of losing the protective barriers around the provinces of knowledge and art that occasioned the most vigorous complaint against the New Sensibility, and even writers who had helped renew social criticism in the late 1950s voiced their discomfort with the cultural mood. Although his *Asylums* seemed like an assault on the institutional regulation of behavior, Erving Goffman showed his dismay at the fraying of the rule-laden social fabric. His own field of public face-to-face interaction had become such a "hot" topic lately, he wrote, because of "a complex unsettling expressed variously in the current unsafety and incivility of our city streets, the new political device of intentionally breaking the ground rules for self-expression during meetings and contacts, the change in rules of censorship, and the social molestation encouraged in the various forms of 'encounter group' and experimental theater."[32] Goffman probably referred to Julian Beck and Judith Malina's acting troupe the Living Theatre, which tempted or hectored members of the audience to participate in the performances, for the sake of "breaking down the barriers that exist between art and life."[33] Goffman feared the erosion of civilizing boundaries and thus shared Bell's concern over an "eclipse of distance." Such observers recoiled from new terms of engagement threatening to level barriers marking the provinces of thought and culture.

The views of the communitarian critic Paul Goodman by 1970 fit this model of response in some respects. A caustic critic of conventional schools but also a university-trained philosopher with a self-confessed conservative's appreciation of learning, Goodman was appalled by the know-nothing attitudes he found among young rebels. They had no patience for rational discussion of particular problems and no belief in the uses of expert knowledge for social change; rather, they hungered for the soul-satisfying rejection of everything imaginably complicit in the status quo. They had given up politics per se—the hope of creating a community of engaged citizens—and their fanaticism, intolerance, and bloated self-importance failed to nurture moral courage, honesty, or even a healthy hedonism.[34] Yet Goodman refrained from an intemperate repudiation of the young: "When older people, like myself, are critical of wrongheaded activism, we nevertheless almost invariably concede that the young are *morally* justified." There was "pathos" in this radicalism: its flaws reflected the lack of meaningful community, useful knowledge, and fulfilling purposes in contemporary society while protesting against those very conditions; it carried a "metaphysical vitality" that bespoke a religious yearning for renewal in an epochal social impasse. With refined ambivalence, Goodman recognized the faults of young people's diffuse rebellion but would not turn back toward embrace of a social order he knew to be radically insufficient.

Divided Disciplines, Revolutionary Theories

Notwithstanding the inarticulate, anti-intellectual demeanor Goodman saw among alienated youth, the late 1960s also ushered in a radical critique of established knowledge authored by young scholars and activist intellectuals of vigor and sophistication. Radical caucuses germinated in many disciplines during 1967 and 1968, often spearheaded by small groups of graduate students gathered at one or more campuses such as the University of Wisconsin, University of Michigan, and Columbia. Among the first ventures was a meeting of "radicals in anthropology" at the 1967 meeting of the American Anthropological Association, led by Michigan graduate students, including Karen Sachs, later to be a distinctive voice in feminist anthropology. The Caucus for a New Political Science began informally at the September 1967 meeting of the American Political Science Association, condemning what it called the profession's role as "a servant to the government, [a body of] technicians rather than scientists." Activists gathered at the 1968 American Sociological Association meeting to organize a Sociology Liberation Movement. That summer, historian Mark Selden led the formation of the Committee of Concerned Asian Scholars (CCAS), and fall 1968 saw the formation, in Ann Arbor, of the Union for Radical Political Economics (URPE).[35] Although the caucuses had varying degrees of success and longevity, depending on specific traditions in each discipline and the ways it fostered, resisted, or assimilated dissent, these last two were among the most distinguished products of the radical wave.

Concerned Asian Scholars (CCAS) attracted attention due to its engagement with the main political issue of the time, the Vietnam War, and its focus on what was, by the late 1960s, a compelling object of radical fascination—revolutionary China. The field of East Asian studies, built in the 1940s and 1950s by John K. Fairbank, Edwin O. Reischauer, and others, was growing in the late 1960s as a new, large cohort of young scholars joined its ranks. CCAS became the vehicle for a sharp generational critique of the founders. The best-known broadside fired against first-generation East Asia scholars came from James Peck, a 25-year-old graduate student in sociology, in the October 1969 issue of the CCAS *Bulletin*, charging that the old guard had obscured the impact of Western imperialism on China in order to justify American anti-communist policies in Asia, thus "cut[ting] themselves off from modes of questioning which could treat revolutionary situations with genuine under-standing and perhaps even appreciation." Peck's article was more polemical than scholarly—Joseph Esherick's 1972 article "Harvard on China: The Apologetics of Imperialism" made a more refined argument—but in any case, the dispute marked the beginning of a new, first-rate scholarship on the course of revolution in modern China that enlivened the field.[36] Although some CCAS veterans have since scorned the pro-Mao bias of much American China research in the 1970s, that work remains a tribute to the energy galva-nized by political commitment and nurtured by the solidarity of CCAS.[37]

While CCAS became a vehicle for bringing a second generation of scholars into a relatively new field, URPE served as a pole of attraction for radicals in an inhospitable profession. In fall 1968, URPE indicted "the poverty of eco-nomics," a field that "genuflect[s] before the twin deities of marginalism and equilibrium, while the world around us suffers from an extreme disequilib-rium requiring large changes." The URPE name harked back to the early his-tory of the discipline when it was called "political economy," before theories of marginal utility, mathematical models of market equilibrium, and academic professionalization helped narrow the field to an abstract, technical "econom-ics" concerned only with the principles of optimizing behavior by individuals and firms. URPE activists wanted to fashion a discipline that regarded poverty, racism, imperialism, and war as problems rooted in established eco-nomic institutions that were subject to critical analysis and open to change. Some economic research into conditions of the poor (to explain, for instance, the persistent color line in job opportunity) began a few years before URPE emerged, but URPE gave a new impulse to such work. The caucus promoted landmark studies by Stephen Marglin, Heidi Hartmann, Thomas Weisskopf, Samuel Bowles, and others that widened the sway of economic analysis to include issues of workplace authority, gender divisions, historic economic crises, and environmental decay.[38] Although unable to move the discipline as a whole, which remained committed to highly technical studies of market mechanisms, URPE made a mark by its longevity (lasting decades after the 1960s) and its distinctive output.

While the caucuses ushered in a new era in which disciplines, rather than being unified each around a consensual paradigm, were divided, political tur-moil in the late 1960s also fueled attempts to leap over disciplinary bound-aries, especially in new programs of ethnic studies. Soon after the bitter San Francisco State struggle, several universities moved more smoothly to create black studies programs, though these initiatives still came at the instigation of committed students and against the resistance or hesitation of faculty and administrators. At Yale University, where scholars wondered whether black studies was "intellectually defensible" as a scholarly field, Black Student Alliance leader (and later a respected historian of the African American past) Armstead Robinson asked why they could not grant "the possibility that there are things worth teaching of which even most academicians may be unaware."[39] An Alliance-sponsored symposium on black studies persuaded the doubters and paved the way for an independent major in Afro-American studies later that year. The program recruited a distinguished black faculty, including Paule Marshall, who taught "the Black Woman in American Literature," and Larry Neal, who taught courses on ideologies of black identity and culture in work by Léopold Senghor of Senegal, Aimé Césaire of Martinique, and African American writers from the Harlem Renaissance on. Around the same time, the first Department of Mexican American Studies was established at California State College in Los Angeles, and after the April 1969 formation of the Chicano student group MEChA, demands proliferated for Chicano Studies departments, programs, and research centers. Also at the end of the decade, as special disciplinary caucuses such as American Women in Psychology emerged, feminist scholars and students helped build "women's studies," dedicated to merging disciplines and exposing the masculine bias in each one. By 1973 thousands of courses about women in history, society, and culture were offered at American colleges and universities, with hundreds of women's studies programs in the making.[40]

The late-1960s reorientation of academic life included the resurrection of Marxism as an "intellectually defensible" perspective. By 1960 Marxism appeared to have given way to "Marxology," the scholarly endeavor of recounting Marxism's history and its fallacies. Over the course of the 1960s, however, writers and scholars affirming their adherence to Marxist theory and politics became more visible, as indicated by the meeting of the first Socialist Scholars Conference in 1965.[41] "Marxist humanism" or related kinds of neo-Marxist cultural criticism led the revival, denying the economic reductionism ascribed to Marx by pointing to the ethical dimension of his socialism, the more voluntaristic aspects of his historicism, and his philosophical roots in Hegel. Work concerning the formation (or deformation) of personality, community, and lifeways under the pressure of modern capitalism, such as Herbert Marcuse's *One-Dimensional Man* (1964), loomed large in this current, as did work by Jean-Paul Sartre, Leszek Kolakowski, and Marcuse's colleagues of the Frankfurt school, who became more familiar to young intellectuals by decade's end.[42]

By the mid-1960s, a more "classic" Marxist political economy also revived to study the problem of the welfare state: how could Marx's critique still make sense of capitalism when government, qualifying the reign of the free market, helped manage social and economic affairs? The landmark in this field, *Monopoly Capital*, by Marxist elders Paul Baran and Paul Sweezy, argued that the key flaw of the system was no longer, as in the age of competitive capitalism, the tendency of the rate of profit to fall, but rather the tendency of the general "surplus" (revenues exceeding the value of necessary labor) to rise. Unless accumulated surplus was drained off by government transfer payments, military spending, and the apparatus of corporate salesmanship, the economic system would choke; given current expertise in these measures of managed waste, though, the regime could persist almost indefinitely. A few other economists, such as the veteran "council communist" Paul Mattick, held a more orthodox view, arguing that the essential crisis tendencies of capitalism would soon break into the open, despite the appearance of affluence in a "mixed economy."[43]

Major statements and debates of these longtime Marxists gained a new audience, but a younger generation of writers also arose to fashion what might be called a new American Marxism. The keynote was struck by New Left historian Martin J. Sklar in his stunning essay "On the Proletarian Revolution and the End of Political-Economic Society," and by 1970 a group of writers more or less closely associated with him coalesced around a new journal, *Socialist Revolution*.[44] Sklar analyzed what he called "disaccumulationist capitalism," a stage in capitalist development when the trend toward accumulating ever more capital in industrial production reversed itself, and a growing proportion of labor was freed from engagement in manufacturing. Under such conditions, Sklar argued, it was socially necessary to devise new outlets for human activity. Drawing together Marx's most visionary speculations about the role of labor in late capitalism with the postindustrial theory of the 1960s, Sklar argued that the regime of wage labor (or "labor abstracted into a commodity" and paid according to the time it was in production) was obsolete. Even the production of necessities at this stage of development rested on workers able to "recognize, realize, [and] transmute their talents and capacities," rather than merely follow orders or fit into the machinery. Above all, society must be able to "open greater and greater areas for discretionary, voluntary life-activity." That was why, Sklar wrote, a critical intelligentsia had emerged in American life in the 1920s, when signs of disaccumulationist capitalism first appeared. Hostile to the marketplace (or the domination of society by economic criteria) and championing creative work and professional service for their own sake, that intelligentsia prefigured the 1960s student rebellion and counterculture.[45]

The new American Marxism paid relatively little attention to the traditional industrial class struggle, but that is not to say the status and role of the working class went unexamined. Despite the conventional view that American life was classless or that the homogenizing trends of mass society made workers "middle-class," neither popular culture nor the social sciences entirely ignored class divisions and tensions. John Updike's novel *Rabbit, Run* of 1961, for instance, gave an aching portrait of working-class anxieties and discontents, and the "rediscovery" of poverty was accompanied by a substantial body of social research by figures such as S. M. Miller, Lee Rainwater, and Patricia Cayo Sexton, compiled in the volume *Blue-Collar World* (1964), which recognized profound distinctions between working-class and middle-class families.[46] It was not until the end of the 1960s, though, that observers saw that the working class might still play a dynamic role in political action and social change.

Although top AFL-CIO leaders backed Johnson's and Nixon's Vietnam policies, and in one notorious incident construction workers assaulted antiwar students, American workers were neither so hawkish nor so quiescent as blue-collar stereotypes suggested. Government and service workers constituted the fastest-growing element of the union movement, and in cases such as the 1959 New York hospital workers' strike and the 1968 Memphis sanitation workers' strike, unionism became a vehicle for people of color to pursue equality. Measured by the incidence of wildcat walkouts, strikes, and union members' rejection of contract settlements, worker militance stepped up after 1967 in a number of industries. In 1969 and 1970, a League of Revolutionary Black Workers revived direct-action tactics to fight assembly line speedup and deadly work hazards at Detroit auto plants. The nationwide postal workers' wildcat of March 1970 showed that public workers could also be especially bold. That spring, striking Teamsters opposed a contract settlement their leaders had negotiated, and black construction workers struck against racist practices in the building trades. In places, students and workers allied, as in student support for General Electric strikers in fall 1969. Some unionists opposed the Vietnam War, starting with the UAW in 1968 and leading to a June 1970 conference of 1,000 unionists demanding immediate withdrawal from Indochina. Given cases of worker resistance to shop floor authority such as the 1971 strike against General Motors at Lordstown, Ohio, class struggle again seemed to be plausible as a social and political force.[47]

Marxism was not alone in promoting the idea of revolution among the younger American intellectuals. In 1969 one wing of women's liberation resurrected the name "feminist"—with the qualifier "radical"—to insist that the struggle against sex inequality and hierarchy constituted an independent movement that rightfully occupied the center, not the periphery, of revolutionary consciousness. Other currents of women's liberation persisted, particularly the incipient "socialist feminism" influenced by British radicals Juliet Mitchell and Sheila Rowbotham, but radical feminism had greater éclat in the United States. American feminism had a lively but somewhat uncomfortable relation with the revival of Marxism. Karen Sachs, for instance, would rely heavily on Marx and Engels to build an original, compelling anthropological perspective on women's roles in the history of human society. But radical feminism as such, contra Marx, regarded gender domination rather than class interest as the fount of all forms of social exploitation.

Nor would radical feminists trace their ideological roots to liberal feminists such as Betty Friedan. If anything, the radical feminists looked back to French writer Simone de Beauvoir, whose *The Second Sex* (1952) borrowed Hegel's phenomenology of the master and slave to analyze relations of dominance and submission between men and women.[48] They also drew on the trend at large in American intellectual life to broaden the concept of power, beyond conventional political definitions concerning government and the state, to include the uses of influence, control, and domination in civil institutions, interpersonal relations, and the family.[49]

The self-conscious declaration of radical feminism as the central ideology of women's liberation came with the 1970 publication of *Notes from the Second Year* (following a volume of "first-year" writings in 1968).[50] Edited by Shulamith Firestone and Anne Koedt, this large newsprint compilation featured more than 30 articles and manifestos on issues such as the movement's relation to male-dominated left-wing groups, techniques of consciousness-raising, abortion, women's sexuality, and political organizing. (It included Koedt's widely discussed "Myth of the Vaginal Orgasm," which cited the landmark 1966 work on sexual physiology by William Masters and Virginia Johnson, *Human Sexual Response*, while claiming that men's interest in keeping power over women led them to deny the key orgasmic role of the clitoris.)[51] In *The Dialectic of Sex*, an audacious book issued shortly after *Notes* appeared, Firestone sought to integrate and transform both Marx and Freud in "a materialist view of history based on sex itself." In the course of her argument, she managed to synthesize several moods of the 1960s—technological optimism and antipositivism, the erotic imagination of Norman O. Brown and the moral recoil from unbound eroticism.

Unlike most feminists, Firestone claimed that women's subjection was based on biology—their role in childbearing—and that a change in nature itself through new reproductive methods (artificial reproduction outside women's bodies) was needed to establish a genuinely "human" standard. She sought "not just the elimination of male *privilege* but of the sex *distinction* itself: genital differences between human beings [in such a society] would no longer matter culturally."[52] Still, Firestone avoided an unquestioning embrace of technological progress: science and technology, no less than art, had suffered from "the modern symptoms of a long cultural disease based on the sex dualism," resulting in an aggressive science impoverished by its failure to evaluate the social significance of its findings and a self-absorbed, impractical art. The ultimate goal of a new society was a cultural revolution overcoming the gendered breach between "masculine" practicality (science) and "feminine" idealism (art), until aesthetic imagination and realism became one. Like Brown, but with feminist intent, Firestone talked of a return to the omnierotic stance of childlike "polymorphous perversity," a prospect, she wrote, that would actually free people from present-day "erotomania," that is, the pervasive "eroticism" of genital sex and imperious male desire. Eros would become more pervasive *and* better integrated as a part (not the whole) of social relations, "allowing love to flow unimpeded."[53] Yet the book concluded with a schematic outline of future collective households and child-rearing arrangements, making clear that new kinds of social regulation would check the reign of individual impulse.

The other major work of radical feminism in 1970, Kate Millett's *Sexual Politics*, also addressed the cultural and moral issues dividing the American intelligentsia. Devoted mainly to literary analysis, *Sexual Politics* rested on a historical outline: a sexual revolution led by women from 1830 to 1930 had reformed and ameliorated traditional patriarchy only to be greeted by a "sexual counterrevolution" (1930–1960) led by men threatened by women's equality and committed to glorifying (male) sexual liberty. Millett easily showed, with selections from D. H. Lawrence, Henry Miller, and Norman Mailer, that the eroticism of these writers is shot through with blunt assertions or transparent symbols of men's domination of, and violence against, women—that is, because politics refers to "power-structured relationships," with sexual politics. She found a special place, however, for Jean Genet, who recounts merciless practices of domination enacted in categories of "masculine" and "feminine" within communities of men.[54] His depiction of power and violence in criminal and homosexual milieus not only reveals the ordinary tyranny of gendered sexual life, Millett wrote, but also makes a plaintive protest against it, embracing a "woman's" point of view and making way for expressions of affection and tenderness as an ideal of sexual revolution.

Millett admired Genet's desire to subvert onerous relations of power and exploitation in everyday life but also recognized a danger in the "outlaw" mystique he cultivated, just as she criticized Norman Mailer's "existential" egoism. As Millett sought "freedom from prescriptive roles" for men and women, she did not advocate an anti-institutional individualism, finding instead "sober wisdom" in Freud's view that social restraints are necessary and inevitable. Hoping for "a sexual revolution [that] would bring the institution of patriarchy to an end," Millett expected a "re-examination of the traits categorized as 'masculine' and 'feminine,' with a reassessment of their human desirability: the violence encouraged as virile, the excessive passivity defined as 'feminine' proving useless in either sex; the efficiency and intellectuality of the 'masculine' temperament, the tenderness and consideration associated with the 'feminine' recommending themselves as appropriate to both sexes."[55] In such terms, Millett attacked some of the same features the conservative cultural critics identified as part of the "New Sensibility"—antisocial egoism and "pornotopia"—but she mounted her criticism not in defense of an old order but in ways looking ahead to a new, more rewarding way of life.

Unfinished Tasks of Social Reconstruction

At the end of the 1960s, politics, culture, and intellectual life in the United States reached a sharply contradictory juncture as polarized sentiments pointed in different directions. Richard Nixon's presidency signaled a conservative trend, but liberal and radical forces had not yet lost their energy. While the administration and conservative forces in the states sought to suppress dissent and limit new social legislation, reformers remained confident that the coming decade would usher in a new politics of equality and greater public services.[56] Indeed, the last years of the 1960s might be regarded as the acme of reform ideology in modern America. The decade had seen a new party of change emerge, loosely knitting radicals and reformers together in the conviction that modern society tended toward socialized forms of life—in ways that required not the suppression of individuality but rather its fulfillment in acts of personal creativity carried out in common. The center of gravity in public discourse had indeed shifted leftward. In 1969, advocacy of a guaranteed minimum income by the Eisenhower commission on the causes of violence, and its call for a "revolution" putting social spending ahead of military spending as the nation's top priority, showed how far ideas of reform had penetrated the mainstream. A staple demand of left-liberal forces since the mid-1960s and a key plank of Martin Luther King's last major protest venture, the Poor People's Campaign, a guaranteed annual income was endorsed by more than a thousand liberal economists in 1968 and gained enough credence to find its way even into Nixon's anemic (and failed) proposal of a Family Assistance Plan as well as George McGovern's 1972 campaign pledge of an income grant to all Americans.[57] In early 1969, moreover, the Department of Health, Education, and Welfare released the study *Toward a Social Report*, a bellwether of liberal sentiment. Looking forward to an annual social report providing "social indicators" of "how well we have done in providing housing, education, health care, public safety, and opportunities for the upward advancement of all sectors of our population," the study summoned up a vision of expansive "social rights" to be guaranteed by public action and perpetuated the reformist vision of the affluent society.[58]

At the same time, however, there was little unity in the loose-jointed party of change. Deep divisions between the mainstream union movement and the antiwar, black-liberation Left sharply limited the chances that a new political force would arise, capable of building on demands for social rights and a guaranteed income while nurturing perhaps even greater visions of social transformation. In this respect, the decade ended by sharpening the contradiction between broad aspirations for change and the absence of means to realize them.

In intellectual life, too, the breach between radicals and reformers, heightened by campus disruption, was virtually at the breaking point, embittering liberals and making radicals more dogmatic. The dissenting young scholars effectively exposed the blind spots and complacency of the established academy, but they also often misread the record of the liberal social democratic intellectuals who preceded them. A telling example occurred in the field of sociology, between two well-established figures in the field. Having turned sharply "left" in the late 1960s, Alvin Gouldner condemned the discipline's most renowned figure, Talcott Parsons, for promoting a deeply conservative doctrine dedicated above all to maintaining the status quo. Gouldner even hinted darkly at fascist elements in Parsons's early thought of the 1930s. Yet Parsons in fact had always advocated some form of progressive liberalism and aimed to build a grand theory of evolution that saw modern society becoming ever more egalitarian and inclusive, open to individual autonomy and keyed to collective responsibility.[59]

Like other cautious postwar reformers, Parsons defended the virtues of stability and "equilibrium," but this concern did not signal conservative leanings as such. Much of the liberal intelligentsia had come of age with social democratic inclinations, confident that modern society tended naturally toward the gradual evanescence of capitalism. They embraced the virtues of social stability largely because they believed stability itself laid out broad vistas of change. To be sure, their argument that stability meant change, that the system was mutating into something profoundly different, became a powerful ideological argument for maintaining the status quo; on the other hand, potent utopian ideas about the course of social change also remained buried within this view of modernity. Condemning the scholarship of the postwar period as little more than crude rationalizations for corporate power and Cold War aggression, young radicals of the late 1960s often failed to recognize how much their own ideas had been nurtured by the drift of postwar liberal intellectual life, particularly the broad sense that abundance made dynamic social change possible and that modernity moved in the direction of both greater personal autonomy and richer social interconnections. They may also have lost a sense of how reform and revolution potentially work together as the demand for change step-by-step (such as a guaranteed annual income) tests the flexibility of the going order, heightens expectations, and rouses impatience with the obstacles imposed by the status quo.

At the least, the best reformers and radicals recognized the need for a reconstruction of intellectual and cultural life in terms congruent with the socialized character of existence and the decade's emphasis on enhancing democracy. In most realms of thought and culture, an enriched sense of context broke down barriers between disciplines and between knowledge and society. The new philosophy of science saw "scientific method" not as an abstract form sustained in a special preserve but as an inquiry inevitably involved in social processes of communication, conflict, and institution building; contemporary art, as Harold Rosenberg said, was inevitably bound up in a fluid discourse concerning "all aspects of contemporary civilization." In the 1960s, a new realism, a revived antiformalism, and an emphasis on the "relational" character of all phenomena and all knowledge appeared paramount. Writing in 1965, Daniel Bell insisted that a veritable intellectual revolution was necessary to begin grasping the character of a social and technical world marked by the most thorough interconnections: we still "tend to think of *things*, not *relations*, of *dualities* rather than *a field*. Most of our vocabulary is 'soaked' in dualisms such as 'man and environment,' 'history and nature,' ... and lacks 'process' terms which see these in interaction, or as interpenetrating terms ... which [emphasize] interdependencies and patterned interchanges."[60]

A relational, contextual mentality challenged the organization of knowledge in separate disciplines, each with a distinct methodology, or in canonical traditions that perceived a transcendental order to things (such as timeless standards of literary value). This new consciousness denied sharp distinctions setting the university apart from society, or the realm of art from profane experience. Indeed, the conflicts of the late 1960s showed that formulating new terms of engagement with society at large was a project fraught with difficulty. A few writers, however, strove to delineate a new form for academic life that was engaged in the world without utterly dissolving the boundaries that gave the university a measure of autonomy. Thus Christopher Lasch and Eugene Genovese denounced "the myth of scholarly neutrality" while denying "the cynical conclusion that all scholarship is subjective and 'ideological.' " In hopes of helping to train professional and technical workers capable of resisting the demands of bourgeois society, they called for "the restoration of the unity of learning. Science and engineering must become once again a branch of philosophy, a means not simply of solving predefined problems but of raising questions about the ends of human life."[61] Art too might bear a new kind of responsibility without denying its special calling if it persists, wrote Adrienne Rich, as "an unsilenceable voice reminding you 'when and where and how you are living and might live.' "[62]

Nonetheless, there were clear signs by the decade's end that a strong reaction was brewing against the spirit of change. The impulse to restore order appeared in plans to expedite deployment of police and militia to college campuses, in government harassment and prosecution of protest organizers, and in calls for reversing the "excess of democracy" believed to have spurred turmoil.[63] In intellectual life, one manifestation of reactionary sentiment was a resurgence in the idea of biological determinism, the suggestion that hereditary traits—of individuals or the species as a whole—explained social ills such as persistent inequality or war. Thus the limits to change were made to look immovable. Berkeley professor Arthur R. Jensen published an article in a 1969 issue of *Harvard Educational Quarterly* proposing that an average difference in I.Q. scores between blacks and whites might help explain the disparity in their socioeconomic standing. In response to the subsequent furor over Jensen's apparent racism and the fallacious character of I.Q. tests, psychologist Richard Hernnstein weighed in with a September 1971 *Atlantic* essay arguing that the "heritability of intelligence," as reliably indicated by I.Q. tests, made the "biological stratification of society" inevitable.[64]

Ethology, the study of animal behavior, enjoyed a growing audience. Whether welcomed as an exposé of the "natural" ("authentic") roots of human action lying beneath the veneer of civilization, or as a warning of residual instincts that wise policy must control, works such as *The Territorial Impera-tive*, by playwright and amateur anthropologist Robert Ardrey, and *On Aggres-sion*, by the German dean of ethology Konrad Lorenz, suggested that aspira-tions for equality, cooperation, and peace in human society must be strictly checked by "the virtue of humility" before biological fact.

Another kind of reaction, taking the guise of social criticism allied with environmental causes, appeared in stentorian declarations of the "end of afflu-ence." In 1968 Paul Ehrlich's best-selling *Population Bomb* helped to raise pub-lic awareness of human threats to the natural environment, in anticipation of the first Earth Day celebration in 1970. Having condemned the ecologically irresponsible practices of corporate capitalism, Ehrlich seemed to fit roughly in the mild left-wing camp of environmentalism. By the early 1970s, however, the conservative implications of his Malthusian views on population emerged in deeply fatalistic pronouncements. Writing with his wife, Anne Ehrlich, he heralded "the leading edge of the age of scarcity" and described "the nature of the dark age to come." While it still made some apt criticisms of economic "growth-mania," and appeared to be validated by the recession of 1974, their book offered a gospel of resignation, escape, self-reliance, and the repudiation of interdependence: enlightened individuals, they wrote, would now act alone to "improve [their] own chances for survival." For the Ehrlichs, affluence sig-nified not the promise of change but the illusion of grandeur at a time of "soci-ety's decline."[65]

The spirit of reaction also appeared in the discovery by political analysts of both major political parties of a new antiliberal bias in public opinion. Kevin Phillips predicted "a new cycle of national Republican hegemony" based on desertion from Democratic ranks by southern whites, Catholic city dwellers, and affluent migrants to the suburbs and southwestern states. Democrats Richard Scammon and Ben Wattenberg identified a "real majority" of Ameri-cans preoccupied with the new "social issue" of crime, disruption, and eroding "values." In retrospect, these pronouncements are often considered accurate measures of a seismic shift in public sentiment, marking the beginning of a rightward turn in American politics; some current observers find in them a suggestion that the "real" story of the 1960s was not the flourishing of re-formist hopes at all but the incubation of a new conservatism.[66]

Indeed, the conservative intellectual movement begun by William Buckley and Russell Kirk in the mid-1950s showed some signs of growth. By the mid-1960s, this current sought respectability, finally repudiating the far-right John Birch Society, and achieved greater visibility in Buckley's *Firing Line* televi-sion show and Milton Friedman's regular column in *Newsweek*. At around the same time, the movement significantly shifted from its old posture as a minor-ity voice for tradition and property rights toward a "majoritarian" conser-vatism appealing to a popular desire for public order in the face of aggravating protest and disruption. The conservatives sensed that the disarray of the Democratic Party in 1968 offered them an opportunity, but they were not at all certain that they rode the wave of the future. The conservatives believed that the Nixon administration made too many concessions to the liberal bias of public policy. At the turn of the decade, Buckley still held to his view that "victories are not for us," and his *National Review* colleague William Rusher still concluded that conservatism "had not yet had a profound influence on American life." Young Americans for Freedom split between conservatives and radical libertarians in 1969, and polls during 1970 and 1971 still found student opinion drifting leftward.[67]

The disenchanted liberals led by *Commentary*'s Podhoretz and Irving Kristol of *The Public Interest*, embittered by student radicalism and impressed by Edward Banfield's argument in *The Unheavenly City* (1970) that Great Society social programs worsened urban ills, were moving to the right. The neoconservative label for this group had not yet appeared, however, and their decisive choice to align themselves politically with Republican conservatism would come only with the 1972 presidential election and the years afterward.[68] As for popular sentiment, the findings of Phillips, Scammon, and Wattenberg were ambiguous. Phillips perceived widespread impatience with Great Society programs, not antagonism toward basic elements of the New Deal order; Scammon and Wattenberg found strong popular support for antipoverty programs of the 1960s (excepting "welfare" payments) alongside concern over rising crime and "irresponsible" youth. The mood of the country at large indeed suggested a widening cultural divide, with a sharp distaste for "hippies" and "protesters" growing in segments of the middle and working classes. Evidence of liberalized habits nettled considerable numbers of evangelical Protestants and some Catholic families. Here too, however, the politicized movement of conservative church people that would help boost the Republican party right wing had not yet surfaced.[69] Sources of such sentiment were surely present, but the die was not yet cast. The late-twentieth-century rightward lurch, marked by disdain for "big government" and New Deal welfare ideals, rather than being a creature of the late 1960s, must be credited to later trends of the mid- and late 1970s.[70]

It is startling, in any case, to contemplate the falloff from the level set by optimistic goals in the 1960s to our own day in visions of what is possible in social life. Writers on automation hoped the standard workweek could be dramatically reduced—perhaps cut in half—by the end of the century, but it has actually increased.[71] Hopes for development in the poor, postcolonial world have been followed, excepting the few cases of aggressive "newly industrialized countries" such as South Korea and Singapore, by stagnation, ruinous poverty, and political decay in Africa, growing polarization of wealth in Latin America, and demands placed by worldwide lenders that poor countries squeeze their social services to make way for foreign investment. Hope for the creation of new social institutions that would revive communities and sustain networks of interpersonal cooperation has yielded to a cynical distrust of everything but individualist strategies of success. In the late twentieth century, capitalism declares triumph but dims any promise of the good life it has to offer as it praises the virtue of toil and attacks social entitlements. In that context, aspirations aroused in the 1960s, rather than being outmoded, remain a worthy challenge to what exists.

The 1960s was an age of contradiction, a period in which the tensions between developments toward a more socialized existence and the concentrated private powers of a bourgeois society, between democratization and the power of organized elites, yielded a set of arduous strains that marked the period as one of conflict and contention. Those contradictions were not overcome at that time, leaving the door to a new way of life unopened. Nonetheless, their echoes in American thought and culture effectively fractured the kind of consensus, self-confidence, and authority that seemed to characterize intellectual life when the 1960s began. Loss of that consensus need not be mourned. The conflicts of the time posed dilemmas of intellect and art that endure—important questions still to be answered—for what is yet only formally a democratic society. Furthermore, the rupture in intellectual community experienced at the end of the 1960s can never be repaired by fiat. The apparent inability since that time to refashion reasonably consensual standards in the human sciences merely signals the shape of a society stuck in a blind alley, unable to vest popular confidence in any common vision responding to the disabling problems of the present. Restoring intellectual consensus—a basis for renewed confidence in the possibility of truth, the practical relevance of ideas, and the shared purposes of learning—will depend on restoring sense to social relations, and that is a practical task beyond the realm of thought itself.

Chronology

1957   Southern Christian Leadership Conference (SCLC) organized, January. First international Pugwash (Nova Scotia) conference of scientists for nuclear disarmament, July. William Brennan's Supreme Court opinion in *Roth v. the United States* begins to lift censorship. *Womanpower* report notes growing role of women wageworkers. Gaither Report to the National Security Council calls for fallout shelters and more military spending to overtake Soviet advances. Ghana gains independence, first "new state" in sub-Saharan Africa.

1958   John Kenneth Galbraith's *The Affluent Society* published. Ornette Coleman issues his debut recording, *Something Else!* Committee for Non-violent Action sponsors voyage of the sailboat *Golden Rule* into Pacific Ocean nuclear testing sites. Clark Kerr becomes president of the University of California.

1959   Fidel Castro's rebel army enters Havana, Cuba, January 1. Columbia-Princeton Electronic Music Center, directed by composer Milton Babbitt, established at Princeton University with an RCA-built synthesizer. Eleanor Flexner's *Century of Struggle* begins new historical writing on the American women's rights movement.

1960   Observations of quasi-stellar objects, or quasars, appear to confirm astronomer Martin Ryle's "big bang" hypothesis on the origin of the universe. After Greensboro, N.C., lunch counter sit-ins for desegregation, February 1, SCLC's Ella Baker convenes regional meeting of student activists, and Student Nonviolent Coordinating Committee (SNCC) is formed. Daniel Bell's *The End of Ideology* appears. American Enterprise Institute revived to promote free-market policies.

1961   In the wake of a U.S.-backed coup, African nationalist Patrice
        Lumumba is murdered in the Congo, January. First manned U.S.
        spaceflight by Alan Shepard, first manned orbital spaceflight by
        Soviet Union's Yuri Gargarin. Adolph Eichmann tried and convicted
        in Jerusalem. Primo Levi's *Survival in Auschwitz* appears. Delegates of
        90 tribes issue *Declaration of Indian Purpose* in Chicago.

1962   Algerian independence. Students for a Democratic Society (SDS)
        issues *Port Huron Statement*. Cuban Missile Crisis, October 22–28.
        Thomas Kuhn publishes *The Structure of Scientific Revolutions*. Exhibi-
        tion of works by Roy Lichtenstein, Claes Oldenburg, and Andy
        Warhol marks debut of pop art. Rachel Carson's *Silent Spring* pub-
        lished, commencing a new environmentalism. Second Vatican Coun-
        cil opens in Rome.

1963   Limited nuclear test ban treaty signed. Hannah Arendt publishes
        Eichmann in Jerusalem: A Report on the Banality of Evil. Timothy Leary
        and Richard Alpert fired from Harvard University for violating 1961
        pledge not to use undergraduates as subjects in experiments with hal-
        lucinogenic drugs. Self-exiled African American scholar and activist
        W. E. B. Du Bois dies in Ghana at age 95, the night before the March
        on Washington is addressed by Martin Luther King Jr., August 28.
        John F. Kennedy assassinated, November 22. Betty Friedan publishes
        The Feminine Mystique.

1964   Lyndon Johnson declares "War on Poverty." Barry Goldwater rallies
        conservatives in his drive for the Republican presidential nomination.
        SNCC and other civil rights groups organize "Freedom Summer," a
        major campaign for black voting rights relying on young volunteers
        from around the country; three activists are murdered. Warren Com-
        mission issues report on the Kennedy assassination, September 24.
        "October Revolution" concerts, organized in New York City by musi-
        cian Bill Dixon, display "the new thing" in jazz (free jazz). Free
        Speech Movement at University of California—Berkeley. Martin
        Luther King Jr. wins Nobel Peace Prize.

1965   Malcolm X assassinated, February 21. First Teach-In on Vietnam War
        held at the University of Michigan, March 24–25. National Endow-
        ments for the Humanities and the Arts established. Liberal journal
        The Public Interest begins publication with articles on "The Great
        Automation Debate." Conservative writer M. Stanton Evans pub-
        lishes *The Liberal Establishment*, beginning drive to build a network of
        conservative intellectuals, policy advisers, and funders. Sylvia Plath's
        posthumous poems, *Ariel*, published. Second Vatican Council ends,
        calling for new steps to integrate the church and everyday social life.
        Delano grape strike led by Cesar Chavez's Farm Workers Association
        (later UFW) begins. Watts rebellion, August.

1966   Walt Rostow succeeds McGeorge Bundy as Johnson's national secu-
        rity adviser and pursues a hard line, promoting the U.S. war effort in
        Vietnam. J. William Fulbright convenes hearings on Vietnam policy
        for the Senate Foreign Relations Committee. Melvin Tolson's *Harlem
        Gallery* appears. Coleman Report on equality of educational opportu-
        nity issued, July 4. Martin Luther King's open housing campaign in
        Chicago encounters hostile white crowds. First issue of countercul-
        tural newspaper, the *San Francisco Oracle*, September 20. National
        Organization for Women (NOW) formed.

1967   Ronald Reagan sworn in as California governor after campaigning on
        a platform of "clearing up the mess in the universities." Martin Luther
        King Jr. declares his opposition to the Vietnam War at New York's
        Riverside Church, April 4. Muhammad Ali refuses military induction
        on religious grounds and is stripped of his heavyweight boxing title,
        April 28. Defense Secretary Robert McNamara, disenchanted with
        the war in Vietnam, commissions an internal study on the history of
        Vietnam policy (the "Pentagon Papers"), June. John Coltrane dies,
        July 17. Uprisings in American cities, particularly Detroit and
        Newark, summer. First women's liberation groups formed.

1968   Tet Offensive by National Liberation Front, January. National Advi-
        sory Commission on Civil Disorders (Kerner Commission) issues its
        report on racial polarization in the United States. Disturbances in 125
        cities follow assassination of Martin Luther King Jr., April 4. Curator
        William Rubin organizes Museum of Modern Art show, "Dada, Sur-
        realism, and Their Heritage." Columbia University student strike,
        April, followed by student-worker rebellion in France, May, and Mex-
        ican student protests, summer. San Francisco State College student
        strike for an independent black studies program begins in the fall. M.
        Scott Momaday's *House Made of Dawn* wins Pulitzer Prize.

1969   President Richard M. Nixon takes office. Kevin Phillips publishes
        The Emerging Republican Majority. Young Americans for Freedom
        split between traditionalist conservatives and radical libertarians.
        Gay street fighting begins after police raid on the Stonewall Inn,
        June 27, marking inception of gay and lesbian liberation movement.
        My Lai massacre disclosed, November. Fire on Ohio River near
        Cleveland and Santa Barbara, California, oil spill excite environmen-
        talist sentiment.

1970   U.S. invasion of Cambodia, April 30, leads to wave of student
        protests, killings at Kent State University (Ohio) and Jackson State
        College (Mississippi), and national student strike. Art Strike in New
        York City signals new level of protest activity by visual artists. Chi-
        cano Anti-war Moratorium in Los Angeles, with 30,000 marchers,
        attacked by police, leaving 3 dead, August 29. Publication of *Notes*

from the Second Year marks emergence of "radical feminist" ideology. Norman Podhoretz commits *Commentary* magazine to a long attack on "the New Sensibility" of dissenting thought and culture.

Notes and References

Preface

1. G. A. Paul, "Wittgenstein," in *The Revolution in Philosophy*, by A. J. Ayer et al. (London: Macmillan, 1957), 94–95.

Chapter One

1. John Kenneth Galbraith, *The Affluent Society* (Boston: Houghton Mifflin, 1958), 319, 135, 257.

2. Loren Okroi, *Galbraith, Harrington, Heilbroner: Economics and Dissent in an Age of Optimism* (Princeton: Princeton University Press, 1988), 59–60; John Morton Blum, *Years of Discord: American Politics and Society, 1961–1974* (New York: Norton, 1991), 62 (hereafter cited as *Years of Discord*).

3. Galbraith, *Affluent Society*, 284, 115.

4. Robert Theobald, *The Challenge of Abundance* (New York: Clarkson N. Potter, 1961).

5. *Automation: A Report to the UAW-CIO Economic and Collective Bargaining Conference* (Detroit: UAW, 1954) (hereafter cited as *Automation*); Warner Bloomberg Jr., *The Age of Automation: Its Effects on Human Welfare* (New York: League for Industrial Democracy, 1955).

6. *Automation*, 11; Theobald, *Challenge of Abundance*, 36; discussion of "Abundance and Freedom," cited in brochure for 58th Annual LID Conference, 18 May 1965, Tamiment Library.

7. Robert M. Solow, "Technology and Unemployment," and Robert Heilbroner, "Men and Machines in Perspective," *The Public Interest* 1 (Fall 1965): 17–36; Howard R. Bowen and Garth L. Mangum, eds., *Automation and Economic Progress* (Englewood Cliffs, N.J.: Prentice-Hall, 1966).

8. Herbert A. Simon, *The Shape of Automation for Men and Management* (New York: Harper and Row, 1965), xi–xiii; Charles R. Walker, *Toward the Automatic Factory* (New Haven: Yale University Press, 1957), xxi, 17; Larry Hirschhorn, *Beyond Mecha-*

nization: Work and Technology in a Postindustrial Age (Cambridge: MIT Press, 1984), 54–58.

9. Herbert Marcuse, *Eros and Civilization: A Philosophical Inquiry into Freud* (New York: Vintage, 1962), 40–41, 136–39; Herbert Marcuse, "The End of Utopia," in *Five Lectures: Psychoanalysis, Politics, and Utopia,* trans. Jeremy J. Shapiro and Shierry M. Weber (Boston: Beacon Press, 1970); Betty Friedan, *The Feminine Mystique* (New York: Dell, 1983), 67.

10. Galbraith, *Affluent Society,* 197, 335; David Riesman, "Leisure and Work in Post-industrial Society," in *Mass Leisure,* ed. Eric Larrabee and Rolf Meyerson (Glencoe, Ill.: Free Press, 1958), 378 (hereafter cited as "Leisure and Work"); Theobald, *Challenge of Abundance,* 31; Albert O. Hirschman, *Shifting Involvements: Private Interest and Public Action* (Princeton: Princeton University Press, 1982).

11. Michael Harrington, *The Other America: Poverty in the United States* (New York: Macmillan, 1962) (hereafter cited as *Other America*); Gunnar Myrdal, *Challenge to Affluence* (New York: Pantheon, 1963), 7–8, 58, 64–65; Dwight Macdonald, "Our Invisible Poor," *New Yorker,* 19 January 1963, 82–132.

12. Myrdal, *Challenge to Affluence,* 35; Harrington, *Other America,* 21–24; Oscar Lewis, *The Children of Sanchez: Autobiography of a Mexican Family* (New York: Random House, 1961); Oscar Lewis, *La Vida: A Puerto Rican Family in the Culture of Poverty—San Juan and New York* (New York: Random House, 1966); Solow, "Technology and Unemployment."

13. C. L. R. James, Grace C. Lee, and Pierre Chaulieu, *Facing Reality* (Detroit: Correspondence, 1958), 24–28.

14. Karl Marx, *Grundrisse: Foundations of the Critique of Political Economy,* trans. Martin Nicolaus (New York: Vintage, 1973), 705 (emphasis added).

15. Richard Freeland, *Academia's Golden Age: Universities in Massachusetts, 1945–1970* (New York: Oxford University Press, 1992), 76–77, 87–88 (hereafter cited as *Academia's Golden Age*); Christopher Jencks and David Riesman, *The Academic Revolution* (Garden City, N.Y.: Doubleday, 1968), 22; Paula S. Fass, *Outside In: Minorities and the Transformation of American Education* (New York: Oxford University Press, 1989), 157, 165 (hereafter cited as *Outside In*).

16. Freeland, *Academia's Golden Age,* 91; Roger L. Geiger, "Science, Universities, and National Defense, 1945–1970," *Osiris* 7 (1992): 26–48 (special issue titled *Science after '40,* ed. Arnold Thackray); Stuart Leslie, *The Cold War and American Science: The Military-Industrial Complex at MIT and Stanford* (New York: Columbia University Press, 1993) (hereafter cited as *Cold War*); Roger L. Geiger, *Research and Relevant Knowledge: American Research Universities since World War II* (New York: Oxford University Press, 1993).

17. Leslie, *Cold War,* 9, 73–77, 100–101, 133–34, 213, 251.

18. James Allen Smith, *The Idea Brokers: Think Tanks and the Rise of the New Policy Elite* (New York: Free Press, 1991), 122–89; John S. Friedman, ed., *First Harvest: The Institute for Policy Studies, 1963–1983* (New York: Grove Press, 1983) (hereafter cited as *First Harvest*).

19. Fritz Machlup, *The Production and Distribution of Knowledge in the United States* (Princeton: Princeton University Press, 1962), 44, 362, 374, 133–44, 396–97.

20. Sherwin Rosen, "Human Capital," in *The New Palgrave: A Dictionary of Economics,* ed. John Eatwell, Murray Milgate, and Peter Newman, vol. 2 (London: Macmillan, 1987), 681–89; Theodore W. Schultz, "Investment in Human Capital,"

American Economic Review 51 (March 1961): 1–17; Gary Becker, *Human Capital* (New York: Columbia University Press, 1964); Milton Friedman, *Capitalism and Freedom* (Chicago: University of Chicago Press, 1962), 11.

21. Freeland, *Academia's Golden Age*, 108; Jencks and Riesman, *Academic Revolution*, 22–24; Fass, *Outside In*, 165–73; Geiger, "Science, Universities, and National Defense," 45.

22. Nicholas E. Tawa, *Art Music in the American Society* (Metuchen, N.J.: Scarecrow Press, 1987), 18–19; Tawa, *A Most Wondrous Babble: American Art Composers, Their Music, and the American Music Scene, 1950–1985* (New York: Greenwood Press, 1987), 68 (hereafter cited as *Wondrous Babble*); Alice Goldfarb Marquis, *Art Lessons: Learning from the Rise and Fall of Public Arts Funding* (New York: Basic Books, 1995), 81, 234–35, 45–46 (hereafter cited as *Art Lessons*); Clark Kerr, *The Uses of the University, with a "Postscript— 1972"* (Cambridge: Harvard University Press, 1972), 112–13 (hereafter cited as *Uses of the University*); Diana Crane, *The Transformation of the Avant Garde: The New York Art World, 1940–1985* (Chicago: University of Chicago Press, 1987), 9–10 (hereafter cited as *Transformation*).

23. Crane, *Transformation*, 9; Marquis, *Art Lessons*, 63; Diana Crane, *The Production of Culture: Media and the Urban Arts* (Newbury Park, Calif.: Sage Publications, 1992), 111, 148 (hereafter cited as *Production of Culture*).

24. Joseph Horowitz, "Professor Lenny," *New York Review of Books*, 10 June 1993, 39–44.

25. Joseph Papp, quoted in Lawrence Levine, *The Unpredictable Past* (New York: Oxford University Press, 1993), 153; Helen Epstein, *Joe Papp: An American Life* (Boston: Little, Brown, 1994)

26. Quoted in Robert von Hallberg, *American Poetry and Culture, 1945–1980* (Cambridge: Harvard University Press, 1985), 29–30.

27. John Tebbel, *A History of Book Publishing in the United States*, vol. 4 (New York: R. R. Bowker, 1981), 291, 308, 349–50, 712; Edward de Grazia, *Girls Lean Back Everywhere: The Law of Obscenity and the Assault on Genius* (New York: Random House, 1992), 247–51, 293 n, 312 n; James L. Baughman, *The Republic of Mass Culture* (Baltimore, Md.: Johns Hopkins University Press, 1992), 23, 75, 80, 139–40; Gerald Mast, *A Short History of the Movies* (New York: Pegasus, 1971), 315–35, 394–422.

28. Baughman, *Republic of Mass Culture*, 73, 133–34; Crane, *Production of Culture*, 51–54; James Gilbert, *A Cycle of Violence: America's Reaction to the Juvenile Delinquent in the 1950s* (New York: Oxford University Press, 1986), 17–23; Charlie Gillett, *The Sound of the City: The Rise of Rock and Roll* (New York: Outerbridge and Dienstfrey, 1970), 51–58; Fred Goodman, "How a Legend Tapped the Rock Underground," *New York Times*, 29 January 1995, sec. 2, p. 23.

29. On conformity criticism in the 1950s, see Richard Pells, *The Liberal Mind in a Conservative Age: American Intellectuals in the 1940s and 1950s* (New York: Harper and Row, 1985), 183–261.

30. Ann Fulton, "Apostles of Sartre: Advocates of Early Sartreanism in American Philosophy," *Journal of the History of Ideas* 55 (January 1995): 113–27; J. Glenn Gray, "Salvation on the Campus: Why Existentialism is Capturing the Students," *Harper's*, May 1965, 57 (hereafter cited as "Salvation on Campus").

31. Albert Camus, quoted in Jeffrey C. Isaac, *Arendt, Camus, and Modern Rebellion* (New Haven: Yale University Press, 1992), 92.

32. Hazel E. Barnes, introduction to *Being and Nothingness*, by Jean-Paul Sartre, trans. Hazel E. Barnes (New York: Philosophical Library, 1956), xxvi.

33. This paragraph relies heavily on Richard Wolin's *The Terms of Cultural Criticism: The Frankfurt School, Existentialism, Poststructuralism* (New York: Columbia University Press, 1992) and Isaac's *Arendt, Camus, and Modern Rebellion.*

34. Karl Reyman and Herman Singer, "The Origins and Significance of East European Revisionism," in *Revisionism: Essays on the History of Marxist Ideas,* ed. Leopold Labedz (New York: Frederick A. Praeger, 1962), 220; and William E. Griffith, "The Decline and Fall of Revisionism in Eastern Europe," in Labedz, 223–28.

35. Daniel Bell, "The Debate on Alienation," in Labedz, *Revisionism,* 195–211; Erich Fromm, *Marx's Concept of Man* (New York: Frederick Ungar, 1961), 48–49, 57.

36. Moishe Postone, *Time, Labor, and Social Domination* (Cambridge: Cambridge University Press, 1993), 376.

37. Ann Charters, ed., *The Portable Beat Reader* (New York: Penguin, 1992); Norman Mailer, "The White Negro (Superficial Reflections on the Hipster)," *Dissent* 4 (Summer 1957): 276–93. On Mailer's existentialism without responsibility, I am indebted to a communication from George Cotkin.

38. Gray, "Salvation on Campus," 58.

39. Joseph A. Schumpeter, *Capitalism, Socialism, and Democracy* (New York: Harper Colophon, 1975), 269, 295; George Catephores, "The Imperious Austrian: Schumpeter as Bourgeois Marxist," *New Left Review* 205 (May–June 1994), 8–18.

40. Robert Westbrook, *John Dewey and American Democracy* (Ithaca, N.Y.: Cornell University Press, 1991); Seymour Martin Lipset, Martin Trow, and James S. Coleman, *Union Democracy: The Internal Politics of the International Typographical Union* (Garden City, N.Y.: Anchor Books, 1955); Seymour Martin Lipset, *Political Man: The Social Bases of Politics* (New York: Doubleday, 1960).

41. Robert A. Dahl, "Socialist Programs and Democratic Politics: An Analysis" (Ph.D. diss., Yale University, 1940); Dahl, *A Preface to Democratic Theory* (Chicago: University of Chicago Press, 1956), 146, 131–32, 149–50.

42. Daniel Bell, "Is There a Ruling Class in America?" in *The End of Ideology,* rev. ed. (New York: Free Press, 1962), 47–74; Paul Sweezy, "Power Elite or Ruling Class," *Monthly Review* 8 (September 1956): 138–50; Talcott Parsons, "The Distribution of Power in American Society," in *Structure and Process in Modern Society* (New York: Free Press, 1960); Robert A. Dahl, *Who Governs? Democracy and Power in an American City* (New Haven: Yale University Press, 1961), 275.

43. Bazelon, *Power in America: The Politics of the New Class* (New York: New American Library, 1967), 17–19, 20–21, 308, 331–32, 139 (hereafter cited as *Power in America*).

44. Theodore Lowi, *The End of Liberalism: Ideology, Policy, and the Crisis of Public Authority* (New York: Norton, 1969), 84–86, 144–45.

45. Aldon Morris, *The Origins of the Civil Rights Movement: Black Communities Organizing for Change* (New York: Free Press, 1984).

46. Sheldon Wolin, *Politics and Vision: Continuity and Innovation in Western Political Thought* (Boston: Little, Brown, 1960), 429–34.

Chapter Two

1. On modes of intellectual life, see Neil Jumonville, *Critical Crossings: The New York Intellectuals in Postwar America* (Berkeley: University of California Press, 1991), and Steven Biel, *Independent Intellectuals in the United States, 1910–1945* (New York: New York University Press, 1992).

2. Kerr, *Uses of the University,* v.

3. Kerr, *Uses of the University,* 45, 99; Edgar Z. Friedenberg, "L.A. of the Intellect," *New York Review of Books,* 14 November 1963, 11–12.

4. Kerr, *Uses of the University,* 39, 69, 87, 123; on the "engineering model," see Donald N. Levine, "Thought, Action, and the Theory of Action: Departures from the Philosophies of Richard McKeon and Talcott Parsons" (paper presented at Conference on Pluralism and Objectivity in Contemporary Culture, University of Chicago, 13–14 March 1992).

5. Kerr, *Uses of the University,* 90, 116–17; Jencks and Riesman, *Academic Revolution,* 12, 20.

6. Jonathan Kozol, *Death at an Early Age: The Destruction of the Hearts and Minds of Negro Children in the Boston Public Schools* (Boston: Houghton Mifflin, 1967) (hereafter cited as *Death at an Early Age*); James B. Conant, *Slums and Suburbs: A Commentary on Schools in Metropolitan Areas* (New York: McGraw Hill, 1961).

7. Frederick Mosteller and Daniel P. Moynihan, "A Pathbreaking Report," in *On Equality of Educational Opportunity: Papers Deriving from the Harvard University Faculty Seminar on the Coleman Report,* ed. Mosteller and Moynihan (New York: Random House, 1972), 5, 28.

8. Principal works criticizing conventional education were Paul Goodman, *Growing Up Absurd* (New York: Random House, 1960); John Holt, *How Children Fail* (New York: Pitman, 1964); Herb Kohl, *36 Children* (New York: New American Library, 1967); Edgar Friedenberg, *Coming of Age in America* (New York: Random House, 1965); Kozol, *Death at an Early Age.*

9. Christopher Jencks, "The Coleman Report and the Conventional Wisdom," in Mosteller and Moynihan, *Equality of Educational Opportunity,* 105; *Education Watch: The 1996 Education Trust State and National Data Book* (Washington, D.C.: Education Trust, 1996).

10. W. J. Rorabaugh, *Berkeley at War: The 1960s* (New York: Oxford University Press, 1989), 19–38.

11. Louis Menashe and Ronald Radosh, eds., *Teach-Ins: USA* (New York: Frederick A. Praeger, 1967); Vietnam Day Committee, *We Accuse* (Berkeley: Diablo Press, 1965), 37, 159–60.

12. See Todd Gitlin, *The Sixties: Years of Hope, Days of Rage* (New York: Bantam, 1987).

13. Primo Levi, *If This Is a Man* (New York: Orion, 1959), republished as *Survival in Auschwitz: The Nazi Assault on Humanity* (New York: Collier, 1961); Elie Wiesel, *Night* (New York: Hill and Wang, 1960); Raul Hilberg, *The Destruction of the European Jews* (Chicago: Quadrangle, 1961); Martin Marty, ed., *The Place of Bonhoeffer* (New York: Association Press, 1962).

14. Hannah Arendt, *Eichmann in Jerusalem: A Report on the Banality of Evil,* rev. ed. (New York: Viking, 1965), 276, 288, 252.

15. Ibid., 18, 125–26, 232–33; Elisabeth Young-Bruehl, *Hannah Arendt: For Love of the World* (New Haven: Yale University Press, 1982), 337–78.

16. Savio, quoted in Rorabaugh, *Berkeley at War: The 1960s,* 22.

17. Menashe and Radosh, *Teach-Ins: USA,* 12, 17, 25.

18. Karl Mannheim, *Ideology and Utopia,* trans. Louis Wirth and Edward Shils (New York: Harcourt Brace Jovanovich, 1936), 153–64; Lewis Coser, *Men of Ideas* (New York: Free Press, 1970), 263–93.

19. Loren Baritz, *The Servants of Power: A History of the Use of Social Science in American Industry* (Middletown, Conn.: Wesleyan University Press, 1960); Baritz in *Nation*, 21 January 1961; Richard Hofstadter, "A Note on Intellect and Power," *American Scholar* 30 (Fall 1961): 588–98; David Eakins, "Objectivity and Commitment," *Studies on the Left* 1 (Fall 1959): 44–53.

20. Rorabaugh, *Berkeley at War: The 1960s*, 92; Lynd, in *We Accuse*, 153–58.

21. Christopher Lasch, "The Cultural Cold War," in *Towards a New Past: Dissenting Essays in American History*, ed. Barton Bernstein (New York: Pantheon, 1968); Lasch, *The New Radicalism in America* (New York: Vintage, 1965), 299–310.

22. Noam Chomsky, *Syntactic Structures* (The Hague: Mouton, 1957), and *Aspects of the Theory of Syntax* (Cambridge: MIT Press, 1965); John Lyons, *Noam Chomsky*, rev. ed. (New York: Penguin, 1977); Joshua Cohen and Joel Rogers, "Knowledge, Morality, and Hope: The Social Thought of Noam Chomsky," *New Left Review*, no. 187 (May–June 1991): 5–27.

23. Dell Hymes, "Review of *Noam Chomsky*," in *On Noam Chomsky: Critical Essays*, ed. Gilbert Harman, 2d ed. (Amherst: University of Massachusetts Press, 1982), 328–32, and *Foundations in Sociolinguistics: An Ethnographic Approach* (Philadelphia: University of Pennsylvania Press, 1974).

24. Noam Chomsky, *American Power and the New Mandarins* (New York: Pantheon, 1969), 14–16 (hereafter cited as *American Power*).

25. Thomas Molnar, *The Decline of the Intellectual* (New York: World, 1961); Robert Nisbet, *The Degradation of the Academic Dogma: The University in America, 1945–1970* (New York: Basic Books, 1971).

26. Chomsky, *American Power*, 348; Randolph Bourne, *War and the Intellectuals: Essays, 1915–1919* (New York: Harper and Row, 1964).

27. Lasch, *New Radicalism in America*, 74–103; Menashe and Radosh, *Teach-Ins: USA*, 2.

28. Daniel Bell, *The End of Ideology: On the Exhaustion of Political Ideas in the Fifties* (New York: Free Press, 1960); Chaim I. Waxman, ed., *The End of Ideology Debate* (New York: Funk and Wagnalls, 1968).

29. Job Leonard Dittberner, *The End of Ideology and American Social Thought: 1930–1960* (Ann Arbor: UMI Research Press, 1979); Peter Coleman, *The Liberal Conspiracy: The Congress for Cultural Freedom and the Struggle for the Mind of Postwar Europe* (New York: Free Press, 1989); Albert Camus, "Neither Victims nor Executioners," *politics* 4 (July–August 1947): 141–47; Hannah Arendt, *The Origins of Totalitarianism* (New York: Harcourt, Brace, 1951); Edward Shils, "The End of Ideology?" *Encounter* 5 (November 1955): 52–58; Seymour Martin Lipset, "The State of Democratic Politics," *Canadian Forum* 35 (November 1955): 170–71.

30. Dennis Wrong, "Reflections on the End of Ideology," Robert A. Haber, "The End of Ideology as Ideology," Stephen W. Rousseas and James Farganis, "American Politics and the End of Ideology," Henry David Aiken, "The Revolt against Ideology," and Joseph La Palombara, "Decline of Ideology: A Dissent and an Interpretation," in Waxman, *End of Ideology Debate*, 116–25, 185, 213, 229–58, 315–18. Daniel Bell and Irving Kristol, "What Is the Public Interest?" *The Public Interest*, no. 1 (Fall 1965), 3–5.

31. Talcott Parsons, *The Structure of Social Action* (New York: McGraw-Hill, 1937), and *The Social System* (Glencoe, Ill.: Free Press, 1951); Gabriel Almond and Sidney Verba, *The Civic Culture* (Princeton: Princeton University Press, 1963); Louis Hartz, *The Liberal Tradition in America* (New York: Harcourt, Brace, 1955); Lewis Coser, *The*

Functions of Social Conflict (Glencoe, Ill.: Free Press, 1956); Ralf Dahrendorf, *Class and Class Conflict in Industrial Society* (Stanford: Stanford University Press, 1959); Barrington Moore Jr., *The Social Origins of Dictatorship and Democracy* (Boston: Beacon, 1966) (hereafter cited as *Origins of Dictatorship and Democracy*); Randall Collins, *Conflict Sociology* (New York: Academic Press, 1975); John Higham, "The Cult of the 'American Consensus': Homogenizing Our History," *Commentary* 27 (February 1959): 94, 100.

32. Seymour Martin Lipset, "A View from Our Left," Irving Louis Horowitz, "Another View from Our Left," in Waxman, *End of Ideology Debate*, 166–81.

33. H. Stuart Hughes, *Consciousness and Society* (New York: Vintage, 1948); Anthony Giddens, "Positivism and Its Critics," in *A History of Sociological Analysis*, ed. Tom Bottomore and Robert Nisbet (New York: Basic Books, 1978), 236–86; Donald Levine, *Visions of the Sociological Tradition* (Chicago: University of Chicago Press, 1995), 18–22; James S. Coleman, *Introduction to Mathematical Sociology* (New York: Free Press, 1964).

34. George Lichtheim, "Dialectical Methodology," *Times Literary Supplement*, 12 March 1970, 272; Bazelon, *Power in America*, 195, 180; Alvin Gouldner, "Anti-Minotaur: The Myth of a Value-Free Sociology," *Social Problems* 9 (Winter 1962): 199–213.

35. Robert S. Ellwood, *The Sixties Spiritual Awakening: American Religion Moving from Modern to Postmodern* (New Brunswick, N.J.: Rutgers University Press, 1994), 85, 126–33, 137–42, 178, 199, 245, 254, 309–12 (hereafter cited as *Sixties Spiritual Awakening*).

36. James H. Capshew and Karen A. Rader, "Big Science: Price to the Present," in Arnold Thackray, *Science after '40*, 6, 19.

37. Clifford Geertz, "Ideology as a Cultural System," in *Ideology and Discontent*, ed. David Apter (New York: Free Press, 1964), 63–64.

38. Clifford Geertz, "Person, Time, and Conduct in Bali" (1966), reprinted in *The Interpretation of Cultures* (New York: Basic Books, 1973); Steven Weiland, *Intellectual Craftsmen: Ways and Works in American Scholarship, 1935–1990* (New Brunswick, N.J.: Transaction, 1991), 221–46.

39. Baughman, *Republic of Mass Culture*, 117–30; John Tebbel and Mary Ellen Zuckerman, *The Magazine in America, 1741–1990* (New York: Oxford University Press, 1991), 246–50, 314–16.

40. Tom Wolfe, *The Kandy-Kolored Tangerine-Flake Streamline Baby* (New York: Farrar, Straus and Giroux, 1965), introduction (n.p.), 76, 82 (hereafter cited as *Kandy-Kolored*).

41. Tom Wolfe, *The Pump House Gang* (New York: Farrar, Straus and Giroux, 1968), 8; Wolfe, introduction to *Kandy-Kolored*, n.p.

42. Wolfe, introduction to *Kandy-Kolored*, n.p.; *Pump House Gang*, 3–14; *The Electric Kool-Aid Acid Test* (New York: Farrar, Straus and Giroux, 1968); Joe David Bellamy, introduction to *The Purple Decades: A Reader*, by Tom Wolfe (Farrar, Straus and Giroux, 1982), vii–xvi.

43. Wolfe, *Pump House Gang*, 14; Wolfe, *The New Journalism* (New York: Harper and Row, 1973), 30.

44. Wolfe, *New Journalism*, 50, 28–29.

45. Quoted in Tom Wells, *The War Within: America's Battle over Vietnam* (Berkeley: University of California Press, 1994), 24 (hereafter cited as *War Within*).

46. Frederick Suppe, "The Search for Philosophical Understanding of Scientific Theories," in *The Structure of Scientific Theories*, ed. Frederick Suppe (Urbana: Univer-

sity of Illinois Press, 1977), 1–241; Tyler Burge, "Philosophy of Language and Mind: 1950–1990," *Philosophical Review* 101 (January 1992): 3–51.

47. Paul Feyerabend, "Explanation, Reduction, and Empiricism," in *Minnesota Studies in the Philosophy of Science*, ed. Herbert Feigl and Grover Maxwell, vol. 3 (Minneapolis: University of Minnesota Press, 1962), 28–97. This discussion of the rise of a historicist challenge to logical positivism relies largely on Steve Fuller, "Being There with Thomas Kuhn: A Parable for Postmodern Times," *History and Theory* 31 (1992): 242–75 (hereafter cited as "Being There with Thomas Kuhn").

48. Thomas S. Kuhn, *The Structure of Scientific Revolutions* (Chicago: University of Chicago Press, 1962), 91.

49. Thomas S. Kuhn, *The Structure of Scientific Revolutions*, 2d ed., enlarged (Chicago: University of Chicago Press, 1970), 151.

50. Popper's followers convened the 1965 International Colloquium in the Philosophy of Science in London, devoted to a critical examination of Kuhn's work, and published the proceedings as *Criticism and the Growth of Knowledge*, ed. Imre Lakatos and Alan Musgrave (London: Cambridge University Press, 1970).

51. Paul Hoyningen-Huene, *Reconstructing Scientific Revolutions: Thomas S. Kuhn's Philosophy of Science* (Chicago: University of Chicago Press, 1993), 258–64.

52. Isaac, *Arendt, Camus, and Modern Rebellion*, 3.

53. David Hollinger, "Free Enterprise and Free Inquiry: The Emergence of Laissez-Faire Communitarianism in the Ideology of Science in the United States," *New Literary History* 21 (1990): 897–919; Fuller, "Being There with Thomas Kuhn," 259–69.

54. Philip Kitcher, "The Naturalists Return," *Philosophical Review* 101 (January 1992): 53–114.

Chapter Three

1. George Young, "Europeanization," in *Encyclopedia of the Social Sciences*, vol. 5 (New York: Macmillan, 1937), 623–36. On avoidance of historical issues in modern Anglo-American social sciences, see Margaret Schabas, *A World Ruled by Number: William Stanley Jevons and the Rise of Mathematical Economics* (Princeton: Princeton University Press, 1990); Dorothy Ross, *The Origins of American Social Science* (New York: Cambridge University Press, 1991); George W. Stocking Jr., *Race, Culture, and Evolution: Essays in the History of Anthropology* (New York: Free Press, 1968).

2. Richard Swedberg, ed., *Joseph A. Schumpeter: The Economics and Sociology of Capitalism* (Princeton: Princeton University Press, 1991), 31–43.

3. Robert Redfield, *Tepoztlán: A Mexican Village* (Chicago: University of Chicago Press, 1930); Robert Redfield and Alfonso Villa R, *Chan Kom: A Maya Village* (Washington, D.C.: Carnegie Institution of Washington, 1934); Oscar Lewis, *Life in a Mexican Village: Tepoztlán Restudied* (Urbana: University of Illinois Press, 1951), xxvi, 429; Eric Wolf, *Europe and the People without History* (Berkeley: University of California Press, 1982), 14.

4. Bert Hoselitz, "The Dynamics of Marxism: What Remains Valid," *Modern Review* 3 (1949): 11–23.

5. Douglas G. Webb, "Philip Selznick and the New York Sociologists" (paper presented at Annual Convention of the Canadian Historical Association, 9–11 June 1982), 66 n. 159.

6. Marshall Sahlins and Elman R. Service, eds., *Evolution and Culture* (Ann Arbor: University of Michigan Press, 1960), 2.

7. Blum, *Years of Discord,* 35–37; Stephen G. Rabe, "Controlling Revolutions: Latin America, the Alliance for Progress, and Cold War Anti-Communism," in *Kennedy's Quest for Victory,* ed. Thomas G. Paterson (New York: Oxford University Press, 1989), 105–22 (hereafter cited as "Controlling Revolutions"); Douglas J. Macdonald, *Adventures in Chaos: American Intervention for Reform in the Third World* (Cambridge: Harvard University Press, 1992), 187, 191 (hereafter cited as *Adventures in Chaos*).

8. Walt W. Rostow, *Stages of Economic Growth* (Cambridge: Cambridge University Press, 1960), 100–101, 106–7, 119, 121, 133, 134, 154, 164; Paul A. Baran and E. J. Hobsbawm, "The Stages of Economic Growth," *Kyklos* 14 (1961): 234–42.

9. Alex Inkeles, "Understanding and Misunderstanding Individual Modernity," in *The Uses of Controversy in Sociology,* ed. Lewis A. Coser and Otto N. Larsen (New York: Free Press, 1976), 104–5, 117–18; Daniel Lerner, *The Passing of Traditional Society: Modernizing the Middle East* (Glencoe, Ill.: Free Press, 1958), 45 (hereafter cited as *Passing of Traditional Society*); David Apter, *Rethinking Development* (Newbury Park, Calif.: Sage, 1987), 48.

10. Rose Laub Coser, *In Defense of Modernity: Role Complexity and Individual Autonomy* (Stanford: Stanford University Press, 1991), 86 (hereafter cited as *In Defense of Modernity*); Redfield, *Tepoztlán: A Mexican Village,* 8–10; Lerner, *Passing of Traditional Society,* 74–75; Arjun Guneratne, "A Dialogue of Civilizations: Robert Redfield and the Development of Language and Area Studies at the University of Chicago" (Regenstein Library exhibition, University of Chicago, 1992).

11. See Parsons, *Social System.*

12. Coser, *In Defense of Modernity,* 67; David McClelland, *The Achieving Society* (Princeton, N.J.: Van Nostrand, 1961); Nicholas Lemann, "Is There a Science of Success?" *Atlantic Monthly,* February 1994, 83–98; Apter, *Rethinking Development,* 39, 24.

13. Anne Firor Scott, ed., *Jane Addams: Democracy and Social Ethics* (Cambridge: Harvard University Press, 1964); Jill Ker Conway, *True North: A Memoir* (New York: Knopf, 1994), 64–66, 148–54.

14. Ellen Fitzpatrick, "Forward," in *Century of Struggle: The Women's Rights Movement in the United States,* by Eleanor Flexner and Ellen Fitzpatrick, enlarged edition (Cambridge: Harvard University Press, 1996); Daniel Horowitz, "Rethinking Betty Friedan and *The Feminine Mystique:* Labor Union Radicalism and Feminism in Cold War America," *American Quarterly* 48 (March 1996): 1–42; Amy Swerdlow, "The Congress of American Women: Left-Feminist Peace Politics in the Cold War," in *U.S. History as Women's History,* ed. Linda K. Kerber et al. (Chapel Hill: University of North Carolina Press, 1995), 306.

15. Mirra Komarovsky, *Women in the Modern World* (Boston: Little, Brown, 1953), and *Blue-Collar Marriage* (New York: Random, 1964); see essays reprinted in William J. Goode, ed., *Readings on the Family and Society* (Englewood Cliffs, N.J.: Prentice-Hall, 1964).

16. William J. Goode, *World Revolution and Family Patterns* (Glencoe, Ill.: Free Press, 1963), 7–26, 54–70, 99, 147, 202, 368, 373, 380.

17. Alice S. Rossi, "Equality between the Sexes: An Immodest Proposal," in *The Woman in America,* ed. Robert Jay Lifton (Boston: Houghton Mifflin, 1965), 99, 132, 136.

18. Friedan, *Feminine Mystique,* 68, 282–309; Wini Breines, *Young, White, and Miserable: Growing Up Female in the Fifties* (Boston: Beacon Press, 1992), 167–95.

19. Lerner, 1964 preface to *Passing of Traditional Society,* vii; S. N. Eisenstadt, "Breakdowns of Modernization," *Economic Development and Cultural Change* 12 (July 1964): 345–67; Carter Goodrich, "Argentina as a New Country," *Comparative Studies in History and Society* 7 (1964–1965): 80–81; Rabe, "Controlling Revolutions"; Macdonald, *Adventures in Chaos,* 187–248; Walt W. Rostow, "Two Views of America's Task Abroad," *New Republic* 152 (29 May 1965): 17; Ithiel de Sola Pool, letter to the editors, *New York Review of Books,* 13 February 1969, 31; Noam Chomsky, foreword to *Prevent the Crime of Silence: Reports from the Sessions of the International War Crimes Tribunal Founded by Bertrand Russell,* ed. Peter Limqueco, Peter Weiss, and Ken Coates (London: Allen Lane, 1971), 11 (hereafter cited as *Prevent the Crime of Silence*).

20. Leonard Binder, "The Natural History of Development Theory," *Comparative Studies in Society and History* 28 (1986): 14–18.

21. Immanuel Wallerstein, *Africa: The Politics of Independence* (New York: Vintage, 1961), 12, 153–67; Wallerstein, *Africa: The Politics of Unity* (New York: Random House, 1967), 223, 247–49; Charles Ragin and Daniel Chirot, "The World System of Immanuel Wallerstein: Sociology and Politics as History," in *Vision and Method in Historical Sociology,* ed. Theda Skocpol (New York: Cambridge University Press, 1984), 280; Wallerstein, "Modernization: Requiescat in Pace," in Coser and Larsen, *Uses of Controversy in Sociology,* 131–35.

22. Robert A. Packenham, *The Dependency Movement: Scholarship and Politics in Development Studies* (Cambridge: Harvard University Press, 1992), 24; Andre Gunder Frank, *Capitalism and Underdevelopment in Latin America* (New York: Monthly Review Press, 1967); Frank, "Sociology of Development and the Underdevelopment of Sociology," in *Dependence and Underdevelopment: Latin America's Political Economy* (Garden City, N.Y.: Doubleday, 1972).

23. Moore, *Origins of Dictatorship and Democracy;* E. P. Thompson, *The Making of the English Working Class* (New York: Vintage, 1963), 195; Herbert Gutman's essays (most originally published 1966–1969) were collected in *Work, Culture, and Society in Industrializing America* (New York: Knopf, 1976).

24. Friedan, *Feminine Mystique,* 43.

25. Quoted in Paul Jacobs and Saul Landau, eds., *The New Radicals* (New York: Vintage, 1966), 231.

26. Riesman, "Leisure and Work," 363–85.

27. David Riesman and Staughton Lynd, preface to *Thorstein Veblen,* by David Riesman (New York: Scribner's, 1960), xvi (emphasis added).

28. Riesman, "Leisure and Work," 377.

29. Daniel Bell, "The Post-Industrial Society," in *Technology and Social Change,* ed. Eli Ginzberg (New York: Columbia University Press, 1964).

30. "The Triple Revolution," *Liberation,* April 1964, 9–15; also in Priscilla Long, ed., *The New Left: A Collection of Essays* (Boston: Porter Sargent, 1969), 339, 352, 348 (emphasis added).

31. Students for a Democratic Society, *The Port Huron Statement* (New York: Students for a Democratic Society, 1962), 61–63.

32. Massimo Teodori, ed., *The New Left: A Documentary History* (Indianapolis: Bobbs-Merrill, 1969), 90.

33. Greg Calvert and Carol Neiman, *A Disrupted History: The New Left and the New Capitalism* (New York: Random House, 1971), 58–59, 22–23, 64, 174.

34. Daniel Bell, *The Reforming of General Education* (New York: Columbia University Press, 1966), 70–88.

35. "Triple Revolution," 347.

36. Alain Touraine, *The Post-Industrial Society*, trans. Leonard F. X. Mayhew (New York: Random House, 1971), 54, 84–85, 220–22.

37. Riesman, "Leisure and Work," 379–81.

38. Bell, "Post-Industrial Society," 52.

39. Daniel Bell, *The Coming of Post-Industrial Society* (New York: Free Press, 1973), 481.

40. Touraine, *Post-Industrial Society*, 4–6, 25.

41. Richard Chase, "The Fate of the Avant-Garde," *Partisan Review* 24 (Summer 1957): 363–74; Irving Howe, "Mass Society and Postmodern Fiction," in *The Decline of the New* (New York: Harcourt, Brace and World, 1970), 190–207; Harry Levin, "What Was Modernism?" in *Refractions: Essays in Comparative Literature* (New York: Oxford University Press, 1966), 271–95; Leslie Fiedler, "The Death of Avant-Garde Literature," in *The Collected Essays of Leslie Fiedler*, vol. 2 (New York: Stein and Day, 1971), 454–60; Malcolm Bradbury, "Neorealist Fiction," in *The Columbia Literary History of the United States*, ed. Emory Elliot (New York: Columbia University Press, 1988), 1126–41.

42. Howe, "Mass Society and Postmodern Fiction," 207, and "The New York Intellectuals," in *Decline of the New*, 211–65, especially 248–65; Fiedler, "The New Mutants," in *Collected Essays*, 379–400; Ihab Hassan, *The Dismemberment of Orpheus: Toward a Postmodern Literature* (New York: Oxford University Press, 1971), 256.

43. Andreas Huyssen, *After the Great Divide: Modernism, Mass Culture, Postmodernism* (Bloomington: Indiana University Press, 1986) (hereafter cited as *After the Great Divide*).

44. Alexander Trocchi, Terry Southern, and Richard Seaver, eds., *Writers in Revolt* (New York: F. Fell, 1963); Maurice Girodias, ed., *The Olympia Reader* (New York: Grove, 1965); Tony Hendra, *Going Too Far* (New York: Doubleday, 1987).

45. Sally Banes, *Greenwich Village 1963: Avant-Garde Performance and the Effervescent Body* (Durham, N.C.: Duke University Press, 1993), 57–58 (hereafter cited as *Greenwich Village 1963*); William C. Seitz, *Art in the Age of Aquarius, 1955–1970* (Washington, D.C.: Smithsonian Institution, 1992), 47 (hereafter cited as *Age of Aquarius*); Allan Kaprow, *Some Recent Happenings* (New York: Something Else Press, 1966).

46. Banes, *Greenwich Village 1963*, 60–61, 66–67.

47. Ibid., 75–76; John Tytell, *The Living Theatre: Art, Exile, and Outrage* (New York: Grove Press, 1995) (hereafter cited as *Living Theatre*).

48. Robert Venturi, *Complexity and Contradiction in Architecture* (New York: Museum of Modern Art, 1966, 1977), 16; Huyssen, *After the Great Divide*, 195–216; Gerald Graff, "The Myth of the Postmodern Breakthrough," in *Literature against Itself: Literary Ideas in Modern Society* (Chicago: University of Chicago Press, 1979), 31–62.

49. Luc Ferry and Alain Renaut, *French Philosophy of the Sixties: An Essay on Antihumanism*, trans. Mary H. S. Cattani (Amherst: University of Massachusetts Press, 1990); John Barth, "The Literature of Exhaustion," *Atlantic*, August 1967, 29–34, and "The Literature of Replenishment: Postmodernist Fiction," *Atlantic*, January 1980, 65–71; Graff, "Myth of the Postmodern Breakthrough," 55.

50. Jonathan Miller, *Marshall McLuhan* (New York: Viking, 1971); Jay P. Corrin, *G. K. Chesterton and Hilaire Belloc: The Battle against Modernity* (Athens: University of Ohio Press, 1981).

51. George Nash, *The Conservative Intellectual Movement in America: Since 1945* (New York: Basic Books, 1976), 137, 144, 156, 188–92, 200, 304 (hereafter cited as *Conservative Intellectual Movement in America*); John A. Andrew III, *The Other Side of the Sixties: Young Americans for Freedom and the Rise of Conservative Politics* (New Brunswick, N.J.: Rutgers University Press, 1997); Harry Ausmus, *Will Herberg: From Right to Right* (Chapel Hill: University of North Carolina Press, 1987), 171, 199.

52. Marshall McLuhan, *The Gutenberg Galaxy: The Making of Typographic Man* (Toronto: University of Toronto Press, 1962), 17–18, 21, 31, 37–43, 63, 141, 230–31.

53. Ibid., 25, 220, 222, 223, 235–37.

54. Huyssen, *After the Great Divide*, 175.

55. Michael Löwy, *The Politics of Combined and Uneven Development* (London: Verso, 1981), 87–88.

56. Wolf, *Europe and the People without History,* 73–100.

57. For a defense of "developmental logic," see Larry Hirschhorn, "The Social Crisis: The Crisis of Work and Social Services: An Approach to the Grammar of Post-industrial Revolution, Part II" (Working Paper 252, Institute of Regional and Urban Development, University of California—Berkeley, 1975).

58. See for instance Talcott Parsons, "Kinship and Associational Aspects of Social Structure," in *Kinship and Culture*, ed. Francis L.K. Hsu (Chicago: Aldine, 1971), 409–38.

Chapter Four

1. Susan Sontag, "Against Interpretation" and "Notes on 'Camp,' " in *Against Interpretation and Other Essays* (New York: Dell, 1969), 17, 277–93.

2. Marshall Berman, *The Politics of Authenticity: Radical Individualism and the Emergence of Modern Society* (New York: Atheneum, 1970), 22, 44–45, 57, 84; Philip Rieff, *The Triumph of the Therapeutic: Uses of Faith after Freud* (New York: Harper and Row, 1966), 3 n, 19, 242–59.

3. James Baldwin, *The Fire Next Time* (New York: Dial Press, 1963), 119.

4. Ibid., 132–33.

5. Janet Malcolm, "The Silent Woman," *New Yorker,* 23 and 30 August 1993, 89.

6. "Editorial," in *Notes from the Second Year,* ed. Shulamith Firestone and Anne Koedt (New York: n.p., 1970), 2; Florence Howe, ed., *No More Masks! An Anthology of Poems by Women* (Garden City, N.Y.: Anchor, 1973).

7. Erving Goffman, *Relations in Public: Microstudies of the Public Order* (New York: Harper and Row, 1971), 107 n (hereafter cited as *Relations in Public*).

8. Hazel E. Barnes, "Translator's Introduction," in Sartre, *Being and Nothingness,* xxxii.

9. Ibid., xix.

10. Erik Erikson, *Childhood and Society,* 2d ed. (New York: W.W. Norton, 1963), 261–63, and *Identity and the Life Cycle* (New York: International Universities Press, 1959); Ellen Herman, *The Romance of American Psychology: Political Culture in the Age of Experts* (Berkeley: University of California Press, 1995), 264–75 (hereafter cited as *Romance of American Psychology*); Frederick Perls, Ralph E. Hefferline, and Paul Goodman, *Gestalt Therapy: Excitement and Growth in the Human Personality* (New York: Dell, 1959), viii, 230, 246–47 (hereafter cited as *Gestalt Therapy*).

11. Forrest G. Robinson, *Love's Story Told: A Life of Henry A. Murray* (Cambridge: Harvard University Press, 1992), 211–65; Herman, *Romance of American Psychology,*

269–73; Barbara Ehrenreich, *The Hearts of Men* (Garden City, N.Y.: Doubleday, 1983), 92.

12. Goodman, *Gestalt Therapy*, 242, and Goodman, *Growing Up Absurd;* David Riesman, with Nathan Glazer and Reuel Denney, *The Lonely Crowd,* abr. ed. (New Haven: Yale University Press, 1961), 239–307.

13. Louis Ginsberg, letter to Allen Ginsberg, 29 February 1956, in *Howl: Original Facsimile, Transcript, and Variant Versions,* by Allen Ginsberg (New York: Harper and Row, 1986), 150.

14. Hallberg, *American Poetry and Culture*, 13–14.

15. Ibid., 53, 101; Maxine Kumin, "How It Was," in *Anne Sexton: The Complete Poems* (Boston: Houghton Mifflin, 1981), xxvii; James E. B. Breslin, "Poetry," in *The Columbia Literary History of the United States,* ed. Emory Elliot (New York: Columbia University Press, 1988), 1083, 1087–88; Paul Breslin, *The Psycho-Political Muse: American Poetry since the Fifties* (Chicago: University of Chicago Press, 1987), 55–56 (hereafter cited as *Psycho-Political Muse*).

16. Paul Breslin, *Psycho-Political Muse,* 53–60, 102.

17. Ted Hughes, introduction to *The Journals of Sylvia Plath,* by Sylvia Plath (New York: Dial Press, 1982), xii.

18. Elizabeth Hardwick, "On Sylvia Plath," *New York Review of Books,* 12 August 1971, 3.

19. Sylvia Plath, "Lady Lazarus," in *Ariel* (New York: Harper Perennial, 1965), 6–9.

20. Poet and Plath biographer Anne Stevenson commented on emotional "extremism" as a feature of the confessional ethos, quoted in Janet Malcolm, "The Silent Woman," *New Yorker,* 23 and 30 August 1993, 113; Paul Breslin, *Psycho-Political Muse,* 103.

21. Seitz, *Age of Aquarius,* 7–8, 10, 25, 66, 79; Lawrence Alloway, "The Development of British Pop," in *Pop Art,* by Lucy Lippard et al. (New York: Oxford University Press, 1966), 32–33, 48, 60.

22. Alloway, "Development of British Pop," 48; Gerald Laing quoted in Seitz, *Age of Aquarius,* 79.

23. Quoted in Crane, *Transformation,* 77.

24. John Updike, "Big, Bright, and Bendayed," *New York Review of Books,* 16 December 1993, 6.

25. Lucy Lippard, "New York Pop," in Lippard et al., *Pop Art,* 78; John McCole, *Walter Benjamin and the Antinomies of Tradition* (Ithaca, N.Y.: Cornell University Press, 1993), 3–7.

26. Crane, *Transformation,* 68, 78.

27. John Bowlby, *Attachment and Loss,* vol. 1 (New York: Basic Books, 1969), xiii; Rollo May, *Love and Will* (New York: Dell, 1969), 16–17.

28. Heinz Kohut, "Forms and Transformations of Narcissism," in *The Search for the Self: Selected Writings of Heinz Kohut,* vol. 1 (Madison, Conn.: International Universities Press, 1978), 427–60.

29. May, *Love and Will,* 26, 326 n. 16.

30. Walker Percy, *The Moviegoer* (New York: Ballantine, 1961), 195–96, 199–200.

31. Nash, *Conservative Intellectual Movement in America,* 220–27; Allen J. Matusow, *The Unraveling of America* (New York: Harper, 1984), 146.

32. Marshall Berman, review of *Relations in Public,* by Erving Goffman, *New York Times Book Review,* 27 February 1972, 10.

33. Alvin Gouldner, *The Coming Crisis of Western Sociology* (New York: Basic Books, 1970), 380–81; Kenneth Cmiel, *Democratic Eloquence* (Berkeley: University of California Press, 1991), 92, 255–56; Goffman, *Relations in Public*, x.

34. Tom Burns, *Erving Goffman* (London: Routledge, 1992), 11, 23.

35. Will Herberg, "Personalism against Totalitarianism," *politics*, December 1945, 369–74; Dwight Macdonald, "The Root Is Man: Part Two," *politics*, July 1946, 210–14; Max Horkheimer, *Eclipse of Reason* (New York: Oxford University Press, 1947; Seabury Press, 1974).

36. Erving Goffman, "Communication Conduct in an Island Community" (Ph.D. diss., University of Chicago, December 1953), 103, 345, 360 (hereafter cited as "Communication Conduct").

37. Goffman, "Communication Conduct," 174, 175, 191, 256–57.

38. See also Goffman, "On Face-Work" (1955) and "The Nature of Deference and Demeanor" (1956), in *Interaction Ritual* (New York: Doubleday, 1967), 5–95.

39. Erving Goffman, *Behavior in Public Places: Notes on the Social Organization of Gatherings* (New York: Free Press, 1963), 243, 247–48 (emphasis added) (hereafter cited as *Behavior in Public Places*).

40. Howard S. Becker, "Labeling Theory Reconsidered," in *Outsiders: Studies in the Sociology of Deviance* (New York: Free Press, 1963, 1973).

41. R. D. Laing, *The Divided Self: An Existential Study in Sanity and Madness* (London: Penguin, 1965, 1990), 11–12.

42. Thomas Szasz, *The Manufacture of Madness: A Comparative Study of the Inquisition and the Mental Health Movement* (New York: Harper and Row, 1970), xviii, quoted in Uta Gerhardt, *Ideas about Illness: An Intellectual and Political History of Medical Sociology* (New York: New York University Press, 1989), 85.

43. Erving Goffman, *The Presentation of Self in Everyday Life* (New York: Doubleday, 1959), 252–53 (emphasis added) (hereafter cited as *Presentation of Self*).

44. Erving Goffman, "Role Distance," in *Encounters: Two Studies in the Sociology of Interaction* (Indianapolis: Bobbs-Merrill, 1961), 133, 152, 141–42.

45. Goffman, *Behavior in Public Places*, 207.

46. Erving Goffman, *Forms of Talk* (Philadelphia: University of Pennsylvania Press, 1981), 2.

47. Goffman, *Presentation of Self*, 215, 155–56: "Hotel maids learn that male guests who make passes at them upstairs are not quite what the seemliness of their downstairs conduct suggests."

48. Goffman, "Normal Appearances," in *Relations in Public*, 289–90n.

49. Goffman, "Communication Conduct," 339 n; *Presentation of Self*, 133; "Role Distance."

50. Goffman, *Stigma: Notes on the Management of Spoiled Identity* (Englewood Cliffs, N.J.: Prentice-Hall, 1963), and *Gender Advertisements* (New York: Harper and Row, 1976).

51. Steve Reich, *Come Out*, on *New Sounds in Electronic Music* (Odyssey, issue no. 32-16-0160, 1967); Truman Nelson, *The Torture of Mothers* (Boston: Beacon Press, 1965).

52. Martin Duberman, *Stonewall* (New York: Dutton, 1993).

53. "State Department Acts on 212 Risks," *New York Times*, 8 June 1963, 8.

54. John D'Emilio, *Sexual Politics, Sexual Communities: The Making of a Homosexual Minority in the United States, 1940–1970* (Chicago: University of Chicago Press, 1983),

18–21 (hereafter cited as *Sexual Politics*); Lillian Faderman, *Odd Girls and Twilight Lovers: A History of Lesbian Life in Twentieth-Century America* (New York: Penguin, 1991), 308 (hereafter cited as *Odd Girls*).

55. Robert Trumbull, "Homosexuals Proud of Deviancy, Medical Academy Study Finds," *New York Times*, 19 May 1964, 1.

56. Duberman, *Stonewall*, 108, 110–11, 163; Barbara Gittings, interview by Jonathan Katz, *Gay American History: Lesbians and Gay Men in the U.S.A.: A Documentary* (New York: Harper and Row, 1976), 427, 432; Barry Adams, *The Rise of a Gay and Lesbian Movement* (Boston: Twayne, 1987), 70–71; D'Emilio, *Sexual Politics*, 146, 227.

57. Duberman, *Stonewall*, 60–61; Lanford Wilson, *The Madness of Lady Bright*, in *Eight Plays from Off-Off Broadway*, ed. Nick Orzel and Michael Smith (Indianapolis: Bobbs-Merrill, 1966), 57–92; D'Emilio, *Sexual Politics*, 136–37.

58. Howard Taubman, "Modern Primer: Helpful Hints to Tell Appearances vs. Truth," *New York Times*, 28 April 1963, sec. 2, p. 1.

59. Benjamin DeMott, " 'But He's a Homosexual ... ,' " in *New American Review* (New York: New American Library, 1967), 166–82; Fiedler, "New Mutants," 379–400; Sontag, "Notes on 'Camp,' " 292.

60. Christine Riddiough, "Culture and Politics," in *Pink Triangles: Radical Perspectives on Gay Liberation*, ed. Pam Mitchell (Boston: Alyson, 1980), 14–33.

61. See Ann Koedt, "Lesbianism and Feminism," in *Radical Feminism* (New York: Quadrangle, 1973), and Adrienne Rich's critique of gay male sexuality, quoted in Faderman, *Odd Girls*, 211–12; Barry Adams, *Rise of a Gay and Lesbian Movement*, 94, 98; Duberman, *Stonewall*, 149.

62. John Rechy, *City of Night* (New York: Grove Weidenfeld, 1963, 1988), 106; Duberman, *Stonewall*, 225.

63. Lippard, "New York Pop," 87.

64. "The Snooty Dame at the Block Party," *New York Times*, 24 October 1993, sec. 6, p. 121.

65. J.C. Thomas, *Chasin' the Trane: The Music and Mystique of John Coltrane* (New York: DaCapo, 1975), 143, 148 (hereafter cited as *John Coltrane*); Frank Kofsky, *Black Nationalism and the Revolution in Music* (New York: Pathfinder Press, 1970), 167 (hereafter cited as *Revolution in Music*).

66. Thomas, *John Coltrane*, 169–70, 219; Kofsky, *Revolution in Music*, 191–94.

67. Robert Shelton, quoted in Robbie Woliver, *Hoot: A Twenty-Five-Year History of the Greenwich Village Music Scene* (New York: St. Martin's Press, 1986), 31; Anthony Scaduto, *Dylan: An Intimate Biography* (New York: New American Library, 1973), 110, 74–75, 135.

68. Scaduto, *Dylan: An Intimate Biography*, 25, 139–40, 204–5, 209, 293.

69. Jonathan Cott, *Dylan* (Garden City, N.Y.: Doubleday, 1984), 158; Scaduto, *Dylan: An Intimate Biography*, 305.

70. Myra Friedman, *Buried Alive: The Biography of Janis Joplin* (New York: William Morrow, 1973), 123–24, 198; Ellen Willis, "Janis Joplin," in *Rolling Stone Illustrated History of Rock and Roll*, ed. Jim Miller (New York: Rolling Stone, 1980), 275–79.

Chapter Five

1. Martin Luther King Jr., "Nonviolence and Racial Justice," in *A Testament of Hope: The Essential Writings and Speeches of Martin Luther King, Jr.*, ed. James M. Washington (New York: HarperCollins, 1986), 8 (hereafter cited as *Testament of Hope*); Lyndon

Johnson, quoted in Frederick F. Siegel, *Troubled Journey: From Pearl Harbor to Ronald Reagan* (New York: Hill and Wang, 1984), 175 (hereafter cited as *Troubled Journey*); *The Documents of Vatican II* (New York: Herder and Herder, 1966), 230–31, 283–84.

2. On protest against development and urban renewal, see Robert Caro, *The Power Broker* (New York: Knopf, 1974), 868–75, and Marshall Berman, *All That Is Solid Melts into Air* (New York: Simon and Schuster, 1982), 326; "Prologue: Florence Scala, 47," in *Division Street, America,* by Studs Terkel (New York: Pantheon, 1967), 1–10; *The Last Tenement: Confronting Community and Urban Renewal in Boston's West End* (Boston: Bostonian Society, 1992). On the Woodlawn Organization, see Robert Fisher, *Let the People Decide: Neighborhood Organizing in America* (New York: Twayne, 1994), 141–44, and John Hall Fish, *Black Power/White Control: The Struggle of the Woodlawn Organization in Chicago* (Princeton: Princeton University Press, 1973); on white anti-integration campaigns, see Arnold R. Hirsch, "Massive Resistance in the Urban North: Trumbull Park, Chicago, 1953–1966," *Journal of American History* 82 (September 1995): 522–50; Thomas J. Sugrue, "Crabgrass-Roots Politics: Race, Rights, and the Reaction against Liberalism in the Urban North, 1940–1964," *Journal of American History* 82 (September 1995): 551–78.

3. Charles Abrams, "The Case for the City: Washington Sq. and the Revolt of the Urbs," in *The Village Voice Reader,* ed. Daniel Wolf and Edwin Fancher (Garden City, N.Y.: Doubleday, 1962); Jane Jacobs, *The Death and Life of Great American Cities* (New York: Vintage, 1961), 4, 409, 14–15.

4. Jane Jacobs, *Death and Life of Great American Cities,* 149, 154, 167–68.

5. Lewis Mumford, "Mother Jacobs' Home Remedies," *New Yorker,* 1 December 1962, 148–79; Mumford, *The Highway and the City* (New York: Harcourt Brace Jovanovich, 1963).

6. Percival Goodman and Paul Goodman, *Communitas: Means of Livelihood and Ways of Life* (New York: Vintage Books, 1960), 10.

7. Fred Matthews, *Quest for an American Sociology: Robert E. Park and the Chicago School* (Montreal: McGill-Queens University Press, 1977).

8. James B. Gilbert, *A Cycle of Outrage* (New York: Oxford University Press, 1986), 134–39; Mark Gould, *Revolution in the Development of Capitalism* (Berkeley: University of California Press, 1987), 71–82; Matusow, *Unraveling of America,* 97–127; James T. Patterson, *America's Struggle against Poverty, 1900–1985* (Cambridge: Harvard University Press, 1986), 138–40.

9. Michael Katz, *In the Shadow of the Poorhouse: A Social History of Welfare in America* (New York: Basic Books, 1986), 254–56.

10. Daryl Michael Scott, "The Politics of Pathology: The Intellectual Origins of the Moynihan Controversy," *Journal of Policy History* 8 (1996): 81–105 (hereafter cited as "Politics of Pathology"); Scott, *Contempt and Pity: Social Policy and the Image of the Damaged Black Psyche, 1880–1996* (Chapel Hill: University of North Carolina Press, 1997), 337–60.

11. Jo Ann Robinson, *The Montgomery Bus Boycott and the Women Who Started It* (Knoxville: University of Tennessee Press, 1987); Mark Gerson, *The Neoconservative Vision: From the Cold War to the Culture Wars* (New York: Madison Books, 1996), 91–102; Nash, *Conservative Intellectual Movement in America,* 278–79. Moynihan, *Maximum Feasible Misunderstanding* (New York: Free Press, 1969).

12. Frank Riessman, quoted in Scott, "Politics of Pathology," 100.

13. Statement by Elizabeth Wickenden in 1964, quoted in James T. Patterson, *America's Struggle against Poverty*, 150.

14. Matusow, *Unraveling of America*, 121–26, and James T. Patterson, *America's Struggle against Poverty*, 135, 143.

15. Casey Hayden, "Raising the Question of Who Decides," *New Republic* 154 (22 January 1966), quoted in Sara Evans, *Personal Politics* (New York: Random House, 1979), 126; Wini Breines, *Community and Organization in the New Left, 1962–1968* (New York: Praeger, 1982).

16. Evans, *Personal Politics*; Jennifer Ann Frost, "Participatory Politics: Community Organizing, Gender, and the New Left in the 1960s" (Ph.D. diss., University of Wisconsin—Madison, 1996); Guida West, *The National Welfare Rights Movement: The Social Protest of Poor Women* (New York: Praeger, 1981).

17. Sterling Stuckey, *Slave Culture: Nationalist Theory and the Foundations of Black America* (New York: Oxford University Press, 1987).

18. Martin Staniland, *American Intellectuals and African Nationalists, 1955–1970* (New Haven: Yale University Press, 1991), 178–213; George Breitman, ed., *Malcolm X Speaks: Selected Speeches and Statements* (New York: Grove Press, 1965), 217 (emphasis added).

19. Quoted in George Breitman, *The Last Year of Malcolm X: The Evolution of a Revolutionary* (New York: Pathfinder, 1967), 49–50.

20. Richard H. King, *Civil Rights and the Idea of Freedom* (New York: Oxford University Press, 1992), 86.

21. Clayborne Carson, *In Struggle: SNCC and the Black Awakening of the 1960s* (Cambridge: Harvard University Press, 1981), 93 (emphasis added).

22. Bayard Rustin, "From Protest to Politics: The Future of the Civil Rights Movement," *Commentary* 39 (February 1965): 25–31.

23. Stokely Carmichael and Charles V. Hamilton, *Black Power* (New York: Vintage, 1967).

24. Larry Neal, "And Shine Swam On" (1968), in *Visions of a Liberated Future: Black Arts Movement Writing*, ed. Michael Schwartz (New York: Thunder's Mouth Press, 1989), 14.

25. Roy Innis, quoted in William Van Deburg, *New Day in Babylon: The Black Power Movement and American Culture, 1965–1975* (Chicago: University of Chicago Press, 1992), 137 (hereafter cited as *New Day in Babylon*); Nikki Giovanni, quoted in Van Deburg, *New Day in Babylon*, 282–83; LeRoi Jones, "Black Art," in *Black Fire*, 302–3.

26. Harold Cruse, *The Crisis of the Negro Intellectual* (New York: Morrow, 1967), 329.

27. LeRoi Jones and Larry Neal, *Black Fire: An Anthology of Afro-American Writing* (New York: Morrow, 1968).

28. Cruse, *Crisis of the Negro Intellectual*, 452, 455, 541–43.

29. Michael Bérubé, *Marginal Forces/Cultural Centers* (Ithaca, N.Y.: Cornell University Press, 1992); James Farmer, *Lay Bare the Heart: An Autobiography of the Civil Rights Movement* (New York: Arbor House, 1985), 117–42.

30. Bérubé, *Marginal Forces*, 177–78; Rita Dove, "Telling It Like It I-S *IS*: Narrative Techniques in Melvin Tolson's *Harlem Gallery*," *New England Review and Bread Loaf Quarterly* 8 (1985): 109–17.

31. M. B. Tolson, *Harlem Gallery: Book I, The Curator* (New York: Twayne Publishers, 1965), 60, 72, 146, 77, 91, 101, 167, 136, 102, 173, 146.

32. Mary Schmidt Campbell and Sharon Patton, *Memory and Metaphor: The Art of Romare Bearden, 1940–1987* (Oxford University Press, 1991), 21–22, 24, 12–15, 8, 69–70.

33. Ibid., 44, 30, 36, 9, 16.

34. W. E. B. Du Bois, *The Souls of Black Folk* (New York: NAL, 1969), 45.

35. Albert Stone, *The Return of Nat Turner: History, Literature, and Cultural Politics in Sixties America* (Athens: University of Georgia Press, 1992).

36. Larry Neal, "The Social Background of the Black Arts Movement," *Black Scholar* 18 (January–February 1987), 22.

37. Neal, *Visions of a Liberated Future*, 180.

38. Ibid., 53, 85–86.

39. Larry Neal, *The Glorious Monster in the Bell of the Horn*, excerpted in *Visions of a Liberated Future*, 150–67.

40. Paule Marshall, *Brown Girl, Brownstones* (New York: Avon, 1959), 70.

41. Toni Cade, *The Black Woman* (New York: NAL, 1970); Toni Morrison, *The Bluest Eye* (New York: Plume, 1994), 209–16.

42. Ronald Radano, *New Musical Figurations: Anthony Braxton's Cultural Critique* (Chicago: University of Chicago Press, 1993), 103 n (hereafter cited as *New Musical Figurations*).

43. Citations of Schiller and Shelley appear in Thaddeus Ashby and Rita Ashby, "On the Possibilities of an LSD Utopia," *The Oracle of Southern California*, no. 3 (June 1967), and Frederick Adams, "The Love-In of the Spring Equinox," *Oracle*, no. 1 (March 1967).

44. D. T. Suzuki, *What Is Zen?* (New York: Harper and Row, 1972), and *An Introduction to Zen Buddhism* (New York: Grove Press, 1964); Watts, *Beat Zen, Square Zen, and Zen* (San Francisco: City Lights, 1959), and *The Joyous Cosmology* (New York: Vintage, 1962).

45. John Gruen, *The New Bohemia: The Combine Generation* (New York: Shorecrest, 1966), 6–18. See also Banes, *Greenwich Village 1963*, 7.

46. Scaduto, *Dylan, An Intimate Biography*, 209, 254.

47. Jay Stevens, *Storming Heaven: LSD and the American Dream* (New York: Atlantic Monthly Press, 1987), and Martin A. Lee and Bruce Shlain, *Acid Dreams: The Complete Social History of LSD: The CIA, the Sixties, and Beyond* (New York: Grove Weidenfeld, 1992).

48. Stan Russell, "Maslow's Model Mutant," *Oracle of Southern California* (hereafter cited as *Oracle*), no. 2 (April–May 1967): 10; Liza Williams, untitled letter to Allen Ginsberg, *Oracle*, no. 1 (March 1967): 11; "How to Start Your Own Religion," *Oracle*, no. 3 (June 1967); Frederick Adams, "The Love-In of the Spring Equinox," *Oracle*, no. 1 (March 1967): 11; "Peter Bergman on the Hopi Indian," *Oracle*, no. 1 (March 1967): 6; Lawrence Lipton, "I Ching (The Book of Changes)," *Oracle*, no. 1 (March 1967): 17; Gridley Wright, interview, *Oracle*, no. 3 (June 1967): 3–5; Alan Watts, interview by Nat Freeland, *Oracle*, no. 2 (April–May 1967): 3.

49. Lipton, "I Ching (The Book of Changes)," *Oracle*, no. 1 (March 1967): 17.

50. This characterization of the late-emerging counterculture is indebted to conversations with Joseph G. Fracchia. For a slightly different perspective, see Doug

Rossinow, "The New Left in the Counterculture: Hypotheses and Evidence," *Radical History Review*, no. 67 (Winter 1997): 79–120.

51. Theodore Roszak, *The Making of a Counter Culture: Reflections on the Technocratic Society and Its Youthful Opposition* (Garden City, N.Y.: Doubleday, 1969), 2, 49.

52. Gary Snyder, "A Curse on the Men in Washington, Pentagon," *San Francisco Oracle* (1967); Glenn W. Jones, "Gentle Thursday," in *Sights on the Sixties*, ed. Barbara Tischler (New Brunswick, N.J.: Rutgers University Press, 1992), 87; Ellwood, *Sixties Spiritual Awakening*, 20.

53. Frederick Adams, "Love-In of the Spring Equinox," 11.

54. Kenneth Keniston, *Young Radicals: Notes on Committed Youth* (New York: Harcourt Brace Jovanovich, 1968); Amitai Etzioni, *The Active Society* (New York: Free Press, 1968); Philip Slater, *The Pursuit of Loneliness* (Boston: Beacon Press, 1970); David Steigerwald, *The Sixties and the End of Modern America* (New York: St. Martin's Press, 1995), 154, 184–86.

55. Joan Didion, *Slouching toward Bethlehem* (New York: Dell, 1968), 122–23, 120–21.

56. Lippmann, quoted in Siegel, *Troubled Journey*, 176.

57. Parsons, "Kinship and Associational Aspects of Social Structure," 409–38.

58. Larry Hirschhorn, "The Counter-Culture in the Transition to Post-Industrialism," in "Two Essays on the Transition to Post-Industrialism," Working Paper 170 (Berkeley: Institute for Urban and Regional Development, University of California, 1972), 19–36.

59. Ellwood, *Sixties Spiritual Awakening*, 37.

60. David Colburn and George E. Pozzetta, "Race, Ethnicity, and the Evolution of Political Legitimacy," in *The Sixties: From Memory to History*, ed. David Farber (Chapel Hill: University of North Carolina Press), 137–38.

61. Carlos Muñoz, *Youth, Identity, Power: The Chicano Generation* (New York: Verso, 1989); Stephen Cornell, *The Return of the Native: American Indian Political Resurgence* (Oxford: Oxford University Press, 1988).

62. D'Arcy McNickle, *The Indian Tribes of the United States: Ethnic and Cultural Survival* (New York: Oxford University Press, 1962); Vine Deloria Jr., *Custer Died for Your Sins: An Indian Manifesto* (New York: Macmillan, 1969).

63. Ramón A. Gutiérrez, "Community, Patriarchy, and Individualism: The Politics of Chicano History and the Dream of Equality," *American Quarterly* 45 (March 1993): 44–47.

64. George Sánchez, *Becoming Mexican American* (Berkeley: University of California Press, 1993), 9.

65. Rudolfo Anaya, *Bless Me, Ultima* (New York: Warner Books, 1972), 249.

66. Coser, *In Defense of Modernity*, 168.

67. James Tully, *Strange Multiplicity: Constitutionalism in an Age of Diversity* (Cambridge: Cambridge University Press, 1995).

Chapter Six

1. Daniel Bell, preface to *The Age of Automation*, by Leon Bagrit (New York: NAL, 1965), xii; William S. Burroughs, *Naked Lunch* (New York: Grove Weidenfeld, 1992), 148–49.

2. The flagship journal of Ludwig von Bertalanffy's scientific circle, *General Systems,* began publishing in the late 1950s. See also Bertalanffy, *General System Theory—Foundations, Development, Applications* (New York: Braziller, 1968); Ervin Laszlo, *Introduction to Systems Philosophy* (New York: Gordon and Breach, 1972).

3. Anatol Rapoport, "General Systems Theory," in *International Encyclopedia of the Social Sciences,* ed. David L. Sills, vol. 15 (New York: Macmillan, 1968), 452–55.

4. Norbert Wiener, *The Human Uses of Human Beings* (New York: Avon Books, 1954, 1967), 38.

5. Robert Boguslaw, *The New Utopians: A Study of System Design and Social Change* (Englewood Cliffs, N.J.: Prentice-Hall, 1965), 29 (hereafter cited as *New Utopians*).

6. David Halberstam, *The Best and the Brightest* (New York: Ballantine, 1992), 213–50.

7. Boguslaw, *New Utopians,* 126, 159, 178.

8. On systems theory as a technocratic worldview, see Robert Lilienfeld, *The Rise of Systems Theory: An Ideological Analysis* (New York: John Wiley and Sons, 1978).

9. "An Editorial," *Journal of Conflict Resolution: A Quarterly for Research Related to War and Peace* 1 (March 1957): 2.

10. Howard Gardner, *The Mind's New Science: A History of the Cognitive Revolution* (New York: Basic Books, 1985), 3–45.

11. Donald Worster, *Nature's Economy* (New York: Cambridge University Press, 1985), 304.

12. Jim O'Brien, "Environmentalism as a Mass Movement: Historical Notes," *Radical America* 17 (1983): 7–27; Roger Gottlieb, "Reconstructing Environmentalism: Complex Movements, Diverse Roots," *Environmental History Review* 17 (1993): 1–19 (hereafter cited as "Reconstructing Environmentalism"); H. Patricia Hynes, "Ellen Swallow, Lois Gibbs, and Rachel Carson: Catalysts of the American Environmental Movement," *Women's Studies International Forum* 8 (1985): 291–98; Kirkpatrick Sale, *The Green Revolution* (New York: Hill and Wang, 1993); Rachel Carson, *Silent Spring* (Boston: Houghton Mifflin, 1962); Lewis Herber [Murray Bookchin], *Our Synthetic Environment* (New York: Knopf, 1962).

13. Barry Commoner, *The Closing Circle: Nature, Man, and Technology* (New York: Knopf, 1971), 35 (hereafter cited as *Closing Circle*); Daniel J. Kevles, "Greens in America," *New York Review of Books,* 6 October 1994, 35–40; Gottlieb, "Reconstructing Environmentalism," 11–13; David M. Gates, "Toward Understanding Ecosystems," *Advances in Ecological Research* 5 (1968): 2.

14. Gottlieb, "Reconstructing Environmentalism," 12; Kevles, "Greens in America"; Barry Commoner, "Feasibility of Biological Recovery from Nuclear Attack," *Ramparts,* December 1966, 20–26; Commoner, *Closing Circle,* 11–44.

15. Norbert Wiener, *Human Uses of Human Beings,* 153–55, 164, 170, 176.

16. Ibid., 70–71, 167, 254, 166, 72, 179, 129.

17. Ibid., 130.

18. Gregory Bateson, "From Versailles to Cybernetics" (1966), in *Steps to an Ecology of Mind* (Northvale, N.J.: Jason Aronson, 1972, 1987), 485.

19. Gregory Bateson, "Form, Substance, and Difference" (1970), in *Steps to an Ecology of Mind,* 454–71.

20. See Jacob Neusner, *History of the Jews in Babylonia,* vol. 3, *From Shapur I to Shapur II* (Leiden: E. J. Brill, 1968), *The Idea of Purity in Ancient Judaism* (Leiden: E. J. Brill, 1973), *The Transformation of Judaism: From Philosophy to Religion* (Urbana: University of

Illinois Press, 1992), and "Holy Writing: The Social Setting," *Method and Theory in the Study of Religion* 3 (1991): 84–99; Wendy Doniger O'Flaherty, *Siva: The Erotic Ascetic* (New York: Oxford University Press, 1973); Jonathan Z. Smith, *Map Is Not Territory: Studies in the History of Religion* (Chicago: University of Chicago Press, 1978).

21. Bateson, *Steps to an Ecology of the Mind*, 467–68.

22. Bertalanffy, quoted in *Encyclopedia Britannica*, 15th ed., s.v. "Religious Experience—the Experience of Mysticism," by Sisirkumar Ghose.

23. Potter, quoted in James Miller, *"Democracy Is in the Streets": From Port Huron to the Siege of Chicago* (New York: Simon and Schuster, 1987), 232 (hereafter cited as *Democracy Is in the Streets*).

24. Paul Buhle, ed., *History and the New Left: Madison, Wisconsin, 1950–1970* (Philadelphia, Pa.: Temple University Press, 1990).

25. Robert Wiebe, *The Search for Order, 1877–1920* (New York: Hill and Wang, 1967); Michael B. Katz, *The Irony of Early School Reform* (Cambridge: Harvard University Press, 1968); David Rothman, *Discovery of the Asylum: Social Order and Disorder in the New Republic* (Boston: Little, Brown, 1971).

26. Martin Jay, *The Dialectical Imagination* (Boston: Little, Brown, 1973), 277.

27. Sontag, *Against Interpretation and Other Essays*, 278, 288; Sontag, *Styles of Radical Will* (New York: Farrar, Straus and Giroux, 1969), 74–95.

28. Norman O. Brown, *Love's Body* (New York: Vintage, 1966), 217, 243, 262.

29. Ibid., 235.

30. Norman O. Brown, "A Reply to Herbert Marcuse," *Commentary* 43 (March 1967): 83.

31. Emmett Grogan, *Ringolevio: A Life Played for Keeps* (Boston: Little, Brown, 1972), 300–303.

32. Tawa, *Wondrous Babble*, 57.

33. Milton Babbitt, "Who Cares If You Listen?" 38–40; Benjamin Boretz, "A Note on Discourse," *Perspectives on New Music* 4 (1966): 79; James A. Davis, "Philosophical Positivism and American Atonal Music Theory," *Journal of the History of Ideas* (1995): 501–22.

34. Richard D. Burbank, *Charles Wuorinen: A Bio-Bibliography* (Westport, Conn.: Greenwood Press, 1994), 1–25.

35. Cage, "Experimental Music" (Winter 1957), in *Silence: Lectures and Writings* (Middletown, Conn.: Wesleyan University Press, 1961), 7–12.

36. Quoted, in notes by Richard Teitelbaum to Cage's *Variations II* on the LP *New Electronic Music from Leaders of the Avant-Garde*, Columbia Masterworks, Music of Our Time Series, Stereo MS 7051.

37. Ibid. See also Marjorie Perloff and Charles Junkerman, eds., *John Cage: Composed in America* (Chicago: University of Chicago Press, 1994), 10, 12.

38. Tawa, *Wondrous Babble*, 93.

39. Quoted in notes by Richard Teitelbaum, *New Electronic Music*. See also Michael Chanan, "A Quartet for Our Times," *New Left Review* 201 (September—October 1993), 106–7.

40. Tawa, *Wondrous Babble*, 15–16.

41. Perloff and Junkerman, *John Cage: Composed in America*, 6, 9.

42. Steve Reich, interview by Edward Strickland, in *American Composers*, by Edward Strickland (Bloomington: Indiana University Press, 1991), 33–50.

43. Radano, *New Musical Figurations*, 107–8.

44. In 1967 and 1968, *Ramparts* gave extensive coverage to conspiracy theories of the Kennedy assassination. See also Richard H. Popkin, "The Second Oswald: The Case for a Conspiracy Theory," *New York Review of Books*, 28 July 1966, 11–22; Thomas G. Paterson, *Kennedy's Quest for Victory;* Max Holland, "After Thirty Years: Making Sense of the Assassination," *Reviews in American History* 22 (June 1994): 191–209.

45. Lawrence Daw, quoted in Michael Bérubé, *Marginal Forces,* 307.

46. Thomas Pynchon, *Gravity's Rainbow* (New York: Viking, 1973), 75, 412.

47. Michael Bérubé makes a similar point in *Marginal Forces,* 269.

48. Bersani, quoted in Bérubé, *Marginal Forces,* 231.

49. On Pynchon's early reading of Wiener, see *Slow Learner: Early Stories* (Boston: Little, Brown, 1984), 3–23.

50. Pynchon, *Gravity's Rainbow,* 434.

51. David Leverenz, "On Trying to Read Gravity's Rainbow," quoted Bérubé, *Marginal Forces,* 276.

52. On the "redemptive vision" in Pynchon's work, see Paul Morris, "Beyond the Zero: *Gravity's Rainbow* and Modern Critical Theory" (Ph.D. diss., City University of New York, 1982).

53. Mike Davis, *City of Quartz: Excavating the Future in Los Angeles* (New York: Vintage, 1992), 66–67.

54. Herbert Marcuse, "Love Mystified: A Critique of Norman O. Brown," *Commentary* 43 (February 1967): 73.

55. John Cage, *Diary: How to Improve the World (You Will Only Make Matters Worse) Continued, Part Three* (West Glover, Vt.: Something Else Press, 1967).

Chapter Seven

1. Richard Hofstadter, "Reflections on Violence in the United States," in *American Violence: A Documentary History,* ed. Richard Hofstadter and Michael Wallace (New York: Alfred A. Knopf, 1970), 3.

2. Lawrence Freedman, "The First Two Generations of Nuclear Strategists," in *Makers of Modern Strategy from Machiavelli to the Nuclear Age,* ed. Peter Paret (Princeton: Princeton University Press, 1986), 735–78 (hereafter cited as "First Two Generations").

3. Marc Trachtenberg, "Strategic Thought in America, 1952–1966," *Political Science Quarterly* 104 (Summer 1989): 307.

4. Albert Wohlstetter, "The Delicate Balance of Terror," *Foreign Affairs* 37 (January 1959): 211–34.

5. Fred Kaplan, *The Wizards of Armageddon* (New York: Simon and Schuster, 1983), 285, 319–20.

6. Quoted in Freedman, "First Two Generations," 757–58.

7. Kenneth Heinemann, *Campus Wars: The Peace Movement at American State Universities in the Vietnam Era* (New York: New York University Press, 1993), 18–19 (hereafter cited as *Campus Wars*).

8. "The University on the Make," *Ramparts* 4 (April 1966): 11–22. Charles Waugh, "Two Worlds Collide: Michigan State in South Vietnam," (M.A. thesis, University of Oregon, June 1996).

9. Amy Swerdlow, *Women Strike for Peace: Traditional Motherhood and Radical Politics in the 1960s* (Chicago: University of Chicago Press, 1993); Charles DeBenedetti, with Charles Chatfield, *An American Ordeal: The Antiwar Movement of the Vietnam Era*

(Syracuse, N.Y.: Syracuse University Press, 1990), 55 (hereafter cited as *American Ordeal*).

10. Milton S. Katz, *Ban the Bomb: A History of SANE, the Committee for a Sane Nuclear Policy, 1957–1985* (New York: Greenwood Press, 1986), 1–64.

11. Joseph Rotblat, *Scientists in the Quest for Peace: A History of the Pugwash Conferences* (Cambridge: MIT Press, 1972), 1–10, 141–47.

12. H. Stuart Hughes, "The Strategy of Deterrence: A Dissenting Statement," *Commentary* 31 (March 1961): 185–92 (hereafter cited as "Strategy of Deterrence").

13. Maurice Isserman, *If I Had a Hammer . . . The Death of the Old Left and the Birth of the New Left* (New York: Basic Books, 1987), 125–69; A.J. Muste, "Politics on the Other Side of Despair," in *Seeds of Liberation*, ed. Paul Goodman (New York: George Braziller, 1964), 63–73.

14. Hughes, "Strategy of Deterrence," 192; Irving Kristol and H. Stuart Hughes, "Controversy: Deterrence," *Commentary* 32 (July 1961): 64–67; Erich Fromm, "The Case for Unilateral Disarmament," *Daedalus* 89 (Fall 1960): 1015–28.

15. Tom Wells, *War Within*, 146; John S. Friedman, *First Harvest*.

16. Martin Luther King Jr., *Testament of Hope*, 60.

17. Greg Moses, *Revolution of Conscience: Martin Luther King, Jr., and the Philosophy of Nonviolence* (New York: Guilford, 1997), 21, 58, 60, 148, 152–55, 158–63, 176.

18. Bernard Fall, *The Two Viet-Nams: A Political and Military Analysis* (New York: Praeger, 1963); Marcus Raskin and Bernard Fall, *The Vietnam Reader* (New York: Random, 1965); Bernard Fall, *Viet-Nam Witness, 1953–1966* (New York: Praeger, 1966). Paul Mus, a former diplomat and student of Southeast Asian culture, published *Viet Nam: sociologie d'une guerre* (Paris: Editions du Seuil) in 1952, but because his work was not translated into English, it was largely unknown, except to a small number of Yale students, until one of them published an English-language version of Mus's writings: John T. McAlister and Paul Mus, *The Vietnamese and Their Revolution* (New York: Harper and Row, 1970).

19. Daniel C. Hallin, *The "Uncensored War": The Media and Vietnam* (New York: Oxford University Press, 1986); Kirkpatrick Sale, *SDS* (New York: Vintage, 1973), 213–14.

20. David Levy, *The Debate over Vietnam* (Baltimore, Md.: Johns Hopkins University Press, 1991), 133–34; Wells, *War Within*, 71, 98–99, 114; Robert McNamara, *In Retrospect: The Tragedy and Lessons of Vietnam* (New York: Times Books, 1995).

21. William A. Williams, *The Tragedy of American Diplomacy* (Cleveland, Ohio: World, 1959; 2d ed., New York: Dell, 1962); D. F. Fleming, *The Cold War and Its Origins, 1917–1960* (New York: Doubleday, 1961); and Gar Alperovitz, *Atomic Diplomacy* (New York: Simon and Schuster, 1965).

22. Robert Wuthnow, *The Restructuring of American Religion: Society and Faith since World War II* (Princeton: Princeton University Press, 1988), 132–72 (hereafter cited as *Restructuring of American Religion*); Mitchell K. Hall, *Because of Their Faith: CALCAV and Religious Opposition to the Vietnam War* (New York: Columbia University Press, 1990).

23. Cabral, in Walter Lowenfels, ed., *Where Is Vietnam? American Poets Respond* (Garden City, N.Y.: Anchor, 1967), 20–21 (hereafter cited as *Where Is Vietnam?*); Dan Georgakas, "19??" in Lowenfels, *Where Is Vietnam?*, 41; Allen Ginsberg, *Wichita Vortex Sutra* (London: Housmans, 1966).

24. Galway Kinnell, "How Many Nights," from *The 1968 Peace Calendar*, ed. Denise Levertov for the War Resisters League, 1967; and Marge Piercy, "Community,"

in *Hard Loving* (1969), quoted in James Mersmann, *Out of the Vietnam Vortex: A Study of Poets and Poetry against the War* (Lawrence, Kans.: University Press of Kansas, 1974), 238, 236.

25. Lowenfels, *Where Is Vietnam?*, xi–xii.

26. Sheehan Sullivan, "Protest Art and the Vietnam War" (unpublished paper, University of Oregon, fall 1995).

27. Arthur Danto, "Edward Kienholz," *Nation*, 10 June 1996, 33–35.

28. Heineman, *Campus Wars*, 44–45.

29. Wells, *War Within*, 91.

30. DeBenedetti, *American Ordeal*, 115.

31. Wells, *War Within*, 148.

32. Levy, *Debate over Vietnam*, 85; Nash, *Conservative Intellectual Movement in America*, 267–73; Paul L. Montgomery, "Vietnam Debated by Intellectuals," *New York Times*, 16 January 1966, 5, and "A Talk-In on Vietnam," *New York Times*, 6 February 1966, sec. 6, p. 12.

33. Rorabaugh, *Berkeley at War*, 93.

34. "A Call to Resist Illegitimate Authority," *New York Review of Books*, 12 October 1967; see also Sandy Vogelgesang, *The Long Dark Night of the Soul: The American Intellectual Left and the Vietnam War* (New York: Harper and Row, 1974), 125 (hereafter cited as *Long Dark Night*).

35. Robert Jay Lifton, "Beyond Atrocity," in *Crimes of War: A Legal, Political-Documentary, and Psychological Inquiry into the Responsibility of Leaders, Citizens, and Soldiers for Criminal Acts in Wars*, ed. Richard A. Falk, Gabriel Kolko, and Robert Jay Lifton (New York: Random House, 1971), 17.

36. Robert Jay Lifton, *Death in Life: Survivors of Hiroshima* (New York: Random House, 1968; Durham, N.C.: University of North Carolina Press, 1991), 14, 32–34.

37. Rapoport, in Menashe and Radosh, *Teach-Ins: USA*, 180.

38. Sol Stern, "War Catalog of the University of Pennsylvania," *Ramparts*, August 1966, 32–40.

39. Vogelgesang, *Long Dark Night*, 136.

40. Chomsky, *Prevent the Crime of Silence*, 21.

41. Sartre, in John Duffett, ed., *Against the Crime of Silence: Proceedings of the Russell International War Crimes Tribunal* (New York: O'Hare Books, 1968), 45.

42. Terry Anderson, *The Movement and the Sixties* (New York: Oxford University Press, 1995), 216; George Katsiaficas, *The Imagination of the New Left: A Global Analysis of 1968* (Boston: South End Press, 1987), 131 (hereafter cited as *Imagination of the New Left*); Siegel, *Troubled Journey*, 196.

43. *Violence in the City—an End or a Beginning: A Report by the Governor's Commission on the Los Angeles Riots* (McCone Report, December 1965), 23–24 (hereafter cited as *Violence in the City*).

44. Gerald Horne, *Fire This Time: The Watts Uprising and the 1960s* (Charlottesville: University Press of Virginia, 1995) (hereafter cited as *Watts Uprising and the 1960s*).

45. *Violence in the City*, 26, 28, 1, 4–5; Paul Jacobs, *Prelude to Riot: A View of Urban America from the Bottom* (New York: Random, 1967), 254–79, 293–95 (hereafter cited as *Prelude to Riot*).

46. Nelson, *Torture of Mothers*, 49–50, 67–68.

47. Horne, *Watts Uprising and the 1960s;* Sidney Fine, *Violence in the Model City: The Cavanaugh Administration, Race Relations, and the Detroit Riot of 1967* (Ann Arbor: University of Michigan Press, 1989).

48. Thomas Pynchon, "A Journey into the Mind of Watts," *New York Times Magazine,* 12 June 1966, 84.

49. John A. Williams, *The Man Who Cried I Am* (Boston: Little, Brown, 1967), 389.

50. Stokely Carmichael, "What We Want," *New York Review of Books,* 22 September 1966, 5.

51. Quoted in Hugh Pearson, *The Shadow of the Panther: Huey Newton and the Price of Black Power in America* (Reading, Mass.: Addison-Wesley, 1994), 96, 101, 140 (hereafter cited as *Shadow of the Panther*).

52. Tom Hayden, *Rebellion in Newark: Official Violence and Ghetto Response* (New York: Random, 1967), 69–71.

53. See Pearson, *Shadow of the Panther,* and Samuel Farber, "The Black Panthers Reconsidered," *Against the Current* 11 (September–October 1996): 22–31.

54. Wells, *War Within,* 297.

55. Pynchon, "Journey into the Mind of Watts," 84.

56. Saul Bellow, *Herzog* (New York: Viking, 1964, 1967), 316–17, 289–90.

57. Williams, *Man Who Cried I Am,* 387.

58. Sontag, quoted in Vogelgesang, *Long Dark Night.*

59. Hannah Arendt, *On Violence* (New York: Harcourt, Brace and World, 1970), 56.

60. Nancy Cott, Juliet Mitchell, and Ann Oakley, eds., *What Is Feminism?* (New York: Pantheon, 1986).

61. Alice Echols, *Daring to Be Bad: Radical Feminism in America, 1967–1975* (Minneapolis: University of Minnesota Press, 1989), 130–34 (hereafter cited as *Daring to Be Bad*).

62. Susan Griffin, "Rape: The All-American Crime," *Ramparts,* September 1971, 26–35.

Chapter Eight

1. William O'Neill, *Coming Apart: An Informal History of America in the 1960s* (Chicago: Quadrangle, 1971); Matusow, *Unraveling of America.*

2. *Report of the President's Commission on Campus Unrest* (New York: Arno Press, 1970), 1, 5.

3. George Breitman, "The Current Radicalization Compared with Those of the Past," *International Socialist Review,* October 1970, 7–9, 25–31.

4. Gitlin, *The Sixties: Years of Hope, Days of Rage,* 306–9; James Miller, *Democracy Is in the Streets,* 290–92; Jerry L. Avorn et al., *Up against the Ivy Wall* (New York: Atheneum, 1969); Ronald Fraser et al., *1968: A Student Generation in Revolt* (New York: Pantheon Books, 1988), 195–202; Christopher Brooks Phelps, "An Intellectual History of the Political Crisis of the University in the 1960s" (thesis, Reed College, 1988).

5. Lawrence E. Eichel et al., *The Harvard Strike* (Boston: Houghton Mifflin, 1970).

6. William Barlow and Peter Shapiro, *An End to Silence: The San Francisco State College Student Movement in the '60s* (New York: Pegasus, 1971); Kay Boyle, *The Long Walk at San Francisco State and Other Essays* (New York: Grove Press, 1970).

7. Katsiaficas, *Imagination of the New Left*, 127–30; Frank Boehm et al., *May 1970: Birth of the Antiwar University* (New York: Pathfinder Press, 1971).

8. Sidney Hook, "The Long View," in *In Defense of Academic Freedom*, ed. Sidney Hook (New York: Pegasus, 1971), 15; James McEvoy and Abraham Miller, eds., *Black Power and Student Rebellion* (Belmont, Calif.: Wadsworth, 1969), 5.

9. Richard Hofstadter, "The 214th Columbia University Commencement Address," *American Scholar* 37 (Autumn 1968): 587–88, 586.

10. Michael Wreszin, *A Rebel in Defense of Tradition: The Life and Politics of Dwight Macdonald* (New York: Basic Books, 1994), 455–56.

11. Jesse Lemisch, *On Active Service in War and Peace: Politics and Ideology in the American Historical Profession* (Toronto: New Hogtown Press, 1975) (hereafter cited as *On Active Service*).

12. Eugene Genovese, *In Red and Black: Marxian Explorations in Southern and Afro-American History* (New York: Pantheon, 1971), 4, 10–14.

13. Cheyney Ryan, interview by the author, Eugene, Oregon, 27 June 1995.

14. Katsiaficas, *Imagination of the New Left*, 125; Douglas M. Knight, *Street of Dreams: The Nature and Legacy of the 1960s* (Durham, N.C.: Duke University Press, 1989), 65.

15. Lucy Lippard, *Changing: Essays in Art Criticism* (New York: Dutton, 1971), 113; Harold Rosenberg, *The De-definition of Art: Action Art to Pop to Earthworks* (New York: Horizon Press, 1972), 212–16, 218–19, 232 (hereafter cited as *De-definition of Art*).

16. Sam Hunter, *American Art in the Twentieth Century* (New York: Harry N. Abrams, 1972), 209–10.

17. Robert Mangold, quoted in Lippard, *Changing: Essays in Art Criticism*, 132.

18. Lippard, *Changing: Essays in Art Criticism*, 102, 153; *Funk* (Berkeley: University Art Museum, 1967); William Rubin, *Dada, Surrealism, and Their Heritage* (New York: Museum of Modern Art, 1968).

19. Andy Warhol, *The Philosophy of Andy Warhol* (New York: Harcourt Brace Jovanovich), 6, 216–17; Rosenberg, *De-definition of Art*, 28–38.

20. Grace Glueck, "Hippies Protest at Dada Preview: 300 in Gentle Demonstration at Museum of Modern Art," *New York Times*, 26 March 1968, 21; Therese Schwartz, "The Politicalization of the Avant-Garde," *Art in America* 59 (November–December 1971): 100.

21. Ann Goldstein and Anne Rorimer, *Reconsidering the Object of Art: 1965–1975* (Cambridge: MIT Press, 1995), 13–15; Nina Felshin, ed., *But Is It Art? The Spirit of Art as Activism* (Seattle, Wash.: Bay Press, 1995), 17–22.

22. Hunter, *American Art in the Twentieth Century*, 391–92, 435; Goldstein and Rorimer, *Reconsidering the Object of Art*, 128–29.

23. Lucy R. Lippard, *Get the Message? A Decade of Art for Social Change* (New York: Dutton, 1984), 31–32.

24. Kramer, "Do You Believe in the Principle of Museums?" *New York Times*, 18 January 1970, D25.

25. Rosenberg, *De-definition of Art*, 28–38, and Nina Felshin, in *But Is It Art?* 22.

26. Quoted in Eva Cockcroft, John Weber, and Jim Cockcroft, *Toward a People's Art: The Contemporary Mural Movement* (New York: E. P. Dutton, 1977), 13 (emphasis added).

27. Rosenberg, *De-definition of Art*, 48.

28. All cited in Lemisch, *On Active Service*, 96, 103, 106–7.

29. Norman Podhoretz, *Breaking Ranks: A Political Memoir* (New York: Harper and Row, 1979), 302–3.

30. Daniel Bell, *The Cultural Contradictions of Capitalism* (New York: Basic Books, 1976).

31. Steven Marcus, *The Other Victorians: A Study of Sexuality and Pornography in Mid-Nineteenth-Century England* (New York: Basic Books, 1966), 242, 266–86.

32. Goffman, *Relations in Public*, x.

33. Tytell, *Living Theatre*, 197–252.

34. Paul Goodman, *The New Reformation: Notes of a Neolithic Conservative* (New York: Random House, 1970), 47–63.

35. See "New University Conference," *Radicals in the Professions Newsletter* [*RiP*], December 1967, 4; Karen Sachs, "At the AAA Meeting," *RiP*, December 1967, 12; David Norris, "Caucus for a New Political Science," *RiP*, June 1968.

36. James Peck, "The Roots of Rhetoric: The Professional Ideology of America's China Watchers," *Bulletin of Concerned Asian Scholars* 2 (October 1969): 59–69; Joseph Esherick, "Harvard on China: The Apologetics of Imperialism," *Bulletin of Concerned Asian Scholars* 4 (December 1972): 9–16; Paul A. Cohen, *Discovering History in China: American Historical Writing on the Recent Chinese Past* (New York: Columbia University Press, 1984), 97–147. Of the new scholarship, see Mark Selden, *The Yenan Way in Revolutionary China* (Cambridge: Harvard University Press, 1971); Joseph Esherick, *Reform and Revolution in China: The 1911 Revolution in Hunan and Hubei* (Berkeley: University of California Press, 1976).

37. Jonathan Mirsky, "The Myth of Mao's China," *New York Review of Books*, 30 May 1991, 19–20. For a more respectful retrospective, see Joseph Esherick, "Ten Theses on the Chinese Revolution," *Modern China* 21 (January 1995): 45–76.

38. "Radical Economics," *RiP* (November–December 1968): 17–19; and Victor D. Lippit, *Radical Political Economy: Explorations in Alternative Economic Analysis* (Armonk, N.Y.: M. E. Sharpe, 1996), 1–16. Examples of URPE-inspired and affiliated work are Stephen A. Marglin, "What Do Bosses Do? The Origins and Functions of Hierarchy in Capitalist Production," *Review of Radical Political Economics* 6 (Summer 1974): 60–112; Heidi I. Hartmann, "The Unhappy Marriage of Marxism and Feminism: Towards a More Progressive Union," in *Women and Revolution: A Discussion of the Unhappy Marriage of Marxism and Feminism*, ed. Lydia Sargent (Boston: South End Press, 1981); Richard C. Edwards, Michael Reich, and Thomas Weisskopf, *The Capitalist System: A Radical Analysis of American Society* (Englewood Cliffs, N.J.: Prentice-Hall, 1972); David M. Gordon, Richard C. Edwards, and Michael Reich, *Segmented Work, Divided Workers: The Historical Transformation of Labor in the United States* (New York: Cambridge 1982).

39. Armstead L. Robinson, preface to *Black Studies in the University*, ed. Armstead L. Robinson, Craig C. Foster, and Donald H. Ogilvie (New Haven: Yale University Press, 1969), viii.

40. Larry Neal papers, Schomburg Center for Research in Black Culture, professional papers, 1966–1981; Carlos Muñoz Jr., *Youth, Identity, Power: The Chicano Movement* (London: Verso, 1989), 127–69; Ellen Carol DuBois et al., *Feminist Scholarship* (Urbana: University of Illinois Press, 1985), 1–37.

41. George Fischer, ed., *The Revival of American Socialism: Selected Papers of the Socialist Scholars Conference* (New York: Oxford, 1971) (hereafter cited as *Revival of American Socialism*).

42. Jean-Paul Sartre, *Search for a Method*, trans. Hazel E. Barnes (New York: Knopf, 1963); Leszek Kolakowski, *Toward a Marxist Humanism: Essays on the Left Today* (New York: Grove Press, 1968); Fischer, *Revival of American Socialism*, 244–321.

43. Paul Baran and Paul Sweezy, *Monopoly Capital* (New York: Monthly Review Press, 1966), and Paul Mattick, *Marx and Keynes: The Limits of the Mixed Economy* (Boston: P. Sargent, 1969).

44. Other contributors to this current were philosopher Richard Lichtman, known for his lectures on Hegel and Marx at Berkeley in the late 1960s; James O'Connor, *The Fiscal Crisis of the State* (New York: St. Martin's Press, 1973); Eli Zaretsky, *Capitalism, the Family, and Personal Life* (New York: Harper and Row, 1976).

45. Martin J. Sklar, "On the Proletarian Revolution and the End of Political-Economic Society," *Radical America* 3 (May–June 1969), 8–9, 11, 34–35.

46. Arthur B. Shostak and William Gomberg, eds., *Blue-Collar World: Studies of the American Worker* (Englewood Cliffs, N.J.: Prentice-Hall, 1964).

47. Katsiaficas, *Imagination of the New Left*, 134–39; Dan Georgakas and Marvin Surkin, *Detroit: I Do Mind Dying* (New York: St. Martin's Press, 1975), 83–127; Kim Moody, *An Injury to All: The Decline of American Unionism* (New York: Verso, 1988), 90–91.

48. Echols, *Daring to be Bad*, 155, 167, 337 n.

49. See Dorwin Cartwright, ed., *Studies in Social Power* (Ann Arbor: University of Michigan Press, 1959); Ronald V. Sampson, *The Psychology of Power* (New York: Pantheon, 1965); the new sociology of deviance by Howard S. Becker and others; and other criticisms of the "helping professions" (including social service agencies), such as Jacobs, *Prelude to Riot*.

50. Shulamith Firestone and Anne Koedt, eds., *Notes from the Second Year: Women's Liberation: Major Writings of the Radical Feminists* (New York: n.p., 1970).

51. William H. Masters and Virginia E. Johnson, *Human Sexual Response* (Boston: Little, Brown, 1966), 27–168; Jane Gerhard, "Feminism, Sexual Liberalism, and Problems of Female Sexuality, 1969–1972" (paper presented at Annual Meeting of the Organization of American Historians, San Francisco, 18 April 1997.

52. Shulamith Firestone, *The Dialectic of Sex: The Case for Feminist Revolution* (New York: Morrow, 1970), 19, 37.

53. Ibid., 162, 224.

54. Kate Millett, *Sexual Politics* (New York: Doubleday, 1970), 215, 233, 343.

55. Ibid., 62.

56. See Michael Harrington, *Toward a Democratic Left: A Radical Program for a New Majority* (New York: Macmillan, 1968).

57. Recent considerations of guaranteed income appear in Philippe Van Parijs, ed., *Arguing for Basic Income: Ethical Foundations for Radical Reform* (London: Verso, 1992). For a history of income plans in the late 1960s, see Gareth Davies, *From Opportunity to Entitlement: The Transformation and Decline of Great Society Liberalism* (Lawrence: University Press of Kansas, 1996).

58. *Toward a Social Report* (Washington, D.C.: GPO, 1969), and Daniel Bell, *The Coming of Post-industrial Society* (New York: Basic Books, 1973), 331.

59. Alvin Gouldner, *The Coming Crisis of Western Sociology* (New York: Basic Books, 1970). See also Howard Brick, "The Reformist Dimension of Talcott Parsons's Early Social Theory," in *The Culture of the Market: Historical Essays*, ed. Thomas L. Haskell and Richard F. Teichgraeber III (New York: Cambridge University Press, 1993).

60. Bell, introduction to Bagrit, *Age of Automation*, xix.

61. Christopher Lasch and Eugene Genovese, "The Education and the University We Need Now," *New York Review of Books*, 9 October 1969, 23.

62. Jan Montefiore, review of *What Is Found There: Notebooks on Politics and Poetry*, by Adrienne Rich, *The Nation*, 7 February 1994, 169.

63. Katsiaficas, *Imagination of the New Left*, 161–64; Carnegie Commission on Higher Education, *Dissent and Disruption: Proposals for Consideration by the Campuses* (New York: McGraw Hill, 1971), 165–66; Michel Crozier, Samuel Huntington, and Joji Watanuke, *The Crisis of Democracy: Report on the Governability of Democracies to the Trilateral Commission* (New York: New York University Press, 1975), 113–14.

64. Richard Herrnstein, "I.Q.," *Atlantic*, September 1971, 43–64.

65. Robert Ardrey, *The Territorial Imperative* (New York: Atheneum, 1966); Konrad Lorenz, *On Aggression* (New York: Harcourt, Brace and World, 1966); Paul R. Ehrlich and Anne H. Ehrlich, *The End of Affluence* (Rivercity, Mass.: Rivercity Press, 1974, 1975), 7, 107, 8, 33–34, 256–57.

66. Kevin P. Phillips, *The Emerging Republican Majority* (New Rochelle, N.Y.: Arlington House, 1969); Richard M. Scammon and Ben J. Wattenberg, *The Real Majority* (New York: Coward-McCann, 1970).

67. Nash, *Conservative Intellectual Movement in America*, 225, 250, 293, 307–8, 314, 342–45.

68. Ibid., 320–28; Irving Kristol, *Neoconservatism* (New York: Free Press, 1995).

69. Wuthnow, *Restructuring of American Religion*, 173–214.

70. Thomas Ferguson and Joel Rogers, *Right Turn: The Decline of the Democrats and the Future of American Politics* (New York: Hill and Wang, 1986).

71. Juliet B. Schor, *The Overworked American: The Unexpected Decline of Leisure* (New York: Basic Books, 1991).

Bibliographic Essay

An excellent place to start in grasping the broad context of American thought and culture in the 1960s is Eric Hobsbawm's *Age of Extremes: A History of the World, 1914–1991* (New York: Pantheon, 1994) and James Patterson's *Grand Expectations: The United States, 1945–1974* (New York: Oxford University Press, 1996). For intriguing essays on a number of topics in social and cultural history of the time, see David Farber, ed., *The Sixties: From Memory to History* (Chapel Hill, N.C.: University of North Carolina Press, 1994). Another collection of essays, focused on debates regarding social policy, is Brian Balogh, ed., *Integrating the Sixties* (University Park: Pennsylvania University Press, 1996). The most comprehensive study of 1960s social movements is Terry Anderson, *The Movement and the Sixties: Protest in America from Greensboro to Wounded Knee* (New York: Oxford University Press, 1995). Alexander Bloom and Wini Breines have compiled a useful documentary collection, *"Takin' It to the Streets": A Sixties Reader* (New York: Oxford University Press, 1995).

The distinguished survey of intellectual developments in this period is Morris Dickstein's *Gates of Eden: American Culture in the Sixties* (New York: Basic Books, 1977), focusing on literary affairs and highlighting the emergence of a refreshingly critical, but innocent, disposition. Todd Gitlin's memoir and history, *The Sixties: Years of Hope, Days of Rage* (New York: Bantam, 1987), gives a good sense of the intellectual environment surrounding the activist life. George H. Nash, *The Conservative Intellectual Movement in America: Since 1945* (New York: Basic Books, 1976), examines discontent on the Right.

Loren Okroi's *Galbraith, Harrington, Heilbroner: Economics and Dissent in an Age of Optimism* (Princeton: Princeton University Press, 1988) examines the author most responsible for popularizing the phrase "the affluent society." Jeffrey C. Isaac's excellent *Arendt, Camus, and Modern Rebellion* (New Haven: Yale University Press, 1992) and Richard Wolin's *The Terms of Cultural Criticism: The Frankfurt School, Existentialism, Poststructuralism* (New York: Columbia University Press, 1992) help illuminate the significance of postwar existentialism. A number of informative studies examine the meaning of alienation and democracy for early 1960s activists, particularly James Miller, *"Democracy Is in the Streets": From Port Huron to the Siege of Chicago* (New York: Simon and Schuster, 1987), and Richard H. King, *Civil Rights and the Idea of Freedom* (New York: Oxford University Press, 1992). See also James Farrell's analysis of "personalism" in *The Spirit of the Sixties: The Making of Postwar Radicalism* (New York: Routledge, 1997).

General trends in the organization and administration of universities are examined in Richard Freeland, *Academia's Golden Age: Universities in Massachusetts, 1945–1970* (New York: Oxford University Press, 1992), and Roger L. Geiger, *Research and Relevant Knowledge: American Research Universities since World War II* (New York: Oxford University Press, 1993). More critical views appear in Stuart Leslie, *The Cold War and American Science: The Military-Industrial Complex at MIT and Stanford* (New York: Columbia University Press, 1993). In this vein, see also the informative essays in Noam Chomsky et al., *The Cold War and the University: Toward an Intellectual History of the Postwar Years* (New York: New Press, 1997). Regarding philosophy of science in this era, Paul Hoyningen-Huene provides the best account of Thomas Kuhn's thought in *Reconstructing Scientific Revolutions: Thomas S. Kuhn's Philosophy of Science* (Chicago: University of Chicago Press, 1993).

Margaret A. Rose, in *The Post-Modern and the Post-Industrial: A Critical Analysis* (Cambridge: Cambridge University Press, 1991), provides a historical etymology of these terms. For the rebirth of the avant-garde (often identified retrospectively with the rise of postmodernism), see Sally Banes, *Greenwich Village 1963: Avant-Garde Performance and the Effervescent Body* (Durham, N.C.: Duke University Press, 1993). William C. Seitz, *Art in the Age of Aquarius, 1955–1970* (Washington, D.C.: Smithsonian Institution, 1992), is an excellent survey of the visual arts. Ann Goldstein and Anne Rorimer, eds., *Reconsidering the Object of Art: 1965–1975* (Cambridge: MIT Press, 1995), focuses on the emergence of "conceptual art." For muralism, see Eva Cockcroft, John Weber, and Jim Cockcroft, *Toward a People's Art: The Contemporary Mural Movement* (New York: E. P. Dutton, 1977).

Marshall Berman's contemporaneous book, *The Politics of Authenticity: Radical Individualism and the Emergence of Modern Society* (New York: Atheneum, 1970) provides insight into that ideal of the 1960s. James E. B. Breslin's essay "Poetry," in *The Columbia Literary History of the United States*, ed. Emory Elliott (New York: Columbia University Press, 1988), surveys the various currents in post–World War II American poetry, including the "confessional" poets. Tom Burns's *Erving Goffman* (London: Routledge, 1992) is a good introduction to his studies of personhood in society.

The best scholarly account of an influential musicians' circle in new jazz—Chicago's AACM—is Ronald Radano, *New Musical Figurations: Anthony Braxton's Cultural Critique* (Chicago: University of Chicago Press, 1993). On folk music in the late 1950s and early 1960s, its origins and its spirit, see Robert Cantwell's wonderfully evocative *When We Were Good: The Folk Revival* (Cambridge: Harvard University Press, 1996). An engaging, opinionated account of recent American popular music is Martha Bayles, *Hole in Our Soul: The Loss of Beauty and Meaning in American Popular Music* (New York: Free Press, 1994); see also Robert Palmer's excellent *Rock and Roll: An Unruly History* (New York: Harmony Books, 1995). Nicholas Tawa's *A Most Wondrous Babble: American Art Composers, Their Music, and the American Music Scene, 1950–1985* (New York: Greenwood Press, 1987) covers currents of modern, avant-garde, and "new music."

Robert Fisher, *Let the People Decide: Neighborhood Organizing in America* (New York: Twayne, 1994), offers a wide-ranging survey of traditions in community organizing. James T. Patterson, *America's Struggle against Poverty, 1900–1985* (Cambridge: Harvard University Press, 1986), is the best general account setting Great Society policies in context. On the intellectual context for the Moynihan report and criticism of it, see Daryl Michael Scott's excellent study *Contempt and Pity: Social Policy and the Image of the Damaged Black Psyche, 1880–1996* (Chapel Hill: University of North Carolina Press, 1997). Gareth Davies's *From Opportunity to Entitlement: The Transformation and Decline of Great Society Liberalism* (Lawrence: University Press of Kansas, 1996) provides a thorough, though antagonistic, review of guaranteed income proposals in the late 1960s. For a more favorable view, from the standpoint of social and political theory, see Philippe Van Parijs, ed., *Arguing for Basic Income: Ethical Foundations for Radical Reform* (London: Verso, 1992).

On the long heritage of black nationalism in American life, see Sterling Stuckey, *Slave Culture: Nationalist Theory and the Foundations of Black America* (New York: Oxford University Press, 1987). On Black Power, see Clayborne Carson's consummate movement history *In Struggle: SNCC and the Black Awakening of the 1960s* (Cambridge: Harvard University Press, 1981) and William Van Deburg's *New Day in Babylon: The Black Power Movement and American Culture, 1965–1975* (Chicago: University of Chicago Press, 1992). For a survey of the early Chicano movement, see Carlos Muñoz, *Youth, Identity, Power: The Chicano Generation* (New York: Verso, 1989). For an overview of the Black Arts movement, see the new *Norton Anthology of African American Literature* (New York: Norton, 1997). For an excellent study that examines Chicano poems such as Rodolfo "Corky" Gonzales's "Yo Soy Joaquín" in the light of the evolving Chicano movement, see José Limón, *Mexican Ballads, Chicano Poems: History and Influence in Mexican-American Social Poetry* (Berkeley: University of California Press, 1992). To begin studying the American Indian literary revival of the late 1960s, begin with Andrew Wiget, *Native American Literature* (Boston: Twayne, 1985), and Robert Allen Warrior, *Tribal Secrets:*

Recovering American Indian Intellectual Traditions (Minneapolis: University of Minnesota Press, 1995).

There is no authoritative, synthetic historical study of the counterculture as a whole. For understanding important precursors, see Ann Charters, ed., *The Portable Beat Reader* (New York: Viking, 1992), and Richard Candida Smith's superb *Utopia and Dissent: Art, Poetry, and Politics in California* (Berkeley: University of California Press, 1995). Jon Wiener, *Come Together: John Lennon in His Time* (New York: Random House, 1984), is very useful as a biographical means of grasping stages in the development of a youth culture opposition from the psychedelia of 1966 to a politicized counterculture in 1970. A broad survey of cultural dissent emphasizing the role of an apocalyptic sensibility in American culture is Margot A. Henriksen, *Dr. Strangelove's America: Society and Culture in the Atomic Age* (Berkeley: University of California Press, 1997).

Among historical accounts of the antiwar movement in the 1960s, see Tom Wells, *The War Within: America's Battle over Vietnam* (Berkeley: University of California Press, 1994), and Amy Swerdlow, *Women Strike for Peace: Traditional Motherhood and Radical Politics in the 1960s* (Chicago: University of Chicago Press, 1993). For studies of formal argument and academic life, see David Levy, *The Debate over Vietnam* (Baltimore, Md.: Johns Hopkins University Press, 1991), and David L. Schalk, *War and the Ivory Tower: Algeria and Vietnam* (New York: Oxford University Press, 1991).

On the meaning and influence of nonviolence in the early 1960s, see works by and about Martin Luther King Jr.: James M. Washington, ed., *A Testament of Hope: The Essential Writings and Speeches of Martin Luther King, Jr.* (San Francisco: HarperCollins, 1991); David J. Garrow, *Bearing the Cross: Martin Luther King, Jr, and the Southern Christian Leadership Conference* (New York: Vintage, 1988); and Greg Moses, *Revolution of Conscience: Martin Luther King, Jr., and the Philosophy of Nonviolence* (New York: Guilford, 1997). See also James Tracy, *Direct Action: Radical Pacifism from the Union Eight to the Chicago Seven* (Chicago: University of Chicago Press, 1996).

Robert Wuthnow, *The Restructuring of American Religion: Society and Faith Since World War II* (Princeton: Princeton University Press, 1988), is a broad social history of American religion that covers the 1960s. More focused on theology and particularly countercultural spirituality is Robert S. Ellwood, *The Sixties Spiritual Awakening: American Religion Moving from Modern to Postmodern* (New Brunswick, N.J.: Rutgers University Press, 1994). For left-wing currents in American Catholicism, see Murray Polner and Jim O'Grady's *Disarmed and Dangerous: The Radical Lives and Times of Daniel and Philip Berrigan* (New York: Basic Books, 1997). Patrick Allitt's excellent book *Catholic Intellectuals and Conservative Politics in America, 1950–1985* (Ithaca, N.Y.: Cornell University Press, 1993) describes the alternative trend.

Ronald Fraser et al., *1968: A Student Generation in Revolt* (New York: Pantheon, 1988), a work of nine oral historians covering developments in student protest in six Western countries, is an excellent source for understanding the perspective of the radical activists that year. Daniel Bell's *The Cultural Contradictions of Capitalism* (New York: Basic Books, 1976) reveals a great deal of the cultural politics involved in the intellectual polarization of the late 1960s. There are a growing number of studies regarding "neoconservative" intellectuals, but many are devoted to explicating individual thinkers and focus on the 1970s and 1980s rather than recount the germination of the circle in the 1960s. In this last respect, useful starting points are John Ehrman, *The Rise of Neoconservatism: Intellectuals and Foreign Affairs, 1945–1994* (New Haven: Yale University Press, 1995), and Mark Gerson, *The Neoconservative Vision: From the Cold War to the Culture Wars* (New York: Madison Books, 1996).

Dan T. Carter, *The Politics of Rage: George Wallace, the Origins of the New Conservatism, and the Transformation of American Politics* (New York: Simon and Schuster, 1995), stresses the role of white backlash, Wallace's national campaigns, and Richard Nixon's resulting "southern strategy" in laying the groundwork for the rightward turn of American politics. Quite a different view, focusing on corporate interests turning right in response to global economic pressures of the 1970s, is taken in Thomas Ferguson and Joel Rogers, *Right Turn: The Decline of the Democrats and the Future of American Politics* (New York: Hill and Wang, 1986).

Peter Novick's magisterial *That Noble Dream: The "Objectivity" Question and the Historical Profession* (Cambridge: Cambridge University Press, 1988) provides a thorough view of the disruptive conflicts in one academic discipline. Perry Anderson's *Considerations on Western Marxism* (London: NLB, 1976) and Martin Jay's *Dialectical Imagination* (Boston: Little, Brown, 1973) review the dimensions of Marxist theory that most intrigued young intellectuals in the 1960s. Sara Evans, *Personal Politics: The Roots of Women's Liberation in the Civil Rights Movement and the New Left* (New York: Vintage, 1980), is the basic text on the contribution of radical youth activism toward the revival of feminism. Judith Hole and Ellen Levine, *Rebirth of Feminism* (New York: Quadrangle, 1971), a contemporary account, provides a very useful compendium of movement history, feminist ideas, and political issues in the wake of the movement's first flowering. An excellent secondary account focusing on the intellectual history of radical feminism is Alice Echols, *Daring to be Bad: Radical Feminism in America, 1967–1975* (Minneapolis: University of Minnesota Press, 1989). The best comprehensive study of postwar gay and lesbian politics and culture is John D'Emilio, *Sexual Politics, Sexual Communities: The Making of a Homosexual Minority in the United States, 1940–1970* (Chicago: University of Chicago Press, 1983). For a focus on women, see Lillian Faderman, *Odd Girls and Twilight Lovers: A History of Lesbian Life in Twentieth-Century America* (New York: Penguin, 1991).

Index

AACM. *See* Association for the Advancement of Creative Musicians
abortion, 183
Abrams, Muhal Richard, 140
absurdism, 59, 110, 133–34
abundance, 1–6, 54–55; and growth of social sphere, 1, 7; Lippmann on, 118
academic disciplines: divisions in, 178–79; and interdisciplinary scholarship, 48, 179–80, 187. *See also* radical caucuses
academic freedom: and autonomy of the university, 25, 171; as self-regulation by academic professions, 171–72
Acuña, Rodolfo, 121
Adorno, Theodor, 133
affluence, Ehrlichs on end of, 188 (*see also* abundance; *Affluent Society, The;* Galbraith, John Kenneth)
Affluent Society, The (Galbraith), 2–3
Africa, new states in, 47, 50, 52, 91, 105
African Americans: in age of contradiction, xv; women, 112–13. *See also* black freedom struggle
African culture, image of, 107, 111
Aiken, Henry David, 34
AIM. *See* American Indian Movement
Ainsworth, Mary, 72
Albee, Edward, 82
Ali, Muhammad, 111, 154
alienation, 1, 14–18; in existentialism, 14–15; in Marxism, 15–17. *See also* dissociation

Alinsky, Saul, 99, 101
Alliance for Progress, 47
Alloway, Lawrence, 71
Allport, Gordon, 68
Alpert, Richard, 115
Altizer, Thomas J. J., 36
American Enterprise Institute, 9
American Indian Movement (AIM), 120–21
American Indians, xv, 116, 119, 120; Indian activism, 120–21
American Women in Psychology, 180
anarchism, 69, 76, 115, 128
Anaya, Rudolfo, 120, 122
anthropology: and cultural science, 37; and development theory, 46, 48; radical caucus in, 178
anti-art, 137, 172, 173–74
anticommunism, 33, 35, 47, 81, 156; and academic life, 24, 149, 171, 179; and rupture of left-wing traditions, xiii, 164
anti-form, 173
antihumanism, and postmodernism, 61, 63
anti-imperialism, 45, 153, 158
antipoverty program, xvii, 101–3 (*see also* Community Action Program)
antipsychiatry, 78
anti-Semitism, 107
antiwar movement, 131; and American thought and culture, 152–58; relation to counterculture, 116; weakness of, 165. *See also* Vietnam teach-ins

The Author

Howard Brick is associate professor of history at Washington University in St. Louis. He is working on a book to be entitled *Beyond the Bourgeoisie: Theories of Capitalism and Social Development in the United States, 1920–1970.*